D1140718

RETHINKING
PUBLIC
POLICY-MAKING

RETHINKING PUBLIC POLICY-MAKING

Questioning Assumptions, Challenging Beliefs

Essays in honour of Sir Geoffrey Vickers on his centenary

Edited by

Margaret Blunden
Malcolm Dando

SAGE Publications
London • Thousand Oaks • New Delhi

Originally published as a special issue of the *American Behavioral Scientist* (Volume 38, Number 1, September/October 1994)

Revised edition published as *Rethinking Public Policy-Making* 1995

SAGE Publications Ltd
6 Bonhill Street
London EC2A 4PU

SAGE Publications Inc
2455 Teller Road
Thousand Oaks, California 91320

SAGE Publications India Pvt Ltd
32, M-Block Market
Greater Kailash-I
New Delhi 110 048

British Library Cataloguing in Publication data

A catalogue record for this book is available from the British Library.

ISBN 0 8039 7602 X

Library of Congress catalog card number 95-069026

Printed in Great Britain by The Cromwell Press Ltd,
Broughton Gifford, Melksham, Wiltshire

Contents

Foreword

Governance in the Hollow State

> This stillness of mind
> is not fatigue or old age
> or approach of death.
>
> It is release from
> obsessive purpose, the mad
> blind charioteer
>
> who through these hard weeks
> has driven me to this end
> which is now achieved.
>
> Success? Or failure?
> Who knows? It does not matter
> now the task is done.
>
> (Extract from "Release," Vickers, 1983b, p. 33)

I met Geoffrey Vickers between September 21 and 24, 1973, at the conference "Public Policy Making" held at Wast Hills House, University of Birmingham. It was the only time we met, and, to my continuing regret, he was overshadowed by Aaron Wildavsky. Both men had a major influence on the study of public policy-making and both changed my thinking about the subject. But Geoffrey was quiet and polite to the point of diffidence. Aaron was ebullient, witty, and the dominating presence. I wasted an opportunity, dazzled by the American superstar. So it goes, but I still read Geoffrey's books and articles whenever possible. (For his contribution to the Wast Hills conference, see Vickers, 1974.)

My second contact was with the Vickers family, and it was scarcely more auspicious. I reviewed Adams, Forester, and Catron (1987) and complained, testily, that they had included articles already available in book form and had omitted several articles that either had never been printed or had not been reprinted since their first journal publication. The enthusiasms of this youth knew no bounds. Not only would I persuade a publisher to produce a collection of this material so that all the Vickers's papers were available in book form, but also my then-current university, the University of Essex, would become the home of the Vickers's archive. So, out of the blue, I bombarded Geoffrey's daughter, Pamela Miller, with letters. The offer of a home for Geoffrey's papers was politely declined, although I was encouraged to look for a publisher. (The family wanted to keep the papers for the time being, although the papers are listed in the National Register of Archives and are available to scholars through that source.) From May 1988 to July 1989, I approached innumerable publishers, all of whom also declined politely. Pamela Miller admired my perseverance. I was underwhelmed by my collection of rejection slips.

I received my invitation to contribute this foreword with delight. At last, a chance to do something productive; compensation for my previous omissions and frustrations. Most important, however, it was an opportunity to explain why Geoffrey's work remains relevant, in this case to governing the hollow state.

A worldwide trend of recent years is the new public management (NPM). It has two defining strands. The first strand is *managerialism*, which refers to hands-on, professional management based on private sector management experience that sets explicit standards and measures of performance and emphasizes output controls. The second strand is based on the new institutional economics, also known as rational choice, which argues for disaggregation of public bureaucracies; competition in the public sector (for example, contracting out, quasi-markets); and discipline and parsimony in public spending. (For a more detailed discussion, see Hood, 1991; Pollitt, 1993.) This new orthodoxy continues to have a major impact not only on British public services but also worldwide (e.g., see Boston et al., 1991; Osbourne & Gaebler, 1992; Wanna, O'Faircheallaigh, & Weller, 1992). World Bank loans to developing countries require the recipient nation to implement NPM nostrums (for a discussion, see Leftwich, 1993). In Britain, it is a defining characteristic of the current trend to "the hollow state," a phrase that encompasses:

1. Privatization and limiting the scope and forms of public intervention.
2. The loss of functions by central and local government departments to alternative service delivery systems (such as agencies).
3. The loss of functions by British government to European Union institutions.
4. Limiting the discretion of public servants through the new public management. (Rhodes, 1994, pp. 138-139)

Geoffrey Vickers's work provides a critique of NPM and is a source of lessons on governing the hollow state. The critique can be summarized under the headings of: regulation, appreciation, multivalued choice, and interdependence.

REGULATION

Vickers (1968) relentlessly criticized policy-making as goal setting; as "the pursuit of an endless succession of goals" (p. 31; see also p. 22, n. 4). In place of goal setting and goal seeking, he proposed policy-making as regulation or

> maintaining through time a complex pattern of relationships in accordance with standards or within limits which have somehow come to be set as governing relations. Its regulative function consists partly in maintaining the actual course of affairs in line with these governing relations as they happen to be at the time and partly in modifying these governing relations. (Vickers, 1968, p. 27)

So,

> the goals we seek are changes in our relations or in our opportunities for relating; but the bulk of our activity consists in the "relating" itself. (Vickers, 1968, p. 33)

But NPM preserves the hierarchical view of management, controlling subordinates by target setting. Above all, it fails to recognize proliferating service delivery systems. Management is no longer about intraorganizational control. It is about managing networks of organizations. In Metcalfe and Richards's (1987) memorable phrase, NPM drags "British government kicking and screaming back into the 1950s" (p. 17).

APPRECIATION

Comparing the course of action with the governing norms, and the evolution and modification of these governing relations, is described by Vickers (1968, p. 39) as "appreciation." Policy-making involves appreciations about both the state of the system (reality judgments) and the significance of these facts (value judgments). These judgments about reality and value are "a set of readinesses to distinguish some aspects of the situation rather than others and to classify and value these in this way rather than in that" (Vickers, 1968, p. 67). In everyday language, the spectacles we wear influence what we see and how we interpret it. If they are rose-colored, then we see the good in people and all is for the best in the best of all possible worlds. If they are of darker hue, we see the hurt we inflict on one another and judge humankind as wanting. On a less elevated plane, every policy decision involves the equivalent process of appreciation. For example, British central government departments have distinctive "departmental philosophies" that encompass the effortless superiority of the Treasury and the trench warfare mentality of the Home Office (Bridges, 1950; Jenkins, 1971).

An appreciative system is the glue holding together an institution. NPM and hollowing out dissolve it. Reformers, including the government, reject the legacy of the generalist civil service and assert the need to change its culture. So the Head of the Civil Service, Sir Robin Butler, calls for policies that will maintain "a degree of cohesion across the service as a whole" and "[a] shared sense of the essential values and ethics that make our system work" (Butler, 1993, p. 404) precisely because the emphasis on cost and output not only sacrifices quality to quantity but also undervalues maintaining relationships within and without the service.

MULTIVALUED CHOICE

When seeking to maintain relationships through time, governments have ideas about what these relations should be. These ideas provide the "standards by which to judge what is and what might be" (Vickers, 1970a, p. 126). Thus a government, when setting its budget,

> has not only to balance its budget but also to achieve, within that balanced budget, an optimal or at least acceptable realization of the manifold things it is trying to do. Wildly disparate aims, such as atom bombs and Medicare, highways and higher education, fight for realization, each an expression of the urge to bring some relation up to standard. No built-in hierarchy or order of priorities decides how far each shall have its way. The choice is multi-valued. (Vickers, 1970a, p. 127)

Above all else, "the multi-valued choice is a central, inescapable, irreducible fact of life" (Vickers, 1970a, p. 12) and a defining characteristic of any appreciative system.

By emulating private sector management, NPM downplays the importance of the multivalued choice because it seeks to depoliticize management in the public sector. As Ranson and Stewart (1989) argue, management in the public domain has distinctive tasks, purposes, and conditions. For example, it determines collective values out of the mosaic of conflicting interests. NPM is confined to the values enshrined in the "3Es" of economy, efficiency, and effectiveness, and it does not encompass broader notions, such as the public interest and public accountability.

INTERDEPENDENCE

We live in an "increasingly complex net of interdependence" (Vickers, 1983a, p. 14), whether the level of analysis is the individual, group, organization, or nation state. "A modern nation state is a system so complex as to demand description not only at many levels but in many complementary dimensions" (Vickers, 1970b, p. 91). Human systems are increasingly difficult to maintain, and interdependence is an ever-greater source of constraints. "We are all more often done by than doers" (Vickers, 1983a, p. 176), so we need to be more aware of the consequences of our actions and become more responsible. Yet interdependence erodes existing structures of authority and modes of responsibility. Human systems are subject to escalating instabilities that demand "a concept of universal responsibility such as no Utopian since Plato ever hoped to get even from his 'Guardians' " (Vickers, 1983a, p. 176).

British government continues to make the net of interdependencies more complex. Functions are taken away from elected local authorities and given to ad hoc nominated bodies. Routine tasks are removed from central departments and vested in separate agencies. Functions are contracted out to the private sector. Quasi-markets are created in health, education, and social care. Membership of the European Union has added a new layer of government and fueled the development of transnational policy networks. The effect of these changes is to disaggregate public bureaucracies.

NPM and hollowing out combine hierarchical line management with cultural change, which erodes long-standing values and ethics and ignores the distinctive tasks, purposes, and conditions of public sector management. At the same time, public bureaucracies are disaggregated, creating complex networks of interdependencies, further emphasizing that the private sector, target-setting style of management is inappropriate to interorganizational contexts.

The resulting problems are all too familiar to anyone who has read *Freedom in a Rocking Boat* (Vickers, 1970b) or *Human Systems Are Different* (Vickers, 1983a). Thus line bureaucracies are replaced by institutional fragmentation that erodes the capacity to coordinate, steer, and build consensus. The hollow state erodes accountability, and it is difficult to know who is responsible to whom for what. NPM is "a disaster waiting to happen" (Hood & Jackson, 1991) because it combines fragmentation with hands-off regulation and increased opportunities for "malversation," more popularly known as "sleaze." And there are also lessons. Organizational interdependence is ubiquitous, and the key task of public sector managers is to steer complex sets of organizations. To the classic dichotomy between planning and markets, we must now add networks, and the networking skills of the "reticulist" (Friend, Power, & Yewlett, 1974) are currently scarce. "Governance" is already the next managerial vogue word.

Traditionally, it refers to the activity or process of governing. Now, it refers to *new* processes, especially to "intergovernmental management" (Marando & Florestano, 1990). To be argumentative, it refers to "governing without government" because it covers multiplying service delivery systems that redefine the boundaries of the state (Rhodes, 1995). We are trying to create "self-steering networks," the ultimate in hands-off government, and the challenge is not confined to understanding and managing the new networks but extends to redefining the ways in which we hold these networks to account.

As governments redefine their governing norms, as relationships change in the hollowing out of the state, Vickers reminds us how important it is to maintain relationships through time and to sustain the values that underpin governing norms in an increasingly interdependent, ever more pluralistic world with its emergent, self-steering networks. He did not succeed. He did not fail. He taught us to *appreciate*; to reappraise continuously the ways in which we regulate our relationships.

Rod A.W. Rhodes
University of Newcastle

REFERENCES

Adams, G. B., Forester, J., & Catron, B. L. (Eds.). (1987). *Policy making, communication, and learning: Essays of Sir Geoffrey Vickers*. New Brunswick, NJ: Transaction.

Boston, J. et al. (Eds.). (1991). *Reshaping the state: New Zealand's bureaucratic revolution*. Auckland, New Zealand: Oxford University Press.

Bridges, E. (1950). *Portrait of a profession*. Cambridge: Cambridge University Press.

Butler, R. (1993). The evolution of the civil service. *Public Administration, 71*, 395-406.

Friend, J. K., Power, J. M., & Yewlett, C.J.L. (1974). *Public planning: The intercorporate dimension*. London: Tavistock.

Hood, C. C. (1991). A public management for all seasons? *Public Administration, 69*, 3-19.

Hood, C. C., & Jackson, M. W. (1991). The new public management: A recipe for disaster. *Canberra Bulletin of Public Administration, 64*, 16-24.

Jenkins, R. (1971). A study in Whitehall style. *The Sunday Times*, January 17.

Leftwich, A. (1993). Governance, democracy and development in the Third World. *Third World Quarterly, 14*, 605-624.

Marando, V. L., & Florestano, P. S. (1990). Intergovernmental management: The state of the discipline. In N. Lynne & A. Wildavsky (Eds.), *Public administration: The state of the discipline*. Chatham, NJ: Chatham House.

Metcalfe, L., & Richards, S. (1987). *Improving public management*. London: Sage.

Osborne, D., & Gaebler, T. (1992). *Reinventing government*. Reading, MA: Addison-Wesley.

Pollitt, C. (1993). *Managerialism and the public services* (2nd ed.). Oxford: Basil Blackwell.

Ranson, S., & Stewart, J. (1989). Citizenship and government: The challenge for management in the public domain. *Political Studies, 37*, 5-24.

Rhodes, R.A.W. (1994). The hollowing out of the state. *Political Quarterly, 65*, 138-151.

Rhodes, R.A.W. (1995). *Governance*. London: Royal Society of Arts and ESRC.

Vickers, G. (1968). *The art of judgement*. London: Methuen University Paperback.

Vickers, G. (1970a). *Value systems and social processes*. Harmondsworth: Penguin.

Vickers, G. (1970b). *Freedom in a rocking boat: Changing values in an unstable society*. London: Penguin.

Vickers, G. (1974). Policy making in local government. *Local Government Studies*, February 5-11.

Vickers, G. (1983a). *Human systems are different*. London: Harper & Row.

Vickers, G. (1983b). *Moods and tenses: Occasional poems of an old man*. Privately printed.

Wanna, J., O'Faircheallaigh, C., & Weller, P. (1992). *Public sector management in Australia.* Melbourne, Australia: Macmillan Educational.

A GUIDE TO FURTHER READING

The classic text is
Vickers, G. (1965). *The art of judgement.* London: Harper & Row; London: Methuen University Paperback, 1968.

The best single collection of articles is
Open Systems Group. (Eds.). (1984). *The Vickers papers.* London: Harper & Row.

As a specialist in British government, public administration and public policy, my favorites are
Vickers, G. (1968). *Value systems and social process.* London: Tavistock; Harmondsworth: Penguin Books, 1970.
Vickers, G. (1970). *Freedom in a rocking boat: Changing values in an unstable society.* London: Penguin; Harmondsworth: Penguin, 1972.
Vickers, G. (1973). *Making institutions work.* London: Associated Business Programmes.

The Open Systems Group (1984) contains Vickers's own select bibliography, which is extensive.
There is little material *about* Sir Geoffrey Vickers. The best single piece is
Blunden, M. (1984). Geoffrey Vickers—An intellectual journey. In Open Systems Group (Eds.), *The Vickers papers.* London: Harper & Row.

Other than the articles in this collection, see also
Adams, G. B., Forester, J., & Catron, B. L. (1987). Introduction. In G. B. Adams, J. Forester, & B. L. Catron (Eds.), *Policy making, communication, and learning: Essays of Sir Geoffrey Vickers.* New Brunswick, NJ: Transaction.
Blunden, M. (1985). Vickers' contribution to management thinking. *Journal of Applied Systems Analysis, 12,* 107-112.
Checkland, P., & Casar, A. (1986). Vickers' concept of an appreciative system: A systemic account. *Journal of Applied Systems Analysis, 13,* 3-17.
Johnson, N. (in press). The art of judgement. *Political Studies.*
Sutton, S. B. (1983). Sir Geoffrey Vickers: An affectionate portrait. In G. Vickers, *Human systems are different* (pp. v-xvi). London: Harper & Row.
Subramaniam, V. (1971). Two complimentary approaches to macro-decision making. *Public Administration* (Australia), *30,* 337-348.
Thompson, D.J.C. (1992). A systems model of policy making and the National Health Service. *Political Studies, 25,* 397-403; and the reply by Rudolph Klein on 404-405.

Finally, there is Introduction: Fragments of an autobiography. In Pamela Miller (Ed.), (1992). *The Vickers family letters* (pp. 5-17). Privately published.

Introduction

Sir Geoffrey Vickers

MARGARET BLUNDEN
MALCOLM DANDO

> Having reached my own centenary, I can only say that I wish Geoffrey could be reaching his in 1994, instead of having left us in 1982 at the age of 87. His wisdom and foresight arc sadly needed in today's world, whose problems he clearly predicted. His proposals for dealing with those problems, and for avoiding them where possible, are as valid today as when he made them. One can only hope that his books, with their clear signposts for the future, will reach and enrich present and future generations in the same way they have enlightened those of the past.
> —Adolph Lowe, 1993

Twenty years ago, *American Behavioral Scientist* published an article by Sir Geoffrey Vickers entitled "The Changing Nature of the Professions" (Vickers, 1974; Open Systems Group, 1984).* Characteristically, in this article he argued that

> understanding, designing, advising, and operating with their partly common background of theoretical knowledge and practical experience are the basic abilities of the professional. But in exercising them, he needs to be able to judge the professional requirements of his role in relation to his client, the public, and his fellow professionals. This capacity for *judgment* is his sixth professional ability. (Open Systems Group, 1984, p. 275)

*All quotations throughout this issue of *American Behavioral Scientist* from the works of Sir Geoffrey Vickers are reprinted by the gracious permission of the copyright holder, Jeanne Vickers, and may not be reprinted elsewhere without separate arrangement.

Editors' Note: *The editors would like to thank Janet Dando, Karen Phillips, John Keane, and Ali Tajvidi for their important and varied contributions to this publication. We are also grateful to Adolph Lowe, who corresponded with Geoffrey Vickers for more than 40 years, for the message printed at the beginning of this Introduction. We owe a particular debt to Jeanne Vickers for her support and advice throughout the project and for her unwavering confidence that it would reach a successful conclusion.*

The article reads as if it was written yesterday and is full of the elegance of professional judgment that impressed and delighted so many people who had the opportunity of meeting and working with Sir Geoffrey—sentiments conveyed so clearly in the message from Adolph Lowe[1] that opens this collection of articles.

Yet that 20-year-old article also conveys the point that little could be taken for granted in Geoffrey Vickers's thinking. Using the Buchanan Report, one of his favorite examples, he argued that

> it illustrates the planner's analytic function, the exercise of professional understanding. Whatever threat or aspiration first led him to action, his definition of "the situation", though as simple as it can logically be, will be more complex than was first perceived, and his definition of "the issue" will include costs and benefits more varied than seemed at first to be involved. The result may be embarrassing. (Open Systems Group, 1984, p. 284)

The Buchanan Report *was* embarrassing because it suggested that the issue examined because of an apparent problem with transport in towns went far beyond the ambit of the Ministry of Transport. Sir Geoffrey's approach to the public policy issues that concerned him generally led to definitions of our predicament much more complex than we might first have imagined, and it included much wider considerations of costs and benefits. For this reason we thought it appropriate to entitle this set of articles "Rethinking Public Policy-Making: Questioning Assumptions, Challenging Beliefs."

The contributors to this collection of articles share a critical approach to an intellectual tradition that has been dominant in Europe and the United States since the 18th century. This pervasive worldview focuses on individual entities, rather than interconnections, and on autonomous individuals and individual rights, rather than on the sense of membership, with its associated obligations and responsibilities, which holds society together and helps to maintain stability. Western cultural assumptions, reflecting the long-standing influence of Benthamite utilitarianism, view human nature as characterized by goal seeking and society as an aggregate of individuals each in pursuit of an endless series of private satisfactions. Emphasis on the pursuit of goals rather than the management of relationships pervades approaches to interactions between, as well as within, states, and between states and their physical environment.

The shortcomings of a conceptual framework that focuses on discrete entities rather than systemic interactions, and on goals rather than relationships, have become steadily more evident as the challenges facing public policy at the local, national, and global levels multiply. Increasingly pluralistic societies are required to manage conflicting moral claims and conflicting standards of morality. Technological advances, such as those in genetic engineering, are placing an increasing load on the political system because, once something is technically feasible, the political process has to take on the burden of determining costs and benefits, and deciding who, if anyone, should benefit and at what cost. The ending of the Cold War has released major disintegrative forces, reinforced the

interaction between internal and international disputes, and brought to prominence the threat of new confrontations between ideologies that, unlike capitalism and communism, reinforce ancient divisions between civilizations. The
rapidly rising trajectory of world population growth complicates the management of relations between the developed and the developing world and international agreement on measures that will make possible a sustainable relationship
with the environment.

All the contributors to this collection of articles acknowledge a profound
intellectual debt to the late Sir Geoffrey Vickers, philosopher and epistemologist,
who was born 100 years ago. The collection has been assembled in the belief
that Vickers's writings—nine books and 87 articles between 1955 and 1982—
are essential reading for those concerned with the creation of policies for a
sustainable future. Since his death in 1982, the linear developments that Geoffrey Vickers believed would eventually generate, at great cost, their own
reversals have continued unabated. Increasing levels of family and community
breakup and rising levels of crime testify to continuing erosion of that sense of
belonging, with its associated commitments and constraints that, Vickers argued,
enhanced rather than inhibited individual personality. Meanwhile, intellectual
currents, including many aspects of American and British feminism, have
extended still further the concept of the autonomous individual. The ending of
the Cold War and the dominance in much of the West of conservative governments have greatly reinforced, and indeed left almost unchallenged as a political
philosophy, the use of the market as an overall social and economic regulator.
To use the market as a regulator of human systems is to import concepts derived
from technological and natural systems into human systems; but human systems,
as Vickers early identified, differ from all the others in that they have a vital
ethical dimension.

There are, however, some signs in the United States, Britain, and elsewhere
of a recognition that personal independence and social interdependence are not
limitlessly compatible; that educational systems need to have ethical, as well as
academic, dimensions; that health services involve care, a relationship, as well
as cure, an output; indeed that the market is only an effective regulator of human
systems up to a point. M. Balladur, the conservative French prime minister,
commented in a recent aside: "What is the market? It is the law of the jungle,
the law of nature. And what is civilization? It is the struggle against nature."[2] At
the international level, some dents have been made in the long-observed convention that the internal policies of individual governments, however gross their
impact on their own populations, are no concern of the international community.

Conceptual change has been miniscule and slow, compared with what Vickers
believed was necessary if mankind was to have any hope of a stable future. He
summarized the scale of the task at the end of his last book, *Human Systems Are
Different*, published after his death in 1982:

> If the argument of this book has any validity at all, it is to suggest that all today's
> human populations, perhaps particularly those heirs of the Enlightenment who

have so successfully pioneered the huge cultural changes of the last two hundred years, need now to achieve an even more radical reversal, a change not only in their understanding, as observers, of the developing situations in which they are trapped, but also a change in their appreciation, as agents and as experients, of what these changes require of them. (Vickers, 1983, p. 168)

It is hoped that these articles—so well received when originally published as a special issue of *American Behavioral Scientist* (Volume 38, Number 1) in Sir Geoffrey's centenary year, and which are now republished with a foreword by Professor Rhodes—will make a continuing contribution to that mammoth task.

NOTES

1. The correspondence between Lowe and Vickers from the 1950s through to the 1980s can be followed in Vickers (1991).

2. See *The Financial Times*, 1993, December 31, p. 1.

REFERENCES

Open Systems Group. (Ed.). (1984). *The Vickers papers*. London: Harper & Row.
Vickers, G. (1974). The changing nature of the professions. *American Behavioral Scientist, 18*(2).
Vickers, G. (1983). *Human systems are different*. London: Harper & Row.
Vickers, J. (1991). *Rethinking the future: The correspondence between Geoffrey Vickers and Adolph Lowe*. London: Transaction.

1

Vickers and Postliberalism

MARGARET BLUNDEN

Geoffrey Vickers's critique of liberalism, in both its classical and modern interventionist forms, and his emphasis on individual responsibility, is resonant of philosophic conservatism. However, his systemic insights led him to radical conclusions, and he mounted a powerful argument for major change in what he called the "appreciative system" of the industrialized West. The systems concepts that Vickers developed in this context make a distinctive contribution to political philosophy and should command more serious critical attention than they have yet received.

It is entirely characteristic that Geoffrey Vickers, in his preface to the *Art of Judgment*, should have acknowledged that the names that gratitude first brought to his mind were those of a physicist, a physiologist, a sociologist, an economist, a theologian, and a philosopher-scientist. Vickers defined himself not as an academic—drawing boundaries in whatever way seemed convenient for the pursuit of ever more specialized knowledge—but as a professional, with a different and built-in standard of relevance by which to define the academic knowledge that he needed. The professional, he believed, seeks knowledge where he can find it and generates it himself if no academic discipline is interested or able to meet his need (Vickers, 1983, p. 153).

The overriding need that Vickers identified and set out to meet was nothing less than to think through the changes that would have to be made to extract Western industrialized society from what he believed to be its present predicament and to offer some hope of a sustainable future. Vickers's interpretation of history, like that of Spengler and Toynbee (Spengler, 1919; Toynbee, 1960), led to alarming conclusions. But unlike the political philosopher Michael Oakeshott, whose work resembles his own in important respects, he believed that greater understanding of the present situation and the dynamics of historical change could and should lead to more appropriate behavior at individual and societal levels. Oakeshott's view that "the belief that the state can be improved in terms of some philosophical arguments is the logical mistake of thinking that a concept *entails* a practical conclusion" (Minogue, 1993, p. 46) was the antithesis of Vickers's "professional" approach. The academic knowledge that he defined as relevant to his self-imposed task included all the elements that normally make up political philosophy—history, ethics, epistemology—but was, most unusually, permeated by the concepts that he derived and adapted to his purpose from systems thinking. The systems approach that he developed underpins the most distinctive and most important aspects of his work.

Vickers's critique of the classical liberalism that he traced to the European Enlightenment, and its derivates during the ensuing 200 years, has much in common with philosophic conservatism and his values often have a conservative resonance; however, his conclusions are entirely radical (Vickers, 1983):

> All today's human populations, perhaps particularly those heirs of the Enlighten-
> ment which have so successfully pioneered the huge cultural changes of the last
> two hundred years, need now to achieve an even more radical reversal, a change
> not only in their understanding, as observers, of the developing situation in which
> they are trapped, but also a change in their appreciation, as agents and experients,
> of what these changes require of them. (p. 168)

THE APPRECIATIVE SYSTEM AND LINEAR CHANGE

Vickers's most important concept, the appreciative system, first fully devel-oped in *The Art of Judgment* published in 1965, has explanatory value at the individual, the organizational, and the societal level. Appreciation manifested itself in the exercise through time of mutually related reality judgments (what is the case) and value judgments (what ought to be the case) (Vickers, 1965, p. 67). He described these judgments as a set of readinesses to distinguish some aspects of a situation rather than others and to classify and value them in this way rather than that. These readinesses have to be learned and, like all learning, they are necessarily limiting as well as enabling. They facilitate further learning consis-tent with the pattern they create, but they create "unreadinesses" to see, to value, and to respond in ways inconsistent with those patterns. Vickers described the state of the appreciative system at any one time as its "setting," an analogy drawn from the control mechanisms of a man-made regulator; the appreciative setting describes the governing relations to which the appreciative system is for the time being set to respond.

The concept of an appreciative system provided an explanatory model of how cultures change over time. It did not, by definition, explain how practical conclusions might be drawn from analyzing historical experience. It was Vick-ers's highly original analysis of historical development in terms of systems theory—a powerful set of concepts applied most often in a technological context—that led him to identify an element of predictability in the broad rhythms of historical change. The key systems concept was that of self-limitation, that is, that it was impossible for linear change to continue indefinitely in any one element of a system. All linear developments were basically self-destabilizing; "linear change is bound in time to be self-limiting or self-reversing and may even destroy the form which it has defined" (Vickers, 1983, p. xx).

If it was possible to understand the process by which standards change over time and to detect actual linear changes approaching critical limits, it should be possible to take remedial action. The point of identifying potentially dangerous linear trends, and attempting to control them, was to avoid the enormous costs that their own, unaided, "natural" or systemic reversals were likely to involve. What Vickers believed to be the self-limiting behavior of linear trends in all aspects of human systems convinced him of the need for the conscious exercise of human control—what he called "the power and duty of the human mind to make judgments of value" (Vickers, 1963/1984b, p. 151), rather than leaving what should be deliberately governed to the so-called automatic regulators such as the market, representing the aggregated actions of autonomous individuals each pursuing his or her own self-interest. Vickers was a conservative in the most basic sense of that term, in that his overriding values were those of order and stability but his systemic analysis led to conclusions fundamentally opposed to that brand of modern market conservatism more accurately described as liberalism.

CRITIQUE OF LIBERALISM

It is implicit in Vickers's analysis that the period of the Enlightenment, and the associated propagation of the values and beliefs of classical liberalism, represented a resetting of the appreciative setting of Western societies, particularly those British and American ones that specifically concerned him, and that the resulting linear changes had begun to breed their own reversals that were threatening Western society.

Although Vickers himself undoubtedly oversimplified the ideological discontinuities associated with the Enlightenment, political philosophers broadly agree that it represented a significant cultural shift. John Gray (1993) has identified what he calls four constitutive elements in doctrinal liberalism whose influence dates from this period: universalism, individualism, egalitarianism, and meliorism (p. 284). Vickers's criticism of classical liberalism, which he classified as a self-regulating system dependent on individual judgment and powered by individual self-interest (Vickers, 1980, p. 21), encompassed all these elements, assuming meliorism in this context to be a belief in linear progress.[1] He saw these as interlinked ideas containing within themselves the seeds both of what was later to develop into revisionist, interventionist liberalism and into totalitarianism. The most fundamental change that Vickers associated with the Enlightenment, and implicitly the most damaging, was an epistemological one: the positivist application of concepts drawn from the natural sciences to the human sciences, the restriction of the concept of human reason by identifying it exclusively with the rational and ignoring the intuitive function, and the exaltation of analysis at the expense of synthesis (Vickers, 1980, pp. 19-20). Together, these led to a drastic downgrading of the ethical dimension in human judgment and their influence remained, he believed, as dominant as ever in the second half of the 20th century. In a characteristic letter to Adolph Lowe written in December 1968, he said that "the more I read of science and see of scientists, the more I feel that science has cramped the human spirit conceptually worse than all the dryads and demons put together" (Vickers, 1991, p. 53).

The universalist claims characteristic of Enlightenment thinking and the consequent assumption that linear change could continue indefinitely were still prevalent as Vickers was writing and have been reinforced since his death in 1982 by the ending of the Cold War. In 1989, Francis Fukuyama made his famous announcement of "the unabashed victory of economic and political liberalism" and promised "the end point of mankind's ideological evolution and the universalization of Western liberal democracy as the final form of human government" (Gray, 1993, p. 245). Vickers had pointed out for many years that the lasting influence of universalist assumptions had led to a characteristic "unreadiness" to perceive the vitally important elements of diversity in human culture. He was concerned to

> emphasize the net of cultural and subcultural systems which so diversify both human experience and the different ways in which this is perceived and interpreted in different human societies . . . an unpopular and neglected viewpoint, especially among scientists, who tend to equate successful understanding with the discovery of general laws. (Vickers, 1983, p. 9)

Some other critics of classical liberalism have come to conclusions similar to Vickers about the importance of the specific and the diverse. Isaiah Berlin, for instance, emphasises the plurality of modern society and rejects the "enormous fallacy" of "human history as a single struggle towards the light" (Berlin, 1991, pp. 37-38). John Gray similarly has refuted the idea of membership of a single moral community but he believes that it still animates most moral thought and is especially prominent in contemporary criticisms of liberalism (Gray, 1993, p. 263). No one who had absorbed Vickers's epistemological approach would have been surprised, as so many otherwise sophisticated political observers were, by the explosion of diverse ethnic and religious consciousness set off by the collapse of the Soviet Union and the ending of the Cold War.

A further persistent strand of Enlightenment thinking, and one that Vickers believed peculiarly misguided, was the belief that the sum of individual benefits automatically translated into the general welfare. In this optimistic view of self-regulating systems, individuals' personal motivations and valuations were their own affair. The common good could prosper without common concern. It would prosper *best* without common concern (Vickers, 1980, p. 22). Vickers marveled at the "extraordinary delusion which has dominated the Western world for two hundred years, equating individual liberty with universal peace" (Vickers, 1983, p. 49). He would, one imagines, have been startled by the resurgence, in the 13 years since his death, of the belief in the consequentialist or utilitarian concept of the market as the maximizer of collective or aggregate welfare, automatically promoting the collective good.

Vickers's key concern was the way in which Enlightenment thinking inaugurated linear changes that were ultimately self-destructive, which, in his distinctive systems terminology, "bred their own reversals." No one element in a system could continue indefinitely along a given trajectory; linear changes, if allowed to continue long enough unchecked by human intervention, would ultimately generate their opposites and might well destroy the system of which they formed part in the process. Modern interventionist liberalism was, Vickers suggested, already implicit in the emphasis on equality within classical liberalism. The idea that all men were created equal, although enshrined in the American Declaration of Independence, was neither self-evident nor true; the natural differences, in health or potential talent, among the newborn were very great. Demand for equality of opportunity was bound to be succeeded in time by demands for equality of outcomes that could only be achieved by large-scale political intervention: "Though the potentially successful minority might need no more than equality of opportunity, the 'greatest number' were bound in time to demand an equality of enjoyment which could be provided only by increasing intervention of the political will" (Vickers, 1977/1984g, p. 88). Liberalism also, he argued, contained the seeds of tyranny. Too exclusive an emphasis on equality bred eventually, with a substantial lag, a neglect of the corresponding requirement of responsibility; during the 20th century, the modern concept of the autonomous individual displaced in Western societies the earlier concept of the "responsible person." De Toqueville had predicted that equality paved the way for tyranny because it eroded the tissue of accepted complementary rights and duties that held traditional societies together (quoted in Vickers, 1980, p. 47). In Vickers's terms:

> The reversals bred by the cultural phase which became dominant two centuries ago throw light on the historical process and help us to recognise the cultural dynamics of the present and the cultural needs of the future.
> The age of the individual has bred collectivities on a scale never dreamed before. The age which exalted individual independence has produced a society of which the constituents are interdependent to an unparalleled degree. In consequence a society dedicated to majority rule has become subject to domination by ever smaller minorities. . . . The growth of science has led to a world ever less predictable. The growth of technology has led to a world ever less manageable. (Vickers, 1977/1984g, p. 89)

Political philosophers other than de Toqueville and Vickers have perceived in classical liberalism the seeds of its own destruction. One may, for instance, compare Gray's conclusion that "recent experience supports the . . . fear that, in slowly consuming its pre-individualist foundations, Western civil society may . . . be a self-limiting historical episode" (Gray, 1993, p. 279). Similarly, Oakeshott has commented that "the masses as they appear in modern European history are not composed of individuals; they are composed of 'anti-individuals' united in a revulsion from individuality"; the "civil rights of individuality had been abrogated by the 'social rights' of anti-individuality" (Oakeshott, 1991, pp. 373, 382). What is distinctive about Vickers's explanation, however, is its methodological grounding in systems theory. This provides a generalizable proposition about the impossibility of continuous or permanent development of linear change of any one element in a system, and the inevitability of automatic self-reversal, if unchecked by human intervention. Vickers's specific conclusions about the primary object of his concern, the Western industrialized world at the end of the 20th century, are rooted in this general framework and consequently deserve more attention than most disaster scenarios. Dangerous political and social trends were, he believed, approaching critical limits; the price that would have to be paid for halting them was very great but nothing like the enormous price that would have to be paid for allowing them to continue until they automatically reversed themselves. Identifying the process and selecting the particular linear trends approaching their critical limits that modern society should intervene to reverse are of course two quite different things.

INDIVIDUAL RESPONSIBILITY

As Vickers (1983) explained at the beginning of his last book, *Human Systems Are Different*, his purpose was not to advocate particular policies; his primary focus was not on solving problems but on the primary and underlying task of understanding situations:

> My object is to show the usefulness of systemic thinking as a means to the better understanding of the human condition at the present time. How far that better understanding may lead to wiser policies and more reliable organizations is a question to be answered in the context of particular situations. It does not offer a blueprint for the design of human societies. I hope it will weaken the contemporary urge to regard such activities as akin to engineering rather than (at most) to gardening. It will probably burden us with a livelier consciousness of all those aspects of the contemporary human condition which we deplore but cannot abate. We and the world in general will, none the less, be the better for a clearer understanding of the processes of which we form part and of our real, however limited, scope for intervening in them. (p. 9)

The broad political stance implicit in Vickers's work is a paradoxical one. Here was a man of conservative instincts and values who came to highly radical conclusions, a man whose belief in responsibility, order, and stability mirrors modern conservative philosophers. His conclusions, however, are not only the reverse of modern market capitalism, better described as liberalism, and the entrepreneurial state, as exemplified in the policies of Mrs. Thatcher and President Reagan, but also of that more traditional conservatism, which views government as a limited and quietist activity, expounded in the writings of Gray (1993), Oakeshott (1991), and Selbourne (1994).

Vickers's temper and values, with their emphasis on maintaining relationships, indicate a disposition toward classical conservatism as defined by Oakeshott (1991):

> To be conservative . . . is to prefer the familiar to the unknown, to prefer the tried to the untried, fact to mystery, the actual to the possible, the limited to the unbounded, the near to the distant, the sufficient to the superabundant, the convenient to the perfect, present laughter to utopian bliss.

> Familar relationships and loyalties will be preferred to the allure of more profitable attachments; to acquire and to enlarge will be less important than to keep, to cultivate and to enjoy; the grief of loss will be more acute than the excitement of novelty or promise. (pp. 408-409)

Vickers's own predisposition helps to explain the particular linear trends—an ever-increasing emphasis on personal irresponsibility and exaggerated personal autonomy—that he identified as needing to be intercepted by conscious reversal before they reached their critical limits. His methodology, like his disposition, is a conservative one: His model is an equilibrium-maintaining one that prioritizes the holding to stability and order over time. The model directs particular attention to standards, the criteria that inform the setting of the appreciative system.

When Vickers looked at late 20th-century Western society in terms of this model, he was struck by the multiplication of desirable but mutually inconsistent standards of acceptance and unacceptability. The threat to the maintenance of stability over time came more from lack of order than from lack of liberty. It was not the tyranny of the state but the *anomie* of the autonomous individual that threatened Western cultures. The emphasis on the autonomous individual, rather than on the responsible person, was dangerous because it was peculiarly inappropriate for the highly interdependent technological world of the late 20th century. It was already beginning to breed its own reversals:

> It was no accident that the world . . . which contain[s] so many partial examples amongst its atomised and alienated members should be marked ever more strikingly by the revival of tribal entities, more compelling in their loyalties and fiercer in their mutual hostility than the world has seen since the religious wars of the 16th and 17th centuries. (Vickers, 1977/1984g, p. 92)

The question posed by history seemed to Vickers to be predominantly how and in what form to replace the autonomous individual by the responsible person (Vickers, 1977/1984g, p. 93).

There is of course no logical reason why the autonomous individual should not also be a responsible person. In setting up such a stark antithesis between the two, Vickers may, in fact, have oversimplified the complex movements in value systems within modern Western societies. The European Values Study 1981-1990, a project involving research teams in 29 countries, found no such clear distinction: There was indeed an increasing emphasis on individual achievement and moral autonomy, but the authors concluded that "individualism may involve identification with, and action on behalf of, others." The human rights (of others) and environmental issues were central concerns for the individuals, regardless of political persuasion, who formed the electorates of Europe (Barker, Halman, & Vloet, 1992, pp. 5, 14).

Vickers, like many exponents of modern ethical conservatism, appeared to subscribe to the belief that a higher level of morality existed in earlier centuries, without addressing the many difficulties that this proposition raises. There was, he suggests, an older tradition, predating the Enlightenment, when the prevailing

value had been that of the "responsible person" rather than that of the autonomous individual; it had still been a strong value in the late-Victorian England of
his childhood. He argued that both the parent traditions of Western culture—the
Judeo-Christian and the Greco-Roman—emphasized the responsibility, rather
than the rights, of the human person (Vickers, 1977/1984g, p. 91). Perhaps
because this view is not central to his argument, he did not deal with the massive
qualifications that this generalization requires, including the possibility that the
Judeo-Christian tradition has encouraged an irresponsible attitude to the natural
environment as a bounty created by God to be exploited by man.[2] As far as social
responsibility is concerned, Vickers's views show some passing resemblance to
those of the moral right, including Digby Anderson, who advocates a reassessment of what he calls the "moral basis of individualism" (Anderson, 1992, p. xxii);
Christie Davies, who concludes that "the workable moral order and moral
consensus constructed by previous generations has been dismantled" (Davies,
1992, p. 13); or David Selbourne, who argues for a return to the principle of duty
(Selbourne, 1994).

The similarities are, however, only superficial. In Vickers's view, achieving
that greater degree of individual responsibility that was needed at the end of the
20th century, like any cultural change, would not be merely a reversal to an
earlier state. Individual responsibility could now only be restored by a conscious
resetting of the appreciative system and would be different in character from
that of earlier times. A sense of responsibility adequate for modern circumstances depended on cultivating a deeper sense of past and future, of understanding the extraordinary facts of modern interdependence, and of what this
circumstance required of individuals if any lasting measure of stability was to
be achieved. It involved exacting from everyone an equality of responsibility
corresponding to his or her equality of rights and widening the sense of human
obligation so that it extended not only across the frontiers of nations but across
the temporal boundaries of the generations, including the as yet unborn (Vickers,
1956/1984c, p. 65). This kind of responsibility should be encouraged by teaching children, from the beginning of their school life onward, to appreciate their
systemic dependence on each other and on the shared natural environment of
the planet; that is, on the social and physical systems that support them and
that claim their support, and the obligations that stem from them (Vickers,
1983, pp. 91-105). He believed that the scale of the cultural change that was
needed could hardly be exaggerated.

Vickers argued that individual responsibility, with its associated acceptance
of obligations and constraints, derived from a sense of membership; the strengthening of the latter was necessary to enhance the former. What he believed to be
the current "declining force of membership" was inconsistent with the survival
of a system wholly dependent on the playing of complementary roles by
individuals and subsystems (Vickers, 1983, p. 102). Self-evidently, however,
given this systemic viewpoint, the sense of membership that was required was
a complex one and ruled out any easy, single focus of allegiance and emotional
commitment. Conservative thinkers, much concerned with questions of mem-

bership, tend to stress one overriding loyalty above all others; for Gray, the family may be the ultimate unit on which civil society stands (Gray, 1993, p. 15); for neoliberal conservatives such as Roger Scruton, the nation is the foundation of civil society and political order (Scruton, 1993, p. 299). Vickers placed relatively little emphasis on the family and he suggested that the membership of land and country was a more subtle and more powerful bond than membership of state (Vickers, 1980, p. 30). He personally did not think that belief in God was a necessary basis for morality nor membership of a church an essential component of the social fabric. The membership that modern circumstances required was more austere and more demanding. The modern individual had multiple memberships and needed to balance commitments and obligations as a role-player in a host of overlapping systems. This involved sustaining through time a host of relationships, all partly conflicting and none of which could be wholly satisfied (Vickers, 1972/1984e).

> The mark of a successful individual or a successful society is that it manages to sustain *through time* a host of different relationships, keeping each in accord with some standard of expectation, while containing all within the resources available, and developing all these standards in the process. . . . The making of a reasonably coherent personality is a task which few accomplish in a lifetime. And even those who do experience continual conflict between the demands of the various roles they play, as well as within each of their roles. (Vickers, 1984e, p. 180)

POLITICAL REGULATION

Changes at the individual level, essentially moral changes, were, Vickers argued, a necessary but not a sufficient requirement for a more stable future. The sum of individual behavior did not automatically aggregate up to the collective good. Human systems were by their nature different from natural ones and human governance the antithesis of the law of the jungle. In the jungle, natural selection prevailed and the strong dominated the weak. With the advent of human government, a new selector has been set up "in opposition to the State of Nature," in T. H. Huxley's phrase that Vickers never tired of quoting (Vickers, 1980, p. 14), with the capacity and the obligation to make judgments and to discriminate on the basis of ethical criteria. There was still a residual hope that deliberate human design would supplement or take over from a given social order.

The problems of political regulation confronting the modern industrialized world were, he believed, incomparably greater than those of two centuries earlier. Modern man was dependent on large scale organizations, whose costs in future must become both larger in total and more widespread. The need for deliberate human intervention was particularly great at the end of the 20th century, because so many dangerous linear trends were approaching their critical limits and threatening, if unchecked, to breed at enormous costs their own reversals. In these circumstances, conservative conceptions of the nature of government activity, which involved rolling back the expansionist state, were particularly inappropriate.

The major characteristic of the modern world that he identified was that the environment of every human being, especially in the industrialized West, had become far more an environment of other human beings than an environment of nature and correspondingly far harder for would-be autonomous people to bear with equanimity or to manipulate without conflict (Vickers, 1983, p. 87). Modern technology had created a highly interdependent world, for which the emphasis on personal autonomy and authenticity, ultimately derived from the Enlightenment, was peculiarly unsuited. The ongoing pace of technological change continued to turn what had been acts of God into "acts of man," to fuel rising expectations and thus to further burden the political process: "Increasing human power over the natural environment focuses human expectations on what man should do rather than on what nature will do and thus hugely expands the ethical dimension" (Vickers, 1973/1984f, p. 198). As numbers and interactions multiplied, the task of government became ever more difficult.

Because of great and growing interdependence, and the power of so many actors within the system to alter the social and natural environment, greater stability could only be achieved if there was a large degree of consensus:

> The limits to the stability of western democracies are set, as I believe, by the extent to which they share an appreciative system or compatible appreciative systems and by the aptness of those systems to interpret their contemporary experience, especially when its pattern is changing. (Vickers, 1983, pp. 45-46)

Vickers appears to doubt at times whether this consensus could come about spontaneously: "The political growing point of the world is the manufacture of consensus" (Vickers, 1983, p. 177). There may seem some disturbing implications here. As Scruton (1993) rightly observed, "A core experience of membership, once lost, cannot be recovered by conscription. It is not for the state to manufacture the deeper forms of loyalty, and the attempt to do so is inherently totalitarian" (p. 311). However, the kind of "manufacture" that Vickers had in mind appears to be the encouragement of a more appropriate set of standards, and of individual appreciative systems more appropriate for an interdependent world, not the sinister arts of the totalitarian state. The art of government consisted essentially in maintaining a set of standards "not tolerably unattainable or mutually inconsistent yet real enough and high enough to regulate a society capable of maintaining and constantly improving itself" (Blunden, 1984, p. 37).

The appreciative system, our "supreme social artifact" (Vickers, 1970/1984a, p. 49), was not wholly under human control. However, its content, its changes, and its pathologies were much the most important condition of our lives today and should rightly claim the greatest part of our attention, because the most conspicuous distinction between human societies and other kinds of systems was their capacity to generate and change the settings of their own systems.

The scale of political regulation that Vickers believed was required, necessitating as it did strong institutions and consensual support for government action to halt dangerous linear trends, effectively ruled out any option of a stable future along the lines of Gray's "post-modern liberal conservatism" that sees government "not as the pacemaker for any specific conception of progress, but instead as providing the framework within which different ways of life and styles of thought may compete in peaceful coexistence" (Gray, 1993, p. 315). Gray argued for limited government within the framework of a civil society, enshrining the principle of private property, which would act as an enabling device "whereby persons with radically discrepant goals and values can pursue them without resource to a collective decision-procedure which would, of necessity, be highly conflictual" (p. 315). This may be compared with Oakeshott's (1991) belief or hypothesis that

> governing is a specific and limited activity, namely the provision and custody of general rules of conduct, which are understood, not as plans for imposing substantive activities, but as instruments enabling people to pursue the activities of their own choice with the minimum frustration. (p. 424)

In Vickers's view, the ever-increasing power of man to alter the multiple social, political, and environmental systems on which human life depended, and the unintended consequences of these manifold alterations, precluded that degree of individual freedom of action if there was to be any hope of a stable future.

Strong government was not needed to achieve specific goals; indeed, Vickers rejected the prevailing view of organizations at all levels, including that of the state, as goal-seeking rather than relationship-maintaining entities. The strong government he believed necessary was not the familiar one of conviction politicians, described by Oakeshott (1991) as bent on turning "a private dream into a public and compulsory manner of living" (p. 426). More active government was needed, not to achieve goals but to avoid threats—a very different kind of activity. Human intervention was essential to halt the dangerous linear trends threatening relationships among human beings and between human beings and their natural milieu, before they reached critical limits. The dense environment in which the industrial epoch was enclosing the developed world, created as it now was by the largely unintended results of what everyone did, was becoming too unpredictable to live in and might soon become too unacceptable to live with. If it was to survive, he believed it would have to be controlled—that is, governed—on a scale and to a depth for which there were as yet neither the political institutions to achieve nor the cultural attitudes to accept (Vickers, 1956/1984c, pp. 55-56). The minimal changes, epistemological and ethical, which people 50 years hence would need to have absorbed if they were to enjoy a political and social order even as acceptable and stable as our own, were, he believed, daunting.

It was consequently, he suggested, Utopian to imagine that modern society could enjoy the traditional freedoms of conservative mythology. The individual in the industrialized West was a component in a rapidly increasing number of systems and subsystems. Systems, by definition, both enable—they allow people to do what they otherwise, unorganized, could not do—and constrain.

> "Free individuals," increasingly dependent on each other, were subject to increasing demands to share the commitments, accept the constraints and accord the trust required by the multiplying systems and subsystems to which they belonged and on which they wholly depended. (Vickers, 1983, p. xxvii)

He found "extraordinary" the "belief that the world can accord to its members increasing freedom from constraints, but still be sufficiently orderly to survive" (Vickers, 1983, p. 66).

If public institutions were effectively to provide the "machinery of deliberate control" needed to replace the "machinery of automatic control" (Vickers, 1983, p. 128) to manage limitations and generate more realistic expectations, the level of public confidence they enjoyed would need to increase dramatically. Vickers himself took an optimistic view of the capability of people in organizational or public roles to act in the public interest. He differed from Hayek (1976), who criticized, in *The Road to Serfdom*, the "dangerous idealists" who could not see that those who assumed a moral responsibility for collective decision making were inexorably driven into positions in which it was impossible to behave morally (p. 169), and he wrote to Adolph Lowe of the laissez-faire aspects of Hayek's later book, *The Political Order of a Free People*, that "it is uncanny in 1979 to hear these views being expounded" (Vickers, 1991, pp. 163-164). In spite of revelations after his death of the failure of public planning and public planners under the Soviet system, he would not have followed the influential Virginia Public Choice School to their conclusion that, in modern mass democracies, states tended overwhelmingly to service private interests rather than protect or promote the public good, a position adopted in his turn by Gray who describes the modern state as existing in practice to satisfy the private preferences of collusive interest groups (Gray, 1993, pp. 11-12). Two of Vickers's major works, *The Art of Judgment* and *Making Institutions Work*, examine the personal skills and the social process of organizational and public decision making and are based on a confidence in what he considered to be one of the proud achievements of Western civilization, that of making power accountable without emasculating it in the process (Vickers, 1979/1984d, p. 106). The "gigantic machine" of modern government operated, he believed, more efficiently and less corruptly than the much smaller public organizations had operated in the past (Vickers, 1983, pp. 74-75).

> In my experience public servants, whether in central or local government, are far more dedicated to the responsible performance of their job, less greedy for power, and more widely informed and concerned about the circumstances in which they are acting than the general run of those for whom they are providing service. (Vickers, 1980, p. 46)

The fact that the governed appeared so notably and so regrettably to have withdrawn their confidence from the governors was, he argued, due to their extravagant and conflicting expectations. It was bizarre that a huge institutional effort was required to deliver the "rights" that were demanded on every side, yet these institutions themselves had become as suspect, as hated even, as in the days of the *ancien régime* (Vickers, 1979/1984d, p. 98). There were, however, no biological or psychological reasons why mankind should not support organizations on the scale of which they have now come to depend, but it required an immense cultural change.

CONCLUSION

Geoffrey Vickers's contribution to political philosophy rests essentially on the quality of his conceptual framework. His development of the concept of the appreciative system as an explanatory model of historical change over time and his exploration of the self-reversing nature of linear developments are significant contributions to the philosophy of history. His concept of human organizations, including the state, as relationship-maintaining rather than goal-seeking entities, and his formulation of the consequences for human governance of the key distinction between human and natural systems, are both original and powerful.

In more practical terms, Vickers's contribution as a self-confessed professional was to think through the implications for personal and political behavior of modern human interdependence, of the ever-growing power of a multitude of actors to alter the systems on which they depend, and by the replacement of a natural environment by one made up largely of other people. His analysis of the political consequences of ever-advancing technological capability, inescapably increasing the load on the political process, makes a strong challenge to advocates of a return to limited government. The accuracy of his perception of the constraints necessarily imposed on individuals in a densely interconnected modern industrial society, where the power to alter or to damage is growing with every technological advance, will become steadily more apparent. His argument for the exercise of conscious human government, rather than reliance on the "automatic" regulators, will gain in force as it becomes clearer that we are approaching certain critical limits in the human and natural environments. The case for a new epistemology, incorporating systemic thinking appropriate to a world whose complex interactions are ever multiplying, will increasingly confront politicians and academics, as the unintended consequences of policies designed to achieve change in one department of government manifestly affect all the interlocking systems of which it forms part.

Particular aspects of Vickers's work have been taken up in the 12 years since his death by specialists in public administration, health policy, and systems analysis. However, his contribution to political philosophy and epistemology, a rare attempt to address what modern interdependence means for political activity and individual behavior, has been not so much rebutted as ignored. It should command much greater critical attention than it has yet received.

NOTES

1. If meliorism is, however, interpreted as the doctrine—intermediate between optimism and pessimism—that affirms that the world may be made better by rightly directed human effort, then Vickers is of course a convinced meliorist.

2. In 1967, the American historian Lynn White described Christianity, especially in its Western form, as "the most anthropocentric religion the world has seen" and blamed the medieval church for the problems of modern pollution (Thomas, 1984, pp. 22-23).

REFERENCES

Anderson, D. (Ed.). (1992). *The loss of virtue*. London: Social Affairs Unit.

Barker, D., Halman, L., & Vloet, A. (1992). *The European values study 1981-1990* (Summary Report). Tilburg, Netherlands: Gordon Cook Foundation for European Values Group.

Berlin, I. (1991). *The crooked timber of humanity*. London: Fontana.

Blunden, M. (1984). An intellectual journey. In Open Systems Group (Eds.), *The Vickers papers* (pp. 3-42). London: Harper & Row.

Davies, C. (1992). Moralization and demoralization: A moral explanation for changes in crime, disorder and social problems. In D. Anderson (Ed.), *The loss of virtue* (pp. 1-13). London: Social Affairs Unit.

Gray, J. (1993). *Post-liberalism: Studies in political thought*. London: Routledge & Kegan Paul.

Hayek, F. A. (1976). *The road to serfdom*. London: Routledge & Kegan Paul.

Hayek, F. A. (1979). *Law, legislation and liberty: A new statement of the liberal principles of justice and political economy. Vol. 3. The political order of a free people*. London: Routledge & Kegan Paul.

Minogue, K. (1993). Modes and modesty. In J. Norman (Ed.), *The achievement of Michael Oakeshott* (pp. 43-57). London: Duckworth.

Oakeshott, M. (1991). *Rationalism in politics and other essays*. Indianapolis, IN: Liberty Press.

Open Systems Group. (Eds.). (1984). *The Vickers papers*. London: Harper & Row.

Scruton, R. (1993). *The philosopher on Dover beach*. Manchester: Carcenet.

Selbourne, D. (1994). *The principle of duty*. London: Sinclair-Stevenson.

Spengler, O. (1919). *The decline of the West*. New York: Alfred A. Knopf.

Thomas, K. (1984). *Man and the natural world: Changing attitudes in England 1500-1800*. Harmondsworth: Penguin.

Toynbee, A. J. (1960). *A study of history* (abridgement by D. C. Somervell). London: Oxford University Press.

Vickers, G. (1965). *The art of judgment*. London: Harper & Row.

Vickers, G. (1980). *Responsibility, its sources and limits*. Seaside, CA: Intersystems Publications.

Vickers, G. (1983). *Human systems are different*. London: Harper & Row.

Vickers, G. (1984a). A classification of systems. In Open Systems Group (Eds.), *The Vickers papers* (pp. 43-49). London: Harper & Row. (Original work published 1970)

Vickers, G. (1984b). Ecology, planning and the American dream. In Open Systems Group (Eds.), *The Vickers papers* (pp. 135-151). London: Harper & Row. (Original work published 1963)

Vickers, G. (1984c). The end of free fall. In Open Systems Group (Eds.), *The Vickers papers* (pp. 55-67). London: Harper & Row. (Original work published 1956)

Vickers, G. (1984d). The future of morality. In Open Systems Group (Eds.), *The Vickers papers* (pp. 97-109). London: Harper & Row. (Original work published 1979)

Vickers, G. (1984e). The management of conflict. In Open Systems Group (Eds.), *The Vickers papers* (pp. 177-193). London: Harper & Row. (Original work published 1972)

Vickers, G. (1984f). Values, norms and policies. In Open Systems Group (Eds.), *The Vickers papers* (pp. 194-204). London: Harper & Row. (Original work published 1973)

Vickers, G. (1984g). The weakness of Western culture. In Open Systems Group (Eds.), *The Vickers papers* (pp. 78-96). London: Harper & Row. (Original work published 1977)

Vickers, J. (Ed.). (1991). *Rethinking the future: The correspondence between Geoffrey Vickers and Adolph Lowe*. London: Transaction.

2

Institutions and Human Relations

A Search for Stability in a Changing World

NEVIL JOHNSON

Recent emphasis on performance and output measures in public sector reform in the United Kingdom rests on assumptions of purposeful rationality and a view of man as essentially goal seeking. Geoffrey Vickers's conception of public institutions as concerned with the regulation of relationships rather than the pursuit of goals challenges the implicit downgrading of the qualitative aspects of institutions that is associated with this approach to reform. There is a need to qualify individualism by acknowledging dependence on the social context of regulation.

If, metaphorically speaking, we carried out an exit poll of those leaving what in modern jargon might be called public service delivery points and asked what was wrong with government today, most likely the majority of them would tell us that government too often fails to provide the services they need, is inefficient, and does not produce enough in relation to the costs imposed on the taxpayer. A similar complaint might also be expected about a large number of institutions outside the sphere of government narrowly defined—the health services, the universities, the schools, the trade unions, and even the churches. The burden of the complaint is that the output is not good enough, the results of the work carried on in the organizations or institutions in question are not up to expectations or are just plain unsatisfactory. Some of this dissatisfaction no doubt reflects a long-standing and widespread discontent with relatively high taxation and the feeling that citizens have lost control over what happens to much of what they earn. But at the same time it also expresses in a forcible way the dominance of economic and instrumental criteria in the collective consciousness of most or all of the advanced industrial societies. Goods and services are produced to satisfy needs and demands; they should be produced as efficiently as possible, that is, on a basis that maximizes output in relation to resource inputs, and they should offer customers, or users, what they want to have. We have become pragmatically oriented societies through and through, deeply committed to the maximization of individual consumer satisfactions, an overall objective justified by appeal to a profoundly individualistic ethic. Despite its well-known shortcomings, Benthamite utilitarianism seems to have triumphed: In our secularized society the only widely acknowledged aim is to maximize the happiness, welfare, and prosperity of its individual members. Concurrently, however, the belief that the preferences of consumers can be added up so that we can form a judgment of how much progress has been made on the road toward the utilitarian Utopia has weakened, and it may even have evaporated. Instead, there is simply acknowledgment of an infinity of individual wants and demands, and the success of the system of production as a whole is judged by the extent to which the individuals it serves appear to be content with its outputs.

This evolution of value perceptions is vividly expressed in the language nowadays used to describe and characterize public services and the sphere of public administration. Two of the key words frequently appearing in British comments on public sector reform are *performance* and *output*. Clerks, administrators, managers, teachers, policemen, and so on are all urged to improve their performance, and the organizations in which they work are told to increase their outputs, preferably for constant resource inputs. I shall return later to the obsession with outputs that appears to characterize the contemporary British discussion of public service reform and adaptation. At this stage, however, it is important to stress the rationalistic foundation for this talk of outputs. What it rests on is the conviction that human beings are essentially governed or even determined by an urge toward purpose fulfilment: They exist to discern and achieve purposes and objectives. The link back to utilitarian individualism is then made. The purposes or goals pursued are seen primarily in terms of the satisfactions to be gained from specific acts of consumption: We want certain things, we get them, we are then (it is hoped) "satisfied." But such satisfaction is always strictly transitory and new demands constantly emerge. The modern dynamic market economy represents, so it is argued by many, the best way of coping with this state of affairs.

This contemporary view of the preeminent role of purpose fulfilment is a far cry from Geoffrey Vickers's understanding of human motivation and of the manner in which it relates to varied patterns of social cooperation. In a letter written in 1982, he complained that for nearly 20 years he had not come across any book on administration "which took seriously the primacy of human motivation, still less one which questioned the rational model of action which insisted that no action at human level was possible unless it was explicable as the pursuit of a purpose."[1] There could hardly be a more explicit rejection of one of the leading shibboleths of the present time or a more forceful challenge to what is an increasingly impoverished account of social behavior and cooperation. Moreover, Vickers goes on in the passage just quoted to comment: "The attack on rationality and purpose or rather the effort to place these in relation to more subtle forms of human regulation is a mammoth task."[2]

These remarks about the dangers inherent in allowing the category of purposeful rationality to dominate our thinking about individual behavior as well as social relationships and the varied ways in which they can be organized and sustained may be taken as a suitable starting point for the discussion of Vickers's ideas about institutions that follows. It is a truism that the 20th century has seen most societies throughout the world exposed to an unprecedented rate of change that has accelerated during the past 50 years. In many of them, and most notably the industrialized countries of the West, such change has in general been welcomed, although it also often stimulates anxieties and even hostility in those adversely affected by it. The forces making for change are many and varied, but foremost among them is the immense growth in scientific knowledge that has occurred and the accompanying technological revolution. This has, in turn, had profound consequences for all forms of industrial production and for those interconnected national economies that today constitute the world economy. But alongside what might be called objective factors driving the rate of change, there are social, psychological, and moral elements that function sometimes as causes but often enough appear as effects of the process of change itself. Increasingly, the source of moral legitimacy has been found in the claim to individual autonomy, while society has then been conceived merely as a matrix of relationships acceptable so long as they are held to serve the demands of the individuals constituting such a society. Not surprisingly, in this context, there has been in most Western societies (and indeed in many others too, for rapid economic development is by no means confined to the Western sphere) an unparalleled rise in individual expectations: Most people have, in fact, become better off materially and they expect this improvement to continue. A further crucial and by now very visible consequence of this rapid rate of change is the threat of ecological disaster that it presents. For the first time in their history, human beings have become aware that finite natural resources are being depleted at an alarming rate and that their own productive activities are having an unknown range of negative effects on the natural environment. What many want to see as social progress is, therefore, accompanied by serious doubts about how much longer it can now continue.[3]

VICKERS AND INDIVIDUALISM

All these aspects of the movement of change in the present century were familiar enough to Vickers and preoccupied him greatly, especially in his later years. His starting point was indeed the ubiquity and incalculability of change. Human societies and their steersmen have to navigate in turbulent seas, they are not sure whither they are bound, and the instruments on which they generally have to rely are for the most part unreliable or even useless.[4] Nevertheless, Vickers was by no means passive in the conclusions he drew from this diagnosis of the human condition. In his view, there was no doubt that an outdated and inappropriate notion of individualism was propelling forward the process of change in the industrial societies of the West. Although change could not be halted (and indeed it would be futile to make any such effort), it was urgently necessary to make the process less blind. This could only happen, so he argued, if the underlying individualism were tamed and qualified. But how could this be done? Fundamentally, Vickers found the answer to this question in the possibility that individuals could be brought to recognize far more fully and more intelligently their need for, and dependence on, norms of behavior appropriate to civilized social cooperation. This, in turn, implied the existence of institutions in which such norms are embodied. Thus his main intellectual preoccupation was always with the kind of relationships that should be sought between individuals, and the patterns of social order and cooperation that they need just as much for their survival as for the satisfaction of their material and emotional wants. Our cardinal problem, so he believed, was to find ways of holding our societies together in something like a condition of dynamic balance, allowing the impulses of individualism to be used beneficially and yet at the same time containing them within a framework that recognizes our mutual interdependence.

More will have to be said later about Vickers's understanding of institutions as the necessary means of social regulation and about how this relates to what he had to say about human systems and systems theory. At this stage, the focus needs to remain on individuals. Any social theorist who seeks to distinguish forms of social life—institutions, organizations, established practices, traditions, and so on—from the individuals whose behavior or conduct actually constitutes such forms needs to have some account of individuals as such if his theorizing is to make progress.[5] It cannot be claimed that Vickers presented a clearly defined or fully elaborated view of individual motivation and what we might call human nature. Nevertheless, he made plenty of remarks throughout his writings about what people do, the roles they perform, and the behavioral characteristics they reveal. Additionally, it is possible to deduce from some of his more extended pieces of analysis, and in particular from what he had to say about appreciative judgment, some of his conclusions about the qualities of individuals. Such evidence suggests that on the whole he took a reasonably hopeful and even optimistic view of human beings, notwithstanding the fact that he was often pessimistic about their capacity to learn from experience and to impose limitations on their own selfish demands. For Vickers was convinced through his own varied experience in military service, law and administration, and the business of coal production, that human beings are capable of putting on one side their immediate self-interest and of joining together in shared undertakings once they begin to grasp the reasons for doing so. This is consistent with his belief that human beings are rational, but in a nontechnical sense. This has nothing much to do with rationality as encountered generally in economic theory or in several versions of utilitarian ethics: Man as a calculator in search of the continuous satisfaction of wants and the realization of purposes was not a construction that Vickers found either plausible or attractive, as already noted. What he seems to have meant by *rational* as a term qualifying human nature was that human beings are capable of acting reasonably and of distinguishing fact from value in the making of choices and moral judgments. The whole argument of *The Art of Judgment*, probably Vickers's best remembered work, depends on something like this assumption.

APPRECIATIVE JUDGMENT

Let us recall for a moment the core element in that work. It is the notion of *appreciative judgment*, the term Vickers uses to describe the mental activity we engage in when we seriously consider alternative courses of action and their potential outcomes.[6] Of course, it is possible to envisage conditions under which the scope of appreciative judgment is severely circumscribed. For example, we can imagine people who prefer to reach decisions on impulse, leaving the course of action to be followed dependent on how they feel at the moment when something has to be done. Or, alternatively, we may try to reduce our discretion to a minimum by subjecting ourselves and a range of possible actions to a clearly defined code of rules. Faced with what looks like a choice, we would then look at the rule book and see what it says (or purports to say). Yet another possibility is to try to avoid decisions and choices, perhaps to look to other people to act on our behalf. However, although the scope for reducing the burdens of judgment may be considerable, it is impossible for normal human beings to escape from these burdens altogether, and this is particularly so when they are working together within some framework of social cooperation. In these circumstances, matters are constantly coming up that call for a choice to be made and a decision to be taken. It is Vickers's contention that what then happens is best characterized as an effort at appreciative judgment.

There are two principal constituents of the process of appreciative judgment as it is described by Vickers. One is the attempt to determine what the facts are. What this implies is that we need to know what the situation is, what the conditions are prevailing in it, what claims on resources are at issue, what demands are being presented, and so on. It is true that in contexts of the kind presented abstractly here it is always possible to problematize the notion of "fact" and so to call into question the very possibility of saying anything reasonably objective and accurate about a given state of affairs. Vickers did not share that negative and sceptical position, influenced no doubt in part by his experience as a lawyer and his favorable assessment of the achievements and potentialities of a range of fact-finding and policy analysis committees within the sphere of British government.[7] He believed that it was possible as a rule to present and elucidate the facts relating to complex problems, even though our knowledge might on many occasions be so deficient as to force us to qualify our findings as incomplete or uncertain. Yet it is rare that a satisfactory decision in a situation of any complexity can be made simply on the basis of the "facts." When the position has been described and perhaps even quantified, it will be apparent that there are several options on hand and that any decision or choice might in principle combine elements of some or all of them. What is more, this or that decision will affect those within its effective range differently, and recognition of this "fact" immediately suggests the need for moral discriminations to be made. So along with the effort to decide what the facts are, there goes the necessity of entering into a consideration of values and the weighing of conflicting claims on our attention and support. Facts and values are two sides of the same coin and appear in all judgments on human relationships. But there is nothing arbitrary about the conclusions we reach on questions of value, or at any rate not if we set about reaching these conclusions in a sensible and reflective way. Vickers, whose early experience of life took place in the closing years of the Victorian age, had no doubt that it is possible to justify our normative conclusions, perhaps not in an ultimate or absolute sense, but at least in terms of being able to provide intelligible and persuasive reasons for concluding that one moral or political choice is better than another.

What Vickers said about appreciative judgment can be evaluated from two different perspectives. First, it can be seen as an attempt to set out what mental processes the individual must engage in when he embarks on an act of policy-making and has to take a decision of policy. At first sight, this language seems to be relevant only to large organizations and weighty decisions on matters that deeply affect the lives of many people. It is true that Vickers's account of appreciative judgment was intended to apply to complex public organizations, a point underlined by the amount of evidence drawn from the sphere of governmental activity that is cited in support of his analysis as well as by the subtitle to *The Art of Judgment*, namely *A Study of Policy Making*. Nevertheless, the notion of appreciation that he developed is general rather than specific in its applications. It claims to model processes of fact finding and the weighing of competing moral claims that any normal individual is bound to engage in once he recognizes that a serious choice has to be made and that it is necessary to go in one direction rather than another. Thus the theory of appreciative judgment comes close to being a contribution to the psychology of individual decision making, an account in general terms of the characteristics of decision taking by individuals.[8]

The alternative way of seeing the theory is to treat it as an account of how individuals regulate their lives in association with others. Vickers believed that a society of Robinson Crusoes was a fanciful construction. Individuals live together in social groupings, they need and recognize social bonds, they often wish to pursue their objectives jointly with each other, and they have a capacity to adopt and practice many different roles in society. The regulation of social life is a continuing and indispensable requirement, and much of this is achieved by the processes of appreciative judgment. The components of appreciative judgment imply, at least in some degree, shared experiences, a common language, and purposes that are also shared or compatible with each other. Thus it may be argued that in the theory of appreciative judgment Vickers is spelling out some of the implications of our need for a regulated coexistence. Moreover, he makes it abundantly clear in many passages that he just does not believe that human beings exist as isolated goal-seeking Robinson Crusoes, no matter how powerful has been the emotional and moral impact of this image during the past two centuries and longer. At every step we find that what we do or propose to do depends for its very feasibility on the presence of conditions that others have helped to produce and are sustaining. Equally, it is not so much goals that we pursue as the maintenance of relationships: "The goals we seek are changes in our relations or in our opportunities for relating; but the bulk of our activity consists in the 'relating' itself."[9] Far from taking the isolated individual as our starting point—be he hero or downtrodden and oppressed potential rebel—we ought as a matter of sober realism to begin with our interdependence and the inescapability of social regulation. It is into that context that individuals with their private aims and ambitions should be set. It then becomes possible to recognize how important appreciative judgment is as a method of carrying forward patterns of social regulation in a civilized and discriminating way.

There are plenty of reasons for concluding that Vickers wanted his notion of appreciative judgment to be understood primarily in terms of the second of the possibilities just outlined. He had had in his own life so much experience of what he saw as dependence on others and of the debts he owed to them that he found the model of the aggressively independent "doer" quite implausible. Not that this view implied a depreciation of self-reliance, independence of mind, and a readiness to assume responsibility for what one is doing. He fully accepted the force of the modern preference for individual autonomy and was keen to see people accepting responsibility for their own lives. But the individualism that he favored differed from that of the familiar utilitarian tradition in acknowledging from the outset our dependence on a social context of regulation that we actually need. Nor was this context of regulation anything like what is provided by Hobbes's contract of government. In a sense that was the social bond (or bondage as Vickers might have suggested[10]) reduced to its bare essentials: the means of preventing us from harming each other. But for Vickers regulation was a richer, although looser, concept referring to something much more like a multitiered structure of interdependences, many of them arising naturally from the ties established by the fact that there is so little that we can really do alone. Nor was regulation something to be feared, even though it could take oppressive forms. Vickers regularly used the term in a sense equivalent to something like adjustment, mutual adaptation, responsiveness to external signals. He did not see regulation as always to be equated with an externally generated set of rules, but much more as a continuous process of establishing and maintaining order in societies and in the relationships between individuals. This is so even in those contexts, for example, the production of goods for sale in a market, in which we tend to assume that everything is driven by the final goal, that is, the successful production and disposal of the goods in question. All organized social life reveals patterns of relationships that those involved are likely to wish to maintain, notwithstanding the particular substantive ends pursued in such contexts.

INSTITUTIONS

Both in *The Art of Judgment,* and later in *Making Institutions Work,* Vickers seeks to put what he has to say about appreciative judgment and policy-making into the framework of regulated social life. This means that he has to talk about institutions, and indeed in the title of the second work just mentioned he specifically invokes the idea of institutions and arouses expectations that the matter will be explored in some depth. In truth, however, there remains something elusive about his idea of institutions and what he meant by the term, a point that will be pursued further below. In his earlier life, long before he had the time and opportunity for sustained reflection and writing, he had experienced institutions in many concrete forms. There was the army during the First World War, a disciplined and hierarchical structure in which, nevertheless, individual soldiers depended greatly for their lives and mental equilibrium on mutual support. There was later the experience of a firm of solicitors and of the complex legal problems in the commercial sphere that the practicing lawyer has to try to solve. This can only be achieved when people with the requisite professional skills and appropriate knowledge of the circumstances cooperate in making the right kinds of appreciative judgment. During the Second World War, Vickers had further experience of complex administrative networks, and this was enriched still further after the war when he assumed important responsibilities in the management of the newly established National Coal Board. Nor was this by any means the limit of his varied personal experience of institutional contexts. Through his involvement in medical research and the organizations supporting it, he became familiar with the varied conditions on which the successful pursuit of improved techniques of treatment, especially in relation to mental health, as well as basic medical knowledge, depend. So there was in Vickers's own career plenty of experience of specific institutions and their operating conditions. Yet this is all rather muted when he comes to write of institutions and to describe and analyze them. Certainly, he often emphasizes the ubiquitousness of institutions and affirms on many occasions that the modern world has witnessed an inexorable rise in the number of institutions engaged in necessary tasks of regulation. Our world, he asserts repeatedly, is densely organized and becoming more so:

> We must therefore accept, at least in our society as it now is, an inherent drive towards unlimited institutional growth, and we must accept it not as an aberration or a peculiar disease of bureaucracy, but as an essential element in the dynamics of the system.[11]

However, there remains something elusive, even abstract, about what he has to say about institutions.

This can be illustrated by referring to passages in both *The Art of Judgment* and *Making Institutions Work*. In chapter 9 of the former, entitled "Institutions as Dynamic Systems," he proceeds at first by simply offering a long list of institutions that illustrates the diversity within the category. But almost immediately he makes this remark:

> Lawyers will be interested in this variety of form, economists in this diversity of function; but sociologically, the significant differences are fewer in number, different in character and less in importance. The most striking feature of all these institutions, sociologically, is their similarity. For they are all dynamic systems, dependent for their continuance on the regulation of relations, internal and external, functional and metabolic, such as I have described in various contexts.[12]

There then follows a summary of five dimensions in terms of which organizations may be described, inspired by a definition of organization taken from a then fairly recent book by C. H. Waddington.[13] These dimensions are presented in abstract terms and are intended to enable us to characterize institutions from different perspectives as dynamic systems. No doubt they succeed in this to a limited extent, as illustrated by some of the examples that Vickers briefly deploys. The approach to roughly the same phenomena in *Making Institutions Work* is not all that different. He begins with a discussion of the rise of the individualist and his subsequent demise in an inexorably more interdependent world. This environment is characterized by ever greater density of institutional provision. But this, in turn, prompts resentment and alienation: People want the benefits that all kinds of institutions are expected to provide, but at the same time they kick against the constraints and costs imposed by those very institutions. This is followed by a chapter devoted to institutional and personal roles from which it is not easy to extract a clear line of argument, although Vickers appeared to believe that we have developed a capacity for institutional design and innovation that may have made it easier to reconcile or resolve some of the conflicts that arise between institutional role-playing and personal roles. This line of thought does not, however, sit too comfortably with the point he also makes about the continuous extension of ethical claims, a development that simultaneously may involve a call for new institutional constraints, and an affirmation that individuals should be free to decide for themselves what they will or will not do. This (the second) part of the book concludes with the chapter entitled "Of Bonds and Bondage," the theme of which is that advanced societies are going to have to accept more "bonds" and that much will have to be done if the public is to be educated into appreciating that this need not portend a slide into "bondage." There are grim overtones here and Vickers does not disguise his conviction that the benefits of membership in society can only remain available and reasonably secure so long as we accept the increasing constraints derived from membership. But to some extent the clouds lift as he then moves on to a discussion of the various ways in which conflict can be managed and channeled into useful relationships, and of the role of the educator in building up better understanding of the problems and dilemmas we face. In these directions Vickers seems to perceive at least some real prospects of helping "to make institutions work."

For a theorist who appeared to set great store by institutions, there does seem to be a certain lack of focus, a blurring at the edges, in Vickers's treatment of them. He does not say much about their genesis and evolution, nor does he consider in any detail the implications of the fact that institutions, despite their proliferation, appear now to have lost much of their capacity to bind those nominally subject to them. Indeed, he pays little attention explicitly to the normative functions of institutions, including the possibility that they are the only means known to us for the handing down from one generation to the next of *regulations* in the broad sense he gave to that term. Nor does he explore in detail what kind of distinctions can and should be drawn between institutions and other forms of social organization or cooperation through which a wide range of purposes is served. This too would be an important issue in any developed theory of institutions. So all in all it is perhaps not too severe a judgment to suggest that Vickers often appeared to approach institutions almost like someone primarily concerned with management, that is, with organizational design and effective ways of getting things done. Yet we know too that there is abundant evidence that Vickers really did take institutions seriously. He never falls into that peculiarly British vice of treating them as "machinery,"[14] mechanical devices to be designed and redesigned according to criteria of functional suitability. He had no illusions either about the limitations of a process- and goal-oriented approach to management, and he passionately believed that people are both deeply concerned by the terms on which objectives are being pursued and attach great importance to the values and relationships that are embodied in the institutions of their society. How, therefore, can we best explain a certain haziness in Vickers's presentation of the role and character of institutions, and of the challenge to which they are exposed?

SYSTEMS THINKING

At first sight there is much that is surprising and puzzling in Vickers's failure to be particularly explicit about what institutions are actually like, what they do and the effects they have, how they grow and decay, and so on. After all, he was a widely read man with a deep knowledge of literature and a great sensitivity toward poetry, a fact testified to by his choice of epigraphs and introductory quotations. He was also interested in history and acutely aware of the evolution of the culture and society of which he was part. In addition, he had a keen interest in modern sociological writing, although here his concern seems to have been less with the great historically minded founders of sociology as a distinctive branch of social inquiry than with those who preferred to apply to social forms and relationships a more abstract mode of analysis. This remark offers a clue to a resolution of the puzzle. Vickers became concerned with the broader problems of social analysis chiefly as a result of his preoccupation in the 1930s with the effects of worldwide economic depression, and in particular with what this might portend for the future prospects of liberal societies based on market economies and private property. In the forefront of his mind were questions about the functioning of the economy and why this had gone so seriously wrong. Partly under the influence of his German émigré friend Adolph Lowe,[15] who was in a sense an early exponent of something rather like a theory of the social market economy, Vickers became convinced that economic issues and the economic organization of society cannot be separated from a more comprehensive understanding of how society is structured and fits together. In particular he began to recognize the great importance of information flows in the fashioning of social relationships and of the innumerable ways in which information is generated, exchanged, and used. It was influences of this kind that led Vickers to take an interest in the concept of system and gradually to give it a key position in his thinking. By the time this happened, well on into the 1950s, the notion of system had been firmly established in sociological theory and more generally in quantitative social analysis. In addition there had been considerable advances, most notably in the United States, in the development of a body of generalized "systems theory." This too had a big impact on social scientific analysis, and Vickers seems to have concluded that here at last was a way of thinking that gave him at least some of the purchase he was anxious to secure on the problems that he believed to be crucial to humanity.

Another factor in this context that influenced Vickers was the emergence of cybernetics as something that looked like a theory or science of communication and information exchange. He came to believe that this too was an intellectual development that could provide models that might, with advantage, be applied to the analysis of social relationships. This interest in cybernetics and information theory tied in with his concern for medical research, especially in the fields of psychology and psychiatry. This, in turn, was a reflection of what we might term rather loosely his scientific interests, especially in biology. He had no training or experience in the natural and experimental sciences, but he was deeply fascinated by their achievements and utterly convinced that we need to grasp fully the profound implications of the progress of science and technology for social life and organization. Indeed, Vickers was sure that it was precisely the possibilities offered by the advance of scientific knowledge that explained the unprecedented rate of change in our societies and the attendant prospects of instability and even breakdown. It is not surprising that Vickers had no sympathy for the idea of "two cultures," so widely cited as a problem in Britain at the end of the 1950s. Although having no doubts about the crucial importance of the humanities and the values transmitted by these branches of knowledge and inquiry, he believed it to be self-evident that we should take on board scientific ways of thinking and of doing things. The two cultures, humanistic and scientific, have to be fused into a single culture if we are to understand our world and become capable of tackling its problems. Perhaps it was because this need seemed to be more generally accepted in the United States that Vickers came to feel in later life that he had there a more sympathetic audience for his ideas than he had in Britain. In return, there can be little doubt that his own thinking about the management of complex societies began to reflect the influence of the systems theorizing and systems language that had become so firmly established in American social science, although it must be said that his own prose style remained serenely free of the jargon so often associated with such approaches.

The overall effect of these influences in most of Vickers's later writing is to work in favor of a transition from problem stating and illustrative example on the one hand to the invocation of systems and subsystems on the other. This can be seen in *Making Institutions Work,* where what are often vivid examples of a serious challenge or difficulty are followed by diagnoses and recommendations expressed abstractly and in general terms. Something similar happens in many more of his published collections of articles and lectures, although this effect is less marked in *The Art of Judgment*, partly because, so it seems to me, the concept of appreciative judgment that he expounds there cannot easily be presented in the language of systems without serious damage to the elements in it. In relation to the continuing relevance of Vickers's ideas, this is a point of great importance, as will be argued again below. There are, however, some serious limitations affecting the notion of system and its many forms and applications, and Vickers did not appear to be fully aware of them. These difficulties are rooted in the fact that systems language is abstract and analogical, suited to model building rather than to description and explanation in specific circumstances and conditions. A system or subsystem is an abstraction from a multifaceted reality, and so necessarily is everything that might then be postulated about its internal and external relationships and about the conditions under which it survives. It is not surprising that the notion of a system has been most persuasively developed and applied in various mechanical and biological contexts: Here the quantities involved, the forces at work, and the paths of change or evolution can be most precisely measured, stated, and related one to another. But to apply the model to society, to social behavior and relationships, is to make a very big jump and to take for granted many assumptions that can reasonably be questioned. It is not obvious, for example, that the principle of uniformity of phenomena applies in human social life, and it is by no means clear that there is any conception of human will and choice that can be reconciled in a conclusive way with the acceptance of systems as social realities. This position does not involve a denial of the usefulness and conditional validity of systems language in relation to many contexts and problems in social life. It does imply, however, that we have to recognize that the language allows us to construct analogies and to suggest ways of thinking about social interactions rather than to engage in comprehensive description and specific explanatory judgments. The degree of abstraction required by the notion of system and its application to actual social relationships and experience is what chiefly qualifies its values and reliability when our concern is primarily with diagnosis and recommendation. It is curious that a thinker like Vickers, who was after all in so many respects a moralist in his approach to the understanding and analysis of society, should have become so enthusiastic for an intellectual approach that seeks to subsume the contingent and specific within the recurrent and general, and must logically put something like a question mark over the reality of human agency.

The conclusion to be drawn from the preceding discussion is that, despite the prominence he gave to institutions in his efforts to grasp what he often called the consequences of membership, Vickers did not actually succeed in providing a completely satisfactory account of institutions, still less a theory explaining their role in social life and practical importance. Instead, institutions tend to be assimilated to organizations in society generally, and sometimes to recede into abstractly specified patterns of social relationships. Yet despite these shortcomings, his consideration of the institutional context of modern society does contain some original elements that continue to have a claim on our attention and to be relevant to current arguments about the principles that should apply in the sphere of public administration. It is these matters that will be looked at now in the concluding part of this article.

RELATIONSHIPS AND INTERDEPENDENCE

The most enduring elements in Vickers's treatment of institutions are to be found in *The Art of Judgment,* despite the fact that the book is ostensibly concerned more directly with forms of activity than with structures for action. Something has already been said about appreciation and appreciative judgment, and we shall not go over the same ground again now. But it will be recalled that Vickers goes beyond an account of judgment in policy-making and argues that most public institutions are in the first place concerned with the regulation of relationships rather than with allowing people to pursue specific goals. In reaching this conclusion Vickers drew heavily on what he had experienced in the British system of administration in relation to problem solving and the taking of policy decisions. He had observed that typically there is (or there was[16]) a process of "fact finding," an attempt to determine what the position is, how it is changing, and what difficulties it presents. In relation to very complex matters, this process of fact finding might be entrusted to a body like a royal commission that takes and sifts evidence. But something very like the inquiry of a royal commission into the facts is carried out by individuals confronted with the need to take a decision of policy: They too try to reach a judgment on the character of the circumstances surrounding the matter on which a decision has to be taken. Subsequent to the effort to establish the facts of a situation, there follows an evaluation of the options on offer. This focuses attention on the questions of value that are presented by the decision to be made, and in particular on the likely consequences for a given structure of relationships of a decision that, because it is setting guidelines for the future and charting the direction ahead, has to be regarded as one of policy. But Vickers is here not merely delineating a process within an organization, the steps we might take to get from A to B. He sees appreciative judgment as occurring within a wider network of social relationships that ensure that much that is going on outside any particular institution is brought into the process of appreciation itself. At any rate, in open and democratically ruled societies institutions are rarely "black boxes," sealed off from the environment round about them. Instead, each is involved in a continuing process of the regulation of relationships that has ripple effects throughout the society. To participate in the formation and exercise of appreciative judgment is a necessary aspect of human associations intended to facilitate the pursuit of shared aims. Through such an engagement individuals become obligated to each other; they take on the bonds that are the price of membership in their society. Thus it follows that institutions have both practical and normative justifications: We need them for practical reasons and for the maintenance of tolerably stable social relationships, but additionally they are the means of our own moral development. Without the support of practices and values acknowledged in the institutional structure of a society, there can only be *anomie* and confusion. Although it remains doubtful whether Vickers discerned the full significance of institutions as concrete social phenomena for his own analysis of the challenges facing modern society, he did nevertheless recognize more sharply than most of his generation the ever-increasing de facto importance of our interdependence and the increasing tension between that state of affairs and deeply rooted habits of individualist moral judgment that played up to the ideal of individual autonomy. There is surely a sad irony in the fact that in many parts of the Western industrialized world, including both Britain and the United States, the years since his death have witnessed a reinforcement of such anomic individualism rather than any movement in a contrary direction. One of his major problems— the price of membership—is certainly still with us.

The contemporary relevance of Vickers's ideas is apparent in another way. He saw policy-making far more in terms of the continuous adjustment of relationships than of goal achievement. This does not mean that he ignored the extent to which so many forms of social organization are intended to facilitate the pursuit of objectives, whether by individuals or through collective action that they make possible. But he also recognized as crucial the fact that we associate with each other in particular ways—*this* way rather than *that*—and this always runs in parallel with the pursuit of substantive goals. The experience of how societies cohere points to the conclusion that it is the relationships that hold us together far more than the goals to be achieved, and often enough these relationships (which will themselves change over time) do in some degree at least displace the goals ostensibly set for the organization.[17] The persuasiveness of this judgment of the relatively greater importance of institutional relationships as compared with goal fulfilment is easily demonstrated by appeal to the history of social institutions of many different kinds. Whether we are considering political institutions such as a cabinet or a parliamentary select committee, legal institutions such as a court of appeal or a magistrate's court, educational institutions such as a university or a comprehensive school, advisory institutions such as a royal commission, administrative institutions such as the civil service or some other public bureaucratic organization, in all these and countless other cases what is crucial to the definition of the institution is how it operates rather than what it actually achieves. For it is by establishing relationships that an institution makes a contribution to the ongoing regulation of society. And all serious arguments about institutions are for this reason ultimately arguments about changing the relationships that they sustain.[18]

PROBLEMS OF PUBLIC SECTOR REFORM

This view of the matter was once perfectly familiar in Britain, for example, even though it may not always have been expressed exactly in these terms.

However, if we cast an eye on contemporary preoccupations in administrative reform—or public management improvement as it might now be called—we find that they are concerned chiefly with ways and means of improving performance, securing a larger output, and generally raising the standards of efficiency. Thinking on these matters is overwhelmingly goal oriented, and procedural values—the terms on which relationships are conducted and sustained—are as a result often downgraded. There are, of course, certain points to be made in favor of this approach. It is indeed true that we need to consider carefully the efficiency of public services and sometimes the question whether they should be provided by public bodies at all; it is probable that most of us are concerned more directly with what standard of service we actually receive than with what sometimes appear to be recondite matters of procedure; and there is indeed no reason why those who work for public institutions—officials of one sort or another—should be shielded from some of the measures intended to improve operational performance that would be applied as a matter of course in private organizations, that is, in industry and commerce.

Nevertheless, there is a danger of throwing out the baby with the bathwater if we pursue too thoughtlessly the attempt to raise the performance and output of public organizations by applying models taken over from the sphere of the market. Public services are so designated precisely because they consist of goods and services that cannot be provided by the market, either because they are in the nature of public goods or because we choose to have them provided by public authorities according to nonmarket criteria. Under such conditions moral and political values enter into the relevant public services from the start: Entitlements are at issue and there are legitimate expectations to fulfill. This means that in many and perhaps most public services there is what might be called a relational element: A service is offered or even something like a product supplied, but what is crucial is this relational element, in other words, the manner in which the citizen-user is treated when drawing on the service in question. For example, we will generally expect respect for the principle of equal treatment to be maintained and a proper check made on whether the conditions of entitlement have been met. Equally important is the expectation that public services are ultimately subject to political accountability: If things go wrong, we feel entitled to complain and to expect corrective action. Such conditions have many further implications for the terms on which officials in the public sector carry out their activities and so both for relationships inside the administrative system as well as between officials and the people they serve.

It would be an exaggeration to assert that the advocacy of a managerialist agenda in the current program of public sector reform in Britain has already seriously damaged the prospects of maintaining in public institutions the kind of values to which Vickers attached great importance in all his writing on public management. But there are plenty of signs of a readiness to downgrade the importance of those qualitative aspects of public service provision that have to do with relationships in favor of more emphasis on the amount, costs, and quality of the outputs as such. As an illustration of this approach the tendency to see education at all levels from school to university in terms of purchasers and providers and by so doing to ignore the fact that education consists first and foremost of certain kinds of relationship between teachers and those who are taught may be cited. Another example is to be found in the piecemeal process in train since the early 1980s by which local authorities have gradually lost functions (often to non-elected special purpose organizations) or been required to contract out to the private sector services previously provided directly. There may be—and, indeed, often are—efficiency gains to be made by the use of such methods. But in parallel, there is the political loss involved in the attenuation of democratic government at the local level and the risks to service quality and coverage as a consequence of the dispersion and fragmentation of responsibilities.

These trends have, of course, wide political implications. In any system of responsible government so long established as that of Britain, public interest and concern are often focused on the conduct of those in office. They serve in some degree as lightning conductors, picking up the anger and criticism discharged by people who believe that they have grounds for complaint about the scale and quality of the "outputs" of the public sector. The logic of the call for more and more public services to be provided "as if they were marketable" is that the range of accountability of elected politicians has to be reduced. Instead, if anybody at all is to be held accountable, it will have to be the executive agencies themselves. Yet in reality this is hardly practicable and the risk is, therefore, that the political accountability of ministers will be dismantled with nothing gained in return. Such an outcome would represent a serious threat in the longer term to the authority of parliamentary institutions and the viability of representative government.

Geoffrey Vickers lived through an epoch in the history of his own country in which for much of the time there was great faith in the strength and vitality of the varied institutions through which it was governed. But toward the end of his life circumstances changed in this respect. The moral substance of the society appeared to have fragmented to a great extent, just as it had in many other comparable societies. There was, therefore, and is today, a far less secure foundation for trying to meet that continuous challenge of adapting to an unprecedented rate of social, technical, and environmental change that was Vickers's abiding preoccupation. As a man of firm moral standards and with some confidence in his own capacity for engaging in judgment, he was able to set up signposts to guide people who are trying to face up to this challenge. Even if the message on the signpost was not always quite as clear or sharply defined as we might wish it had been, the signpost nearly always pointed in roughly the right direction. Whatever the weaknesses to be found in his treatment of institutions, there is no doubt that in his approach to them he was on the right track. The self-sufficient autonomous individual represents a dangerous illusion: It is only within the framework of institutions that such an individual finds safety and the possibility of a civilized life. About this Vickers had no illusions at all.[19]

NOTES

1. Letter to Guy Adams (February 23, 1982) cited in Blunden, M. (1984), Geoffrey Vickers—An intellectual journey, in Open Systems Group (Eds.) (1984), *The Vickers papers*. London: Harper & Row.

2. Ibid., p. 29.

3. Relatively early prophets of the limits to growth and material enrichment include Schumacher, E. (1973), *Small is beautiful*, London: Blond & Briggs; and Hirsch, F. (1977), *The social limits to growth*, London: Routledge & Kegan Paul. But Vickers revealed in his writings a remarkable awareness of the issues these writers (and others) were raising well before their books appeared.

4. It is indicative of Vickers's preoccupation with change that his most accessible study of the challenges facing industrialized societies is entitled *Freedom in a rocking boat: Changing values in an unstable society* (1970), London: Penguin.

5. A notable exponent of this view was Michael Oakeshott, especially in his major work, *On human conduct* (1975), Oxford: Oxford University Press. Nowhere in Vickers's work have I come across any reference to Oakeshott and he seems to have been unaware of the relevance of many of Oakeshott's arguments to his own analysis.

6. See especially *The art of judgment* (Vickers, 1965), chapter 2 on "Appreciation" and chapter 4 on "The appreciative system."

7. Chapter 3 of *The art of judgment* is entitled "Three case studies in appreciation." Here Vickers illuminates what he means by appreciation by considering the main appreciative judgments recorded in the reports of Buchanan, C. (1963), *Report on traffic in towns*, London: Her Majesty's Stationery Office (HMSO); Lord Robbins (1963), *Committee on higher education*, London: HMSO; and Gowers, E. A. (1953), *Royal commission on capital punishment*, London: HMSO.

8. Vickers was strongly influenced in his reflections on judgment by Michael Polanyi's (1958) *Personal knowledge*, London: Routledge & Kegan Paul. His views also reveal affinities with those of F. A. von Hayek, at any rate with regard to the latter's analysis of how knowledge is diffused and used in a free society. But there appears to be no evidence that Vickers had read much of Hayek's work.

9. Polanyi, op. cit., p. 33.

10. There is an interesting chapter entitled "Of Bonds and Bondage" in *Making institutions work* (Vickers, 1973), pp. 123-136.

11. *The art of judgment* (Vickers, 1965), op. cit. p. 139; see also *Making institutions work* (Vickers, 1973), for references to the proliferation of organizations and institutions.

12. Vickers, 1965, op. cit., p. 117.

13. See Waddington, C. H. (1960), *The ethical animal*, Chicago: University of Chicago Press.

14. There is doubtless some irony in the fact that it was a Hegelian, the statesman Lord Haldane, who unwittingly enshrined the term *machinery of government* in the British administrative and political vocabulary through his chairmanship of the Haldane Committee on the Machinery of Government that issued a famous report on that matter in 1918.

15. Adolph Lowe, already a professor of economics before 1933, came to Britain to escape persecution by the Nazi regime in Germany. He met Vickers and formed a lasting friendship with him. Lowe (who in 1993 attained the age of 100) has written widely on the connections between the economy and society, for example, *Economics and sociology* (1935), London: Allen & Unwin; *On economic knowledge: Toward a science of political economics* (1965), New York: Harper & Rowe; *Has freedom a future?* (1988), New York: Praeger.

16. It has to be noted that since 1979 British governments have made less regular use of commissions and committees of inquiry than was formerly the case. Instead, there has been a preference for a more executive style of policy-making, the results of which have not always been successful. But even if this change of approach reflects executive preoccupations, it probably mirrors also a general weakening of support in society for sophisticated and often slow exercises in appreciation of the kind cited by Vickers in his analysis.

17. A simple illustration of displacement of institutional purposes is provided by public libraries. Founded in 19th-century Britain primarily to serve the goal of facilitating wider access to books for educational purposes, they have now to be justified mainly by reference to the satisfaction of leisure and entertainment needs. This is, of course, not an example of 100% displacement, because education and the use of leisure time may overlap. The concept of displacement plays a considerable part in the theory of institutions elaborated by Arnold Gehlen (1904-1976), the most notable modern German thinker in this field.

18. The close ties between institutional and constitutional categories derive from the fact that a constitution seeks to define or state institutional relationships that it is desired to establish and maintain. Thus to change a constitution is to change institutions, and this in turn involves some changes in relationships. This argument is illustrated in Johnson, N. (1977), *In search of the constitution: Reflections on state and society in Britain*, Oxford: Pergamon.

19. Op. cit. *The Vickers papers* (Open Systems Group, 1984), p. 33.

REFERENCES

Blunden, M. (1984). Geoffrey Vickers—An intellectual journey. In Open Systems Group, *The Vickers papers* (pp. 3-42). London: Harper & Row.

Buchanan, C. (1963). *Report on traffic in towns*. London: HMSO.

Gowers, E. A. (1953). *Royal Commission on capital punishment*. London: HMSO.

Hirsch, F. (1977). *The social limits to growth*. London: Routledge & Kegan Paul.

Johnson, N. (1977). *In search of the constitution: Reflections on state and society in Britain*. Oxford: Pergamon.

Lowe, A. (1935). *Economics and sociology*. London: Allen & Unwin.

Lowe, A. (1965). *On economic knowledge: Toward a science of political economics*. New York: Harper & Row.

Lowe, A. (1988). *Has freedom a future?* New York: Praeger.

Oakeshott, M. (1975). *On human conduct*. Oxford: Oxford University Press.

Polanyi, M. (1958). *Personal knowledge*. London: Routledge & Kegan Paul.

Robbins, Lord (1963). *Committee on higher education*. London: HMSO.

Schumacher, E. (1973). *Small is beautiful*. London: Blond & Briggs.

Vickers, G. (1965). *The art of judgment*. London: Harper & Row.

Vickers, G. (1970). *Freedom in a rocking boat: Changing values in an unstable society*. London: Penguin.

Vickers, G. (1973). *Making institutions work*. London: Associated Business Programmes.

Waddington, C. H. (1960). *The ethical animal*. Chicago, IL: University of Chicago Press.

3

Communitarianism, Vickers, and Revisioning American Public Administration

GUY B. ADAMS
BAYARD L. CATRON

Classical liberalism and the unrestrained individualism that is of its essence are inappropriate for current ever-increasing interdependence. Recent communitarian thinking in the United States suggests that the exclusive pursuit of private interest is, in fact, inimical in the long run to individual liberty. Sustained policy change depends, however, on a fundamental rethinking of ethics and epistemology; Vickers's concept of appreciation is an important contribution to this task. The authors conclude that there is a need both for more government and for more democracy; greater intrusions on autonomy are inevitable if Western culture in its present form is to survive.

The sanest like the maddest of us cling like spiders to a self-spun web, obscurely moored in vacancy and fiercely shaken by the winds of change. Yet this frail web, through which many see only the void, is the one enduring artifact, the one authentic signature of humankind, and its weaving is our prime responsibility.
                                                                    —Geoffrey Vickers
                                        "The Psychology of Policymaking and Social Change"

The relation between the individual and society has been one of the most fundamental questions of political theory throughout Western history. It can be traced to the ancient Greeks, but it takes on particular significance with the political theory of Thomas Hobbes and John Locke in 17th-century England. For the first time in significant and sustained ways, the individual is set over and against society. Soon afterward, the utilitarian view was articulated in which social welfare is taken to be an aggregate of the satisfaction of individual preferences. This framework for the polity, known widely as classical liberalism, has served us for centuries but may now have reached a breaking point.

Individualism, rooted in the 17th century, has been one of the core values of Western culture in general and of the United States in particular. It has remained so throughout American history. As Bellah, Madsen, Sullivan, Swidler, and Tipton (1986) pointed out, "American cultural traditions define personality, achievement and the purpose of human life in ways that leave the individual suspended in glorious, but terrifying isolation" (p. 6). This is of great practical significance, as these authors stressed: "We are concerned that this individualism may be destroying those social integuments that Toqueville saw as moderating its more destructive potentialities, that it may be threatening the survival of freedom itself" (p. vii).

As the end of the century approaches, two trends seem clear, at least in the United States. First, interdependence is greater than it has ever been—people's fates are deeply intertwined—and this is less recognized than ever; and second, social groups are ever more fractionated and fractious—socially centripetal forces are as powerful as they have ever been. Without the cohesion provided by a much greater sense of community, it is hard to see how American society can be kept from flying apart, except through coercive power. An authoritarian America is a possible scenario that has to be taken seriously.

We will argue that the historic and current emphasis on individualism is pathological, socially and politically, and that it misrepresents basic human experience (Heller, Sosna, & Wellbery, 1986). What Sir Geoffrey Vickers (1965) called the "appreciative system" is what links us one to another. Even at the level of individual consciousness, it is relationships, managed through time, that are central to the human experience. It was one of Vickers's most basic insights that human meaning is constituted through relationships, and that the development and maintenance of relationships through time is the basis of human activity from consciousness to culture. That is the point of the artfully crafted quotation at the beginning of this chapter.

Given the centrality of relationships in the human condition, we have—whether we recognize it or not—the collective, shared experience from which arises the capacity to create and sustain human communities. This shared experience has as its most fundamental constituents epistemology and ethics. We must literally "re-member" our appreciation of these manifold relations and renew our sense of obligation and responsibility within social settings. But the challenge is a paradoxical one: We need to find or create a viable basis for the maintenance of legitimate social bonds even as there is less and less trust and tolerance for the constraints of social life. Out of this paradox must be created a new sense of responsibility and obligation toward community. This is a daunting task, but the American polity has reconstituted itself at more than one critical juncture in the past (Skowronek, 1982), although perhaps never so fundamentally and against such long odds.

The argument of this article proceeds as follows. First, we discuss the cultural pathology of individualism. In the United States, communitarianism has been one response to the problem of an overweening individualism, and we briefly treat this school of thought that has focused primarily on a variety of public policy issues. We argue, however, that a more fundamental rethinking of the problems of individualism is needed. This is the contribution of "appreciation," perhaps the major intellectual legacy left by Sir Geoffrey Vickers. We show how appreciation consists of managing a variety of relations through time in a variety of contexts, and then we show how these relationships cluster into patterns—in the mind, in nature, and in culture. Next, we discuss "technical rationality," as a chief component of the modern age and as the legacy of Enlightenment thinking. Along with individualism, technical rationality and its associated scientific-analytic mind-set remain as the chief obstacles to a fuller appreciation of the revised roles of governance and of public administration necessary to maintain social viability in the coming century. We use the metaphors of the midwife and the gardener to evoke these more appreciative roles. To begin, however, we turn to a discussion of individualism.

INDIVIDUALISM

The essential problem of an unrestrained individualism is captured by Vickers (1980) in the distinction he draws between the "autonomous individual" and the "responsible person." When the emphasis on the autonomous individual is unleavened by a sense of the responsible person, freedom reduces to liberty, and liberty degenerates into license. Vickers uses the example of Martin Luther to convey the freedom of the responsible person—bound by his commitments, he could "do no other" than make public his protest against the church of Rome. The pathology of autonomous individualism at the personal level is isolation, alienation, sociopathy. The pathology at the collective level is manifested in cleavages both along lines of social interests (groups with conflicting economic self-interest) and along lines of individual characteristics (race, religion; what Bellah and his colleagues (1986) call the "lifestyle enclave"). The result, in Vickers's words, is that "the cultures of subgroups dominate the decaying structures of the societies which they constitute" (Vickers, 1980, p. 28).

Responsible people weave the web of culture alluded to in the opening quote, whereas the reductio ad absurdum of the autonomous individual, according to Vickers (1980, pp. 25-28), is Nietzsche's superman, or Sartre's existential man, or Rameau's nephew (Diderot) or Mann's Felix Krull, the self-satisfied parasite on a society he defines as worthless and not meriting his loyalty. Bellah et al. (1986) posed the issue as follows:

> The question is whether an individualism in which the self has become the main form of reality can really be sustained. What is at issue is not simply whether self-contained individuals might withdraw from the public sphere to pursue purely private ends, but whether such individuals are capable of sustaining either a public or a private life. (p. 143)

The implications of autonomous individualism accrue far beyond the level of the individual, however. Vickers (1983) has described how socially pervasive, and how inappropriate, belief in autonomy has become:

> The autonomy sought alike by states, groups and individuals is basically the same. It is freedom from the obligation to accept as given the decisions of other groups and other individuals. Submission . . . to the judgments of others has become almost synonymous with weakness and subservience. On the face of it this seems

a singularly inept response to the obvious situation and trend of our time; for the dependence of men on each other is clearly greater than it has ever been and is obviously bound to become greater still. Each individual depends on others more and more for the basic necessities of life as well as for nearly all its amenities. Each therefore depends more on others for the faithful performance of their roles and should expect that their dependence on him and the faithful playing of his role will be correspondingly increased. (p. 81)

Under a presumption of individual autonomy, all achievements are seen as individually accomplished, and society is often presented as an obstacle rather than an asset. Consider Rousseau's famous observation that "man is born free but is everywhere found in chains." Would it not be more accurate to say that "man is born completely dependent and, with luck and the good will of the people around him, may grow into a free (differentiated) and responsible person"? From a community perspective, "person" is a social creation and rights are socially constructed (Berger & Luckmann, 1967). The fundamental role of the social in enabling any individual achievement at all is little appreciated. There has, however, been some response within the community of scholars in the United States to the problem of individual autonomy in an interdependent society.

COMMUNITARIANISM

Although "individualism lies at the very core of American culture" (Bellah et al., 1986, p. 142), the authors of *Habits of the Heart* found in their interviews an ambivalence about individualism and a recognition of the importance of community life:

We found all the polarities of American individualism still operating: the deep desire for autonomy and self-reliance combined with an equally deep conviction that life has no meaning unless shared with others in the context of community; a commitment to the equal right to dignity of every individual combined with the effort to justify inequality of reward, which, when extreme, may deprive people of dignity; an insistence that life requires practical effectiveness and realism combined with the feeling that compromise is ethically fatal. The inner tensions of American individualism add up to a classic case of ambivalence. We strongly assert the value of our self-reliance and autonomy. We deeply feel the emptiness of a life without sustaining social commitments. Yet we are hesitant to articulate our sense that we need one another as much as we need to stand alone, for fear that if we did we would lose our independence. (pp. 150-151)

This attachment to community—that is, a communitarian political philosophy— has a long history in Western culture. Ancient (Aristotle), medieval (St. Thomas Aquinas), and modern (MacIntyre, 1984; Taylor, 1985) philosophers all have reflected communitarian thinking. In the face of an overweening and obsessive individualism in the United States today, it should have been no surprise that a reaction would occur. Various strands of communitarian thinking were brought together in 1990 by a small group of intellectuals in the United States who formed a self-styled new social movement (Bellah, Madsen, Sullivan, Swidler, & Tipton, 1992; Chapman & Galston, 1992; Elshtain, 1990; Fishkin, 1991; McCollough, 1991; Spragens, 1990). These scholars argue, among other things, that a moral revival in the United States is possible without puritanism or oppression; that people can again live in communities without turning into vigilantes; that self-interest can be balanced by a commitment to the community without requiring austerity, altruism, or self-sacrifice (Etzioni, 1993, pp. 1-2). Interestingly, the communitarian platform argues, not that individualism is wrong, but that the development of social responsibility is necessary if individual liberty and rights are to be preserved over time (Etzioni, 1993):

> Neither human existence nor individual liberty can be sustained for long outside the interdependent and overlapping communities to which all of us belong. . . . The exclusive pursuit of private interest erodes the network of social environments on which we all depend and is destructive to our shared experiment in democratic self-government. For these reasons, we hold that the rights of individuals cannot long be preserved without a Communitarian perspective. . . . A Communitarian perspective recognizes that the preservation of individual liberty depends on the active maintenance of the institutions of civil society where citizens learn respect for others as well as self-respect; where we acquire a lively sense of our personal and civic responsibilities, along with an appreciation of our own rights and the rights of others; where we develop the skills of self-government as well as the habit of governing ourselves and learn to serve others—not just self. (pp. 253-254)

Across a variety of public policy issues, communitarian proposals emphasize rejuvenated social obligations—activities that strengthen community (Etzioni, 1991). In the area of family policy, for example, communitarians tend to promote initiatives that would reduce the "parenting deficit," such as more liberal family leave policies, enabling parents to spend more time with (that is, meet their responsibility to) very young children (Etzioni, 1993, chap. 2). The area of family policy also includes a variety of initiatives to reduce "entertainment violence," which increasingly dominates all areas of television programming, including "news." One of the better known policy initiatives of communitarians is the idea of voluntary or even mandatory national service for young people of high school or college age. A 1- or 2-year public service experience, it is thought, could instill a lifetime appreciation for community and might be rewarded, for example, by tuition credits for further education.

There are other policy initiatives that reflect a more communitarian stance (Barber, 1994; Yankelovich, 1991). However, the introduction of new policies, even the introduction of new values, into the political arena and into social discourse is probably not sufficient by itself to alter the American landscape. A more fundamental rethinking is likely to be necessary to bring about what communitarians refer to as the "change of heart" necessary for sustained policy change. Vickers's concept of appreciation, with its twin roots of ethics and epistemology, makes a major contribution to this task. Linked as it is from the level of individual consciousness through intervening levels to the level of culture, the idea of appreciation provides a system of thought on which a renewed sense of community can be built. The next sections of this article will elaborate how this may be accomplished.

APPRECIATION AND THE FUNDAMENTAL IMPORTANCE OF RELATIONSHIPS

Perhaps Vickers's best known intellectual contribution is the notion of the "appreciative system." Our ability to make sense of contexts—to appreciate—rests on the foundation of our self- and mutual expectations, themselves built by accretion through our experience. Vickers (1970) noted that the set of mutual and self-expectations "is the basic regulator of society. It sets the standard of what ought to be, by which deviance is defined; and it is constantly on the move under the influence of the process which it mediates" (p. 82). The basic human experience, then, is the experience of manifold relations through time. What is uniquely human, according to Vickers, is the ability to situate oneself within a myriad of contexts. A story Vickers liked to tell illustrates this nicely:

In early IQ test days, tests briefly became an English party game. At a party, our host said he would test our intelligences. He then read quickly a number of disconnected statements about three men, driver, "fireman," and guard of a steam railway train, whose names (but in no stated order) were Jones, Smith and Robinson. The last statement was, "Smith beat the fireman at billiards."

Then came the question: "What was the name of the engine driver?" The fireman's name was not Smith. But so what? There were still three possibilities for the driver. Two must have been foreclosed by some information derivable from that jumble of earlier statements but none of the statements, except the last, had specifically attributed or excluded a name to or from anyone.

Nonetheless, in the silence that followed, my wife, Ellen, immediately and confidently said, "Smith." The following dialogue ensued:

Host: You mean Smith was the name of the engine driver?
Ellen: Of course.
Host: How did you do it so quickly?
Ellen: Do what?
Host: Solve the clues.
Ellen: What clues?
Host: (patiently, but painedly, explains what the clues were for).
Ellen: Oh, I didn't understand all that.
Host: (totally puzzled) Then how did you know that the engine driver's name was Smith?
Ellen: (equally puzzled) But of course it would have been the engine driver who was playing billiards with the fireman. They work on the same foot plate; they belong to the same union. The guard is at the other end of the train, a different union, a different promotion ladder. He wouldn't even know the fireman.
(A pause . . . broken by increasing laughter)

Host: He might have done.
Ellen: I suppose. (pause) But Smith was the name of the engine driver, wasn't it?
Host: (glumly) Yes.

To my wife an engine driver was an engine driver, a fireman, a fireman. The rest of us had thrown away all of the information included in their contexts and treated these men as A, B, and C. We knew what was expected of us to show intelligence. She did not. (Vickers, personal communication, 1981)

The appreciative system encompasses two sets of standards or norms, which are only separable conceptually. In everyday thought and action, the two sets of norms—standards of fact and standards of value—are essentially seamless. The first set of norms, standards of fact, represents the way we classify and characterize objects and relations; whereas the second set of norms, standards of value, represents the way in which we judge those objects and relations (Vickers, 1987a): "good or bad, welcome or unwelcome, important or unimportant, acceptable or unacceptable" (p. 85). The appreciative system, then, comprises the criteria, the schemata, by which we make sense of the various contexts we encounter in our experience (Vickers, 1965):

> Even physical perception depends on learning perceptual categories by which to classify experience. The child learns to recognize cows in all their variety by their correspondence with some generalized schema in which "cowishness" has come to reside; yet the very schema was developed by the experience of seeing actual cows and will be amplified and if need be corrected by further use. The medical student cannot read a pulmonary radiograph until experience of many has built up an interpretative schema; nor can he build up a schema except by exposing himself to individual experiences. (p. 68)

Appreciation encompasses a variety of processes, including the ability to discriminate figure from ground, signal from noise; the ability to create and alter organized patterns with great subtlety and interaction of theme and variation; and the ability to harmonize disparate ideas—or failing that, to mute dissonance through selective inattention. These are not simply subjective processes that occur within an individual's head. Rather, they are relational, intersubjective processes that involve communicative interaction with other people.

Unlike the objective detachment emphasized by the "scientific" method, appreciation acknowledges the presence and indeed the investment of the self in the process. The self may be viewed as the instrument, the vehicle, or the medium through which the appreciative process works. Further, appreciation depends on the presence of a caring bond between the self and other, subject and object. The bond may be between two people in a communicative interaction, or it may be the relation between a person and object, as between a sculptor and clay, or even between a scientist and a field of inquiry. Perhaps a verse from Yeats will serve to illustrate this connection:

> O body swayed to music, O brightening glance
> How can we know the dancer from the dance?
>   (from "Among School Children")

APPRECIATION: A VARIETY OF CONTEXTS

This same, fundamentally relational, appreciative process is extended to ever more encompassing systems, to groups and organizations, to political and economic relations within a society, to national cultures and to the most widely shared context of meaning of all—our basic humanity. Thus, for Vickers, the communitarian standpoint is not a choice. It is rather a fact of human existence; it is who we are.

The ideology of individualism takes for granted that each individual's actions are unique, because each individual is supposedly unique and all behavior is a projection of individual personality. The examination of an individual's behavior in isolation often reinforces that notion. However, Western culture's emphasis on individualism often conceals what is shared. Relating is not just an action; rather, it is an essential constituent of what it means to be human.

Some recent feminist literature in the United States has emphasized this point in striving to validate the experience of women, which, at the conscious level, has been far more oriented around relationships than that of men (Belenky, Clinchy, Goldberger, & Tarule, 1986; Gilligan, 1982). In the context of a discussion of moral development, and how it differs for women and men, Gilligan characterizes women's experience of the world as one of relation and connection, whereas men's experience is one of separation and individuation. These different experiences lead to different modes of assertion and response: "[For men] the wish to be alone at the top, and the consequent fear that others will get too close; [for women] the wish to be at the center of connection and the consequent fear of being too far out on the edge" (Gilligan, 1982, p. 62).

This is a useful line of thinking. Exploring a possible "masculine" bias in the emphasis on individualism in Western culture offers an opportunity for reevaluation of individuality and separateness, of interconnections and relatedness.

Vickers clearly stated his conviction that appreciation was a partly tacit process, and one that was not fully describable. It is a regrettable prejudice of modern Western culture that those things that are fully describable are honored with the terms *scientific* and *rational*, whereas those that are not are deemed unscientific or irrational. To say that something is partly tacit is not to relinquish all hope of understanding it or to relegate it to the realm of the mystical. Rationality and appreciation are not conflicting but complementary, not dichotomous but dialectical.

CONSCIOUSNESS AS RELATIONAL

The notion of relationship is even more fundamentally important, characterizing the very structure of consciousness, as revealed through the careful phenomenology of Edmund Husserl (1962) and his followers. Consciousness, as Husserl (1964) carefully explained in the *Phenomenology of Inner Time Consciousness*, is always relational and intentional. The intentionality of consciousness means that consciousness never exists in isolation but is always consciousness of (something). We may be conscious of, or thinking about, a tree or a building, some external object. Or, we may be conscious of an idea, some mental construct, or we may even be reflecting on the processes of consciousness itself, in a moment of reflexivity. In all these cases, there is no thinking without the thought of. Consciousness, in its very nature, is relational.

Another significant characteristic of the structure of consciousness is its partly tacit nature. Indeed, Michael Polanyi (1958) suggested that tacit knowing is more fundamental than explicit knowing: "We can know more than we can tell and we can tell nothing without relying on our awareness of things we may not be able to tell" (p. x). Polanyi elaborates on this assertion, which runs counter to the logic of the scientific-analytic mind-set, by distinguishing between focal and subsidiary awareness. Skilled wielders of paintbrushes, brooms, or indeed, any tool, have as their focal point of awareness the tip of the implement. Yet it is the complex movements of their hands, of which they are only aware in a subsidiary way, that actually guide the tool. If the hand becomes the focal point of awareness, skill with the tool diminishes or even disappears.

Consider the art of riding a bicycle. If we try to focus on each of the actions needed to ride, we would likely fall over. We are not speechless when trying to instruct a child on a bicycle for the first time, but we surely do not provide an analytical list of the components of riding. We are more apt to suggest that a feel for riding is what is important. As Polanyi (1966) said more generally, one "cannot represent the organizing principles of a higher level by the laws governing the isolated particulars" (p. 36).

PATTERNS OF RELATIONSHIPS

Relationships, over time, cluster into patterns. These patterns of relationships comprise symbolic structures and functions within a culture. Moreover, these patterns are isomorphic with the patterns of relationships in the human mind and with the patterns of relationships in nature. The latter point is argued most persuasively by Gregory Bateson (1979), whereas the connections between the patterns of mind and culture have been developed by William Vanderburg (1985):

> The mind's systems acquired on the basis of experience mediate all relationships with reality, converting it into a symbolic universe. Within this universe these structures orient behavior because they imply . . . certain values, myths, beliefs, etc., with the result that they function as a kind of mental map by which we orient ourselves in reality. . . . It now follows that culture as acquired by a process of socialization is a way of living in reality based on a certain organization of the mind. . . . The customs, manners, beliefs, myths, language, and institutions are in part the phenomenal manifestations of these structures. (p. 44)

Although much of social science continues to emulate the mechanistic physics of 85 years ago, much of modern physics is far removed from that past (Bohm, 1980; see also Prigogene & Stengers, 1984). However, it remains difficult for us to think relationally, because mechanistic thinking is still pervasive in Western culture:

> In attempting to conceptualize a non-mechanistic reality, we need to recall that the mechanistic one is constituted of organized wholes that exist independently, each in their own region of space and time, and that interact by external contact. This is exactly what one finds in a machine. In a living whole, on the contrary, there have never existed any independent "parts." Each "part" has emerged within the whole. They do not interact with the other "parts" in the same way, and there exist no distinct boundaries between them. In so far as boundaries do manifest themselves, they are likely to shift with the frame of reference employed by the observer and the paradigm he or she has internalized. . . . It is only on the basis of a mechanistic hypothesis of reality that a society decomposes into functions, mechanisms, systems and structures. When a society is studied on the basis of a non-mechanistic hypothesis, they become dimensions of an undivided whole. Even what to our senses manifests itself as a largely autonomous whole is in fact a part of the undivided whole of a reality, and science must attempt to account for this undivided wholeness. (Vanderburg, 1985, p. 44)

The difficulty that much mainstream social science has in describing relationships derives from its adoption of the reductionist method of the natural sciences. A scientific analytic mind-set, part of an enduring intellectual tradition that may be traced back to the Enlightenment, is still characteristic of modern Western approaches to complex social phenomena.

MODERNITY AND TECHNICAL RATIONALITY: THE LEGACY OF THE ENLIGHTENMENT

Technical rationality is one of the chief constituents of modern culture (Barrett, 1979). Technical rationality is a way of thinking and living that emphasizes the scientific-analytic mind set and the belief in technological progress. In the United States, a confluence of two intellectual currents occurred around the turn of the last century that unleashed a flood of ideas and practices into the social and political world (Wiebe, 1967, pp. 145-163). One of the two currents emerged from the recent development of epistemology in Western culture. This first current was the scientific-analytic mind-set that was the legacy of 17th-century Enlightenment thinking. The second current was the product of the technical transformation of the 19th century and comprised the belief in technological progress characteristic of this period of industrialization with its unparalleled succession of technological developments.

The scientific-analytic mind-set and belief in technological progress that combined nearly 100 years ago unleashed a powerful current of technical rationality and professionalism extending far beyond their original locus. Impressed by the tremendous achievements of science and technology in the physical world, many naturally wanted to apply them in the social and political world, to achieve sciencelike precision and objectivity in these spheres as well (Bendix, 1956).

Technical rationality led irresistibly to specialized, expert knowledge, the very lifeblood of the professional, and then to the proliferation of professional associations in the latter half of the 19th and early part of the 20th centuries (Larson, 1977). Without the legitimacy derived from specialized knowledge, the professional could not have gained either the social status or the autonomy and control over the practice of the profession, which are the ultimate goals, even if sometimes unstated, of every profession. The compartmentalization of knowledge demanded by technical rationality also inevitably led to a contextless, or timeless, practice, including a lack of historical consciousness across the professions and disciplines. The practice of a profession with little or no sense of context has precluded meaningful engagement with the larger ethical and political concerns of a society (Guerreiro-Ramos, 1981).

THE EMERGENCE OF TECHNICAL RATIONALITY

In the context of modernity, technical rationality is the convergence of the scientific-analytical mind-set and belief in technological progress (Turner, 1990). Technical rationality is quite similar to "functional rationality" as described by Karl Mannheim (1940). Mannheim saw functional rationality as the logical organization of tasks into smaller units, originally in the interest of efficiency. Mannheim contrasted this with "substantive rationality," the ability to understand the purposeful nature of the whole system of which a particular task is a part. Technical rationality is also closely akin to the notion of "instrumental reason" discussed by Max Horkheimer (1947). Instrumental reason is the narrow application of human reason solely in the service of instrumental aims. Until the modern era, reason was conceived as a process incorporating ethical and normative concerns as well as the consideration of merely instrumental aims. In the public administration literature, similar points have been made by Alberto Guerreiro-Ramos (1981).

To understand how technical rationality became pervasive in the social and political world, and therefore in the public administration world as well, it is necessary to take a brief look at the recent history of epistemology. By the time of the 17th-century Enlightenment, the developing physical sciences were beginning to exert a powerful influence. Epistemology became preoccupied with a quest for the stubborn and irreducible facts of existence. By the 18th century, the split between European and Anglo-American epistemology and philosophy had begun to be visible (this split has blurred considerably more recently). European philosophy may be represented as a series of attempts to resuscitate epistemology and metaphysics from the problems posed by science and its method of empiricism (Hegel, 1807/1965; Heidegger, 1926/1977; Nietzsche, 1872/1956). Anglo-American philosophy, in contrast, may be represented as a series of attempts to reconstruct the concerns of philosophy according to the insights of science and its method (Whitehead & Russell, 1910; Wittgenstein, 1922). In Anglo-American culture, the scientific-analytic mind-set captured ways of thinking, and the study of epistemology was largely reduced to commentaries on the history of science. The scientific-analytic mind-set, then, represents one part of the confluence that occurred almost a century ago; the impact of technological developments on values and beliefs comprised the other.

The astonishing succession of technological developments during the 19th century reinforced the power of technical rationality (Rabinbach, 1990). What could have been more plausible than to apply technical rationality to the social world to achieve sciencelike precision and objectivity? Technical rationality became the vehicle of hope in the social and political world and created a wave that before World War II impelled new professionals, managers, behaviorists, social scientists, and industrial psychologists toward a worldview in which human conflicts appeared as problems fit for engineering solutions (Bendix, 1956; Ellul, 1954). By the present time, as William Barrett (1979) stated,

> it would be silly for anyone to announce that he is "against" technology, whatever that might mean. We should have to be against ourselves in our present historical existence. We have now become dependent upon the increasingly complex and interlocking network of production for our barest necessities. (p. 229)

THE UNFULFILLED PROMISE OF THE SYSTEMS APPROACH

Beginning shortly after World War II, however, writers such as Norbert Wiener (1967), Ludwig von Bertalanffy (1955), and Ross Ashby (1956) introduced into the intellectual community a contrasting set of ideas about systems and their control that, although they too originated in technical arenas, had very different implications from technical rationality. Although their definition quickly grew problematic, systems were seen as wholes, greater than (or different from) the "sum" of their parts; as composed of interrelated parts; and as depending on some sort of "steering" mechanism to maintain those relationships over time.

For many, including Vickers, the systems metaphor seemed a promising way to resolve nagging questions about organizations and societies. Indeed, Vickers reported the advent of systems thinking as having a profound impact on him (Adams, Catron, & Forester, 1987, p. viii). Some systems theorists became almost immediately preoccupied with the notion of a *general* systems theory, one that would apply to all systems. Unsurprisingly, given the modern, epistemological dominance of technical rationality, this concern was captured by a general theory that fitted best those systems that could be fully described, if not fully designed. Theorizing was reduced to modeling, which, construed in this explicit fashion, could not accommodate processes that are partly tacit, such as appreciation. The concomitant development of the digital computer exacerbated this tendency in systems thinking. Vickers (1977) described the unfortunate outcomes as follows:

> A computer scientist was describing to a possible supporter of his work the result of teaching young children . . . to program a computer to make drawings. They had learned how to program an approximate circle; and they were heard later in

earnest metaphysical debate as to whether there was or could be a real circle. Was not every circle a more or less refined polyhedron?

It seems to me that the concept of circularity is simple and important, easy to teach and rich in implications. No child with a lathe or a compass could conceive itself to be producing polyhedrons. To this computer scientist, however, it evidently seemed an expendable concept. Why bother children in a computer age with concepts foreign to computers? The same argument would justify an effort to persuade children that time is best conceived for all purposes (not merely for mathematical convenience) as a series of moments of no duration. Perhaps this helps to explain today's disastrous contempt for history.

Hence my anxiety that the concept of gestalt recognition may again be stifled, and with it our belief in an essential part of our own mental capacity for judgment. (p. 14)

Over time, the scientific-analytic mind-set effectively narrowed the scope of systems thinking to dimensions that fitted the preexistent parameters of technical rationality. Within organization studies, a similar narrowing of the scope of systems thinking occurred (Smircich & Calas, 1987, p. 231). A similar fate could await communitarian thinking if it fails to broaden its scope to incorporate the centrality of relationships beyond just questions of public policy. Vickers's concept of appreciation, sufficiently expansive to move from consciousness to culture, offers a way to accomplish this broadening of scope.

Contemporary communitarian thinking still faces formidable obstacles. Announcements of the advent of postmodernity notwithstanding, the considerable cultural forces of modernity, technical rationality, and its scientific-analytic mind-set are still omnipresent. Technique is as ready a substitute for communitarian thinking as it was for systems thinking. Consider the so-called electronic town hall. Billed as a way of increasing participation in an electronic age, citizens could be wired through their televisions or home computers and could vote on the issues of the day. As a supplement to community, such technical fixes could be useful. However, as a substitute for community—much like a polyhedron as substitute for a circle—technique is, at best, inadequate, and at worst, simply dangerous.

IMPLICATIONS FOR GOVERNANCE AND PUBLIC ADMINISTRATION

What then are the implications of this discussion for governance? There are at least two. First, the exercise of authority by "governors" of all kinds can only increase as growing interdependence combined with hyperpluralism threatens to destabilize the system as a whole. The crisis of legitimacy this precipitates will require increasing forbearance by the governed as "authority is exercised more frequently, in unfamiliar issues of vital importance, at remote levels and on a widening scale of space and time" (Vickers, 1965, p. 189).

In an individualistic society, the exercise of authority is experienced as a limitation of freedom and sovereignty. It is seen as "making me do what I otherwise would not." Where there is the strong sense of mutuality and belonging to community, authority is more likely to be understood as necessary guidance to ensure effective cooperation toward shared goals (Vickers, 1965):

> The liberal age tended to take for granted the bonds of common humanity or to underrate their importance in containing conflict, because it overrated the extent to which human interests are rationally reconcilable. In the post-liberal age, both doers and done-by will have far more reason to cultivate these bonds; for their practical importance is never so clear as when they are in danger of breaking. (pp. 185-186)

In words echoed by today's communitarians, Vickers (1973) said that the inescapable demands to which we will have to respond

> follow from the need to establish a viable relationship between rights and responsibilities, political, economic and social—in other words between the constraints and assurances of all our memberships. Since everyone is going to depend increasingly on assurances derived from membership, everyone will have to accept increasing constraints derived from membership. (p. 128)

No matter where we are in the cycle of centralization/decentralization, regardless of how we reinvent government or whether we privatize many of its functions, governance itself must be strengthened if the extreme consequences of instability are to be avoided:

> The post-liberal era will depend absolutely on adequate means to make and implement political choices of extreme difficulty. Its first task must be to strengthen the machinery of government, to place at its disposal a larger share of resources, including human resources, and to support it with more confidence. All but the last have been in progress, though reluctantly, for some time. The last lags, partly because of well-founded doubt of the ability of government to handle its new tasks, but equally because the legitimacy of these tasks is not yet fully admitted. (Vickers, 1965, p. 186)

The second implication for governance concerns the practices of democracy. The new communitarians favor "strong democracy" (Etzioni, 1993): "We seek to make government more representative, more participatory, and more responsive to all members of the community. We seek to find ways to accord citizens more information and more say, more often" (p. 253). Vickers agrees on the need for greater public participation at several levels: participation in planning and policy-making at the local level, fortification by emotional involvement in the expected result, and the reshaping of values and priorities. But he is not optimistic: "It involves that free but disciplined dialogue which lies at the heart of the democratic process. Dialogue on this scale has never yet been achieved" (Vickers, 1973, p. 86).

It appears that our democratic practices are woefully out of balance, and our responses too often only exacerbate the problem:

> The ambiguity and ambivalence of American individualism derive from both cultural and social contradictions. We insist, perhaps more than ever before, on

finding our true selves independent of any cultural and social influence, being responsible to that self alone, and making its fulfillment the very meaning of our lives. Yet we spend much time navigating through immense bureaucratic structures—multiversities, corporations, government agencies—manipulating and being manipulated by others. In describing this situation, Alasdair MacIntyre has spoken of "bureaucratic individualism." . . . In bureaucratic individualism, the ambiguities and contradictions of individualism are frighteningly revealed, as freedom to make private decisions is bought at the cost of turning over most public decisions to bureaucratic managers and experts. A bureaucratic individualism in which the consent of the governed, the first demand of modern enlightened individualism, has been abandoned in all but form, illustrates the tendency of individualism to destroy its own conditions. (Bellah et al., 1986, p. 150)

IMPLICATIONS FOR PUBLIC ADMINISTRATION

Appreciation, resting on the twin pillars of ethics and epistemology, offers the foundation for a renewed sense of community. This means a greatly amplified role for governance along with stronger democracy—richer and deeper participation in democratic practices. In public administration, these two requirements have largely been seen as mutually exclusive. Like contemporary American society as a whole, public administration as a field has been dominated by the American regime values of classical liberalism and by the technical rationality that emerged in full scope over the past century. As both Vickers and the contemporary communitarians point out, this has produced a culturally deadly combination. A reform of considerable depth, if not indeed a revolution in thinking and acting, is required to maintain social viability into the first half of the 21st century.

Public administration starts from a position of weakness in American culture, because of the predisposition of classical liberalism for limited government. Some attempts by public administration thinkers to bootstrap the field into a more expansive role have focused on professionalism. Professionalism emerged in the United States in the latter half of the 19th century, at the same time technical rationality came to a dominant cultural position. Unsurprisingly, our understanding of professionalism is that its practitioners bring technical expertise to their area of practice. For public administration, much as other fields, to be professional is to be technically expert.

It follows that the role of public administration is predicated on a weak version of citizenship. In the more extreme versions of technical-rational professionalism, citizen involvement and activity are no more than a diversion and distraction from the exercise of expert decision. Even in the most enlightened versions of professionalism, citizens start from an inferior position in terms of knowledge and expertise. In the most optimistic, if still patronizing versions, citizens should perhaps be listened to—if educated enough.

We suggest that the role of public administration needs to be rethought in far more dramatic terms, if it is not to obstruct attempts to build a communitarian society sufficient to maintain viability in the decades to come. This need is underscored all the more so if *more communitarian* also means *more democratic*.

There is some recent precedent in the field of public administration for such a rethinking. In 1983, a national conference was held in New York City on the relationship between citizenship and public administration; one result of this conference was a special issue of the *Public Administration Review* (vol. 44, March 1984) on this relationship. Perhaps the spirit of this thrust was best captured in the notion of *civism*, defined as an appreciation of civic principles and practices that public administration needed to recapture in its own thought and practice.

In the years since, ideas of citizenship and democracy as they apply to public administration have been further developed (Adams, Bowerman, Dolbeare, & Stivers, 1990; Stivers, 1990). Perhaps most noteworthy in these recent developments is Terry L. Cooper's (1991) vision of a new professionalism based on citizenship. Understanding public administration as a practice, following MacIntyre (1984), Cooper argues for a more public-centered version of public administration, one that strongly emphasizes the tradition of democratic citizenship. Conceptions of public administration that call for stronger democratic practices—drawing both politics and ethics back into the center of discourse—of necessity require major revisions in professionalism as it is understood in American culture in general and in public administration in particular.

THE ROLE OF THE PUBLIC ADMINISTRATION PROFESSIONAL

The concept of "communitarian facilitator" has been suggested as appropriate for the new role of the public administration professional (Catron & Hammond, 1990). The image of midwife may be even more apt. In this perspective, the public administrator, in what seems a paradox, gains power and prestige not through acquiring expertise and knowledge but through giving it away (Box, in press). As Camilla Stivers (1993) has described it:

> The image of the midwife is of a skilled and caring person who facilitates the emergence of new possibilities by means of embodied and embodying action. The good midwife has deep knowledge and vast experience, which she brings to bear on each unique situation, using them to help her sense the nuances of a process that she can only facilitate rather than steer. The process is an embodied, life-or-death affair (no distanced contemplation here!), one on which she brings to bear both her own body and her mind, one that requires *both* connection and a certain level of detachment *in order to be of greatest service*. (p. 132)

The midwife is a highly skilled and trained practitioner, one who approaches the relationship with the mother and baby much differently from the more objective, scientific standpoint of the physician (perhaps the paradigmatic example of a technical-rational professionalism). The midwife typically does more to establish and maintain the relations with the mother and father and with the baby, and often with relatives and friends, than does the physician. In the most specialized example, the patient may see one physician before the birth, a different one during the birth, and a third after the birth. And although each may choose otherwise, all three could be as strangers to the patient. However, midwives are skilled practitioners at managing difficult transitional relations. Such relationships may be expected to become the norm in the public sector in years to come, if they are not already. Moreover, midwifery is far less expensive socially in a variety of ways, not least because it is built more on practice and less on science.

AN APPRECIATIVE FUTURE?

Vickers envisioned that the "doers" in society would progressively be dealing with more difficult and conflict-laden public and social choices. One of the main points of our argument here is that all citizens must become much more active doers than they currently are, and further, that each must in some area of interest or practice become a doer to a large degree. This is the only way to build a sufficient foundation of trust to enable everyone to be "done by" to the extent that will be necessary in the years to come. The gulf between the doers and the done-by can only be narrowed by such reciprocal relationships. This is very different from the notion of everyone being a technical-rational expert in one area, even if such a condition were imaginable. Both a general and a specific increase in participation—in doing—seems the best way, and perhaps the only way, to renewing social integuments to the degree necessary to keep American culture from flying apart as a result of the geometric increase in socially centripetal forces.

One of Vickers's favorite sources was Thomas H. Huxley, the 19th-century biologist and Darwinist. He was particularly fond of citing Huxley's juxtaposition of the metaphors of the garden and the jungle. Nature, as represented by the jungle, has its own regulators; it crowds as much as possible into a given space and creates the struggle for survival. Natural selection happens as a result of a constant, daily test of the fit (or misfit) between a plant and its environment. The gardener, on the other hand, prunes and weeds and thins, using other criteria of selection, namely, normative criteria.

In human culture, as in agriculture, the selection of the normative criteria by which we will govern ourselves (that is, ethics) is to some considerable extent left up to us, within the broad constraints determined by our nature. The first step is to appreciate the nature of the task and the meaning of growing in a culture. Vickers was deeply concerned that we in the West show so little understanding of community and are so disinclined to acknowledge our dependence on it. Community nourishes and sustains us; it is indispensable that we remain deeply rooted in it and sustain and nourish it in return.

From this perspective, the notion of the autonomous individual appears foolish and dangerous—foolish, because autonomy is impossible, and dangerous, because the notion implies that we can neglect our community with impunity. But the untended garden quickly becomes a jungle again, like the Garden of Eden after the Fall. Culture, then, is not something remote and abstract; it is close by and personal and something we share in common—in community—and share by communication. To be a member of a community is to share, in common, certain beliefs, habits of acting, and values. But more fundamentally, the community is the medium on which we depend vitally and through which we act, whether cooperatively or competitively.

Social institutions, including organizations both public and private, which are the most ubiquitous embodiment of culture, therefore require the most tender and the most tenacious ministrations, much like those of the midwife. Vickers's vision was that, if Western culture is to survive in the future in anything like its present form, we will need to acquiesce in greater and greater intrusions on our individual autonomy, submit to greater exercise of authority (even though it will doubtless be abused), and pay ever greater attention and effort to sustaining community against the forces that threaten to destroy it. Perhaps the midwife and the gardener will be able to appreciate such a challenge.

REFERENCES

Adams, G. B., Bowerman, P. V., Dolbeare, K. M., & Stivers, C. (1990). Joining purpose to practice: A democratic identity for the public service. In H. D. Kass & B. L. Catron (Eds.), *Images and identities in public administration*. Newbury Park, CA: Sage.

Adams, G. B., Catron, B. L., & Forester, J. (Eds.). (1987). *Policy making, communication and social learning: Essays of Sir Geoffrey Vickers*. New Brunswick, NJ: Transaction.

Ashby, W. R. (1956). *Introduction to cybernetics*. New York: Wiley.

Barber, B. R. (1994). *An aristocracy of everyone: The politics of education and the future of America*. New York: Oxford University Press.

Barrett, W. (1979). *The illusion of technique*. Garden City, NY: Anchor/Doubleday.

Bateson, G. (1979). *Mind and nature: A necessary unity*. New York: Dutton.

Belenky, M. F., Clinchy, B. M., Goldberger, N. R., & Tarule, J. M. (1986). *Women's ways of knowing*. New York: Basic Books.

Bellah, R. N., Madsen, R., Sullivan, W. M., Swidler, A., & Tipton, S. M. (1986). *Habits of the heart: Individualism and commitment in American life*. New York: Harper & Row.

Bellah, R. N., Madsen, R., Sullivan, W. M., Swidler, A., & Tipton, S. M. (1992). *The good society*. New York: Alfred A. Knopf.

Bendix, R. (1956). *Work and authority in industry*. New York: Harper & Row.

Berger, P., & Luckmann, T. (1967). *The social construction of reality*. Garden City, NY: Anchor/Doubleday.

Bohm, D. (1980). *Wholeness and the implicate order*. London: Routledge & Kegan Paul.

Box, R. C. (in press). Critical theory and the paradox of discourse. *American Review of Public Administration*.

Catron, B. L., & Hammond, B. R. (1990). Epilogue: Reflecting on practical wisdom—enacting images and developing identity. In H. D. Kass & B. L. Catron (Eds.), *Images and identities in public administration*. Newbury Park, CA: Sage.

Chapman, J. W., & Galston, W. A. (Eds.). (1992). *Virtue*. New York: New York University Press.

Cooper, T. L. (1991). *An ethic of citizenship for public administration*. Englewood Cliffs, NJ: Prentice-Hall.

Ellul, J. (1954). *The technological society*. New York: Vintage.

Elshtain, J. B. (1990). *Power trips and other journeys*. Madison: University of Wisconsin Press.

Etzioni, A. (1991). *A responsive society*. San Francisco, CA: Jossey-Bass.

Etzioni, A. (1993). *The spirit of community: Rights, responsibilities, and the communitarian agenda*. New York: Crown.

Fishkin, J. S. (1991). *Democracy and deliberation*. New Haven, CT: Yale University Press.

Gilligan, C. (1982). *In a different voice: Psychological theory and women's development*. Cambridge, MA: Harvard University Press.

Guerreiro-Ramos, A. (1981). *The new science of organization*. Toronto: University of Toronto Press.

Hegel, G.W.F. (1965). Preface to the phenomenology of mind. In W. Kaufmann (Ed. and Trans.), *Hegel: Texts and commentary*. Notre Dame, IN: Notre Dame University Press. (Original work published 1807)

Heidegger, M. (1977). *Basic writings* (D. Krell, Trans.). New York: Harper & Row. (Original work published 1926)

Heller, T. C., Sosna, M., & Wellbery, D. E. (Eds.). (1986). *Reconstructing individualism: Autonomy, individuality and the self in Western thought*. Stanford, CA: Stanford University Press.

Horkheimer, M. (1947). *The eclipse of reason*. New York: Oxford University Press.

Husserl, E. (1962). *Ideas: General introduction to pure phenomenology*. New York: Collier. (Original work published 1913)

Husserl, E. (1964). *The phenomenology of internal time-consciousness*. Bloomington: Indiana University Press.

Larson, M. L. (1977). *The rise of professionalism*. Berkeley: University of California Press.

MacIntyre, A. (1984). *After virtue* (2nd ed.). Notre Dame: University of Notre Dame Press.

Mannheim, K. (1940). *Man and society in an age of reconstruction*. New York: Harcourt, Brace.

McCollough, T. E. (1991). *The moral imagination and public life*. Chatham, NJ: Chatham House.

Nietzsche, F. (1956). *The birth of tragedy and genealogy of morals* (F. Golffing, Trans.). Garden City, NY: Anchor/Doubleday. (Original work published 1872)

Polanyi, M. (1958). *Personal knowledge: Towards a post-critical philosophy*. Chicago, IL: University of Chicago Press.

Polanyi, M. (1966). *The tacit dimension*. Garden City, NY: Anchor/Doubleday.

Prigogine, I., & Stengers, I. (1984). *Order out of chaos: Man's new dialogue with nature*. New York: Bantam.

Rabinbach, A. (1990). *The human motor: Energy, fatigue and the origins of modernity*. New York: Basic Books.

Skowronek, S. (1982). *Building a new American state: The expansion of national administrative capacities, 1877-1920*. Cambridge: Cambridge University Press.

Smircich, L., & Calas, M. B. (1987). Organizational culture: A critical assessment. In F. M. Jablin, L. L. Putnam, K. H. Roberts, & L. W. Porter (Eds.), *Handbook of organizational communication*. Newbury Park, CA: Sage.

Spragens, T. A., Jr. (1990). *Reason and democracy*. Durham, NC: Duke University Press.

Stivers, C. (1990). Active citizenship and public administration. In G. L. Wamsley, R. N. Bacher, C. T. Goodsell, P. S. Kronenberg, J. A. Rohr, C. Stivers, O. F. White, & J. F. Wolf (Eds.), *Refounding public administration*. Newbury Park, CA: Sage.

Stivers, C. (1993). *Gender images in public administration*. Newbury Park, CA: Sage.

Taylor, C. (1985). *Philosophical papers* (2 vols.). New York: Cambridge University Press.

Turner, B. S. (Ed.). (1990). *Theories of modernity and postmodernity*. London: Sage.

Vanderburg, W. H. (1985). *The growth of minds and cultures: A unified theory of the structure of human experience*. Toronto: University of Toronto Press.

Vickers, G. (1965). *The art of judgment*. New York: Basic Books.

Vickers, G. (1970). *Freedom in a rocking boat*. London: Penguin Books.

Vickers, G. (1973). *Making institutions work*. New York: Wiley.

Vickers, G. (1977). Some implications of systems thinking: Presidential address. In A. Rapoport (Ed.), *General systems: Yearbook of the Society for General Systems Research* (Vol. 22). Louisville, KY: Society for General Systems Research.

Vickers, G. (1980). *Responsibility: Its sources and limits*. Seaside, CA: Intersystems.

Vickers, G. (1983). *Human systems are different*. London: Harper & Row.

Vickers, G. (1987a). Communication and ethical judgement. In G. B. Adams, B. L. Catron, & J. Forester (Eds.), *Policy making, communication and social learning: Essays of Sir Geoffrey Vickers*. New Brunswick, NJ: Transaction. (Original work published 1973)

Vickers, G. (1987b). The psychology of policymaking and social change. In G. B. Adams, B. L. Catron, & J. Forester (Eds.), *Policy making, communication and social learning: Essays of Sir Geoffrey Vickers*. New Brunswick, NJ: Transaction. (Original work published 1964)

von Bertalanffy, L. (1955). General systems theory. In A. Rapoport (Ed.), *General systems: Yearbook of the Society for General Systems Research* (Vol. 1). Louisville, KY: Society for General Systems Research.

Whitehead, A. N., & Russell, B. (1910). *Principia mathematica*. Oxford: Oxford University Press.

Wiebe, R. (1967). *The search for order*. New York: Hill and Wang.

Wiener, N. (1967). *The human use of human beings*. New York: Avon.

Wittgenstein, L. (1922). *Tractatus logico-philosophicus*. New York: Harcourt, Brace & World.

Yankelovich, D. (1991). *Coming to public judgment: Making democracy work in a complex world*. Syracuse, NY: Syracuse University Press.

4

Judgment and the Cultivation of Appreciation in Policy-Making

JOHN FORESTER

The periodic irrelevance of social science may be far easier to explain than we have thought. For in the face of ambiguous claims, little time, and unsatisfactory data, most practical people, among them public policy analysts and planners, friends and co-workers, have to learn not only about feasible outcomes and stable relationships of cause and effect but about value in our possible worlds, about potential significance, import, consequentiality. Practical people in our lives help us learn what to want, what to care about, and what we should care for, too. Yet as long as social scientists treat value as essentially irrational, an epiphenomenal dependent variable, or merely the expression of preferences, they will ignore, if not fail to understand entirely, the demands and opportunities of practical judgment and deliberative rationality, the heart of practical inquiry in the applied professions.

For many years now, I have been doing intermittent fieldwork in a setting that my colleagues find anything but thrilling, the staff meetings of a small-city Department of City Planning. My colleagues have a point at times, but more often they are quite wrong: The meetings combine drama, politics, humor, and just enough theater of the absurd to reflect the experience of working in and around city hall. In the past few years, in particular, I have studied the practical rhetoric of city planners, the moral, political, and ethical work that their accounts and "practice stories" (shoptalk) told on the job actually do.

Curiously, only after I saw how my own students were learning from diverse stories in the classroom did I begin to observe the planners' biweekly staff meetings in new ways. Here in front of me all the time had been rich and complex stories, told in sometimes shrewd, sometimes exasperated, sometimes desperate ways. Here, too, I found that not only did staff stories shape agendas and accounts but those stories shaped identities and reputations as well. Telling stories at work, it seemed, inevitably involved revealing oneself to others as much as it involved telling them about the case in hand. Furthermore, telling short stories about last night's city council meeting, for example, was necessarily selective, always value driven in several senses, and thus inevitably and selectively value disclosing, obscuring, or illuminating. Told on particular occasions for particular audiences and for particular purposes, practitioners' stories highlight some aspects of a case (what Jones did when Steiner attacked the budget projections) and distract our attention from others (the basis for the budget projections, for example) (Forester, 1989; Throgmorton, 1993).

At one staff meeting last year, I was preoccupied with a nagging question of politics and ethics: Can planners learn not only about facts and relationships but about the world of value as well? If the power of literature, for example, is in part to make us more ethically attuned to important aspects of human experience, then might not compelling practice stories function in similar ways (Nussbaum, 1991; Forester, 1993b)? When a planner gives a sensitive account of a community's suspicions about city hall motives, might that planner disclose not just the facts of suspicion but an ethical history of promises honored here and betrayed there, of obligations fulfilled or not, of important possibilities realized or squandered? When giving such accounts, then, are planners not disclosing issues of value, teaching their listeners about value?

Even in a staff meeting, might a diverse and professional group of city planners, accordingly, teach each other about important issues, about value in the world, and not just about values and opinions inferred from survey responses? As I listened in that meeting a year ago, I wondered if I could clarify the ways these professionals discussed value and values. Would such discussions differ from those in which they discussed the facts? What I found will stay with me for a very long time: When the staff discussed project proposals, or what happened at the city council subcommittee meeting last night, or the state transportation consultant's report, they were not separating facts here and values there. They were, instead, always searching for, and considering, what we can call the facts that *mattered*. They were exploring both fact and value, or, better, value *in* fact, at the very same time! How different this seemed from the muddy colloquial talk of value freedom, those presumptions of professional practice we periodically hear, "We want the facts, not what you like or don't like, but the facts!"

The planning staff in front of me knew that they would have to make recommendations to the city council, to the planning board, to interested citizens. This responsibility made them first cousins of the broader family of policy analysts and program evaluators. To make those recommendations and to do the analytical work to support them, these planners had to learn not only about factual relationships in the world but also about why and how they would matter. They had to learn not only about consequences but about consequentiality, about which of various matters might really come to matter, to be important—even to an unborn future population of a housing project or neighborhood not yet built. How distant, too, their practice seemed from the world of policy literature that presumes that values, preferences, and interests can be clearly specified in the beginning so that subsequent policy analysts and implementers can do their job competently.

To recognize that such professionals must routinely search for the facts that matter suggests that practicing planners and analysts like them face a daily challenge, not simply of learning about the facts of cases at hand but of exploring and learning about domains of value and different forms of value too. Learning about value here means something quite different from learning about people's deeply held values, preferences at the moment, or desires (Lovibond, 1983). Indeed, planners and policy analysts have to look far beyond expressions of preferences at a given time, for such analysts are routinely put in the all too fantastic position of foreseeing and anticipating problems—threats to value— and, even, trying to ensure that such potential problems never actually occur. Perversely, if these analysts are successful in avoiding problems and in protecting threatened value, they may then have nothing to show for their preventative efforts—quite unlike the proud architect who can point to his or her new edifice and say, "I built that!"

Planners and policy analysts typically try to anticipate both opportunities and threats, value that can be realized in the world (from steady employment to safe drinking water), and value that ought to be protected (from archaeological treasures to view corridors). This work involves much more than setting goals, for the real analysis comes within the broad parameters of whatever goals—*promote economic development* or *protect the environment*—are set. The real analysis requires a kind of learning that the modern social sciences seem peculiarly ill equipped to foster: a learning about value, an essentially reasoned, normative inquiry. Sadly, though, as long as the social sciences presume that claims of value simply reflect intensities of preference or differing irrational commitments, they tie the hands of the public-serving analysts whose very jobs demand a careful concern with what's at stake, what matters, in public policy and planning decisions, popularly recognized and explicitly valued or not.

Several students of public policy, however, have pointed to these problems. For example, Giandomenico Majone (1989) wrote recently,

> It is widely assumed that public deliberation and public policy are primarily concerned with setting goals and finding the means to achieve them. Actually, the most important function both of public deliberation and of policy-making is defining the norms that determine when certain conditions are to be regarded as policy problems. (p. 23)

Majone continues,

> Experts, including policy analysts, are often engaged in setting norms rather than in searching for solutions that satisfy given norms. Empirical methods have no point of attack until there is agreement on norms, since the nature of the problem depends on which norms are adopted. Hence, argument and persuasion play the key role in norm setting and problem definition. (p. 28)

In this article, I would like particularly to discuss Sir Geoffrey Vickers's prescient analysis of these problems of learning about value and, as Majone puts it, "norm-setting."

VICKERS ON ACTION, APPRECIATION,
AND CYBERNETIC SYSTEMS THEORIES

A value-free plan or policy analysis would be literally worthless. This is Sir Geoffrey Vickers's persistent insight, and it suggests the significance of the planning and policy-making skill of "appreciation" that he so extensively elaborated. Vickers (1970b) wrote,

> Facts are relevant, only by reference to some judgment of value and judgments of value are meaningful only in regard to some configuration of fact. Hence the need for a word to embrace the two, for which I propose "appreciation," a word, not yet appropriated by science, which in its ordinary use (as in "appreciation of a situation") implies a combined judgment of value and fact. (p. 198)

Throughout his work, Vickers demonstrated the centrality of human appreciation: in everyday life, planning, and policy-making, with regard to problems of accountability, management, and organizational communication, in our understanding of political and economic systems, and in scientific inquiry more generally. In so doing, Vickers characterized a style of planning and political practice that is factually grounded, ethically attuned, and also politically astute.

If we consider Vickers's friendly but searching criticism of cybernetic feedback models of social action, we can recognize a primary contribution of his work: to pose clearly and pragmatically the problem of how best to inform judgments of value to guide public decision making. Vickers's work is not only alert to the promise of cybernetic systems theories but it insightfully and incisively reveals their flaws as well. His discussion of the concept of the cybernetic feedback signal as it might be used to explain human behavior provides an instructive example.

Feedback is a signal that indicates the difference between a mechanism's actual performance and a preset standard of desired performance. If we set our household thermostat at 68°F but then open our windows on a cold winter day, the thermostat will soon sense the difference between the cooling room temperature, lowered by the cold winter air, and our preset standard, and as a result it will turn on the heat to attempt to bring the room temperature back to the desired standard.

Similarly, cybernetic models of action lead us to understand human behavior in the model of a helmsman's performance on a ship. With a course set, the helmsman monitors wind and sea to adjust the rudder properly to keep the vessel on course. Human actors also, presumably, compare their performance to their standards and adjust their behavior accordingly.

Vickers takes this information-processing view of action and regulation to be a substantial achievement. It shifts our focus from one accounting for the energy expended in action to one keyed to information flows and sensitive to human purposes (Vickers, 1973). Yet Vickers recognizes substantial problems here too.

As anyone living without a California climate knows, if the house windows are open in midwinter, the action of the thermostat is likely to be futile. And as any sailor, automobile driver, skier, or hiker knows, there are times when the environmental conditions are so uncertain—the sea is too stormy, the road too muddy, the hill too icy, the trail too dangerous—that it is time to turn around and go back. New norms come into play.

In such cases, the only sensible, efficient, and safe course of action is not obstinately to try harder, but to wait for another day, for a better opportunity, and thus not to heed the call of the original standard we set. Many times we find it better not to pursue blindly, stubbornly, and foolishly the originally valued ends or standards, but rather to modify those values, ends, or standards, possibly to realize them at another time (Richardson, 1990). Vickers recognizes clearly that this course of action of changing, perhaps supplementing, our values and standards, and not just adopting new means to the same ends, is fundamentally a matter of immediately practical ethics.

Accepting the cybernetician's initial focus on system standards, performance, and the feedback indicating discrepancies between these two, Vickers then asks the cybernetician to address the questions that logically follow: How do human beings change goals, standards, and values? Vickers saw clearly, too, that to refer to such change as a *political* matter risks simply substituting a label for an explanation.

To Vickers's substantial credit, he shows not only the power of cybernetic views of action but also their necessarily ethical and political content—a content, however, that seems not very well elaborated within the cybernetic paradigm itself (Levin, 1994). Recognizing the contribution of communications scientists and students of artificial intelligence to models of human action, Vickers noted acutely:

> They are teaching us to distinguish information from energy, and to seek the explanation of enduring form in a regulator and a programme. But they have not yet provided us with working models to help our thinking about the way we set and reset our own and each other's appreciative systems. And until they do this, the most important aspect of human life is still likely to be ignored and even denied. (Vickers, 1973, p. 334)

Pointing out the radical significance of these yet-to-be explored questions of valuation and appreciation (Forester, 1993b; Nussbaum, 1991), he continued:

> We can thank the communications scientists for having at least defined [the structuring of perception and action by values and standards] as a field of study and provided its first elementary vocabulary. Some of them look improbable revolutionaries. Many of them are unconscious of their revolutionary message. Most of them would hate it if they knew it. (Vickers, 1973, p. 336)

Vickers shows elegantly and vividly, then, that cybernetic theories of action are necessarily ethical theories. Yet to say this does not solve, but rather poses, a deep problem of modern social science tackled by Weberians, Marxians, and Durkheimians as well: How are we to understand social action? Students of Max Weber risk "methodological individualism" and the dangers of explaining action predominantly as the result of individual choice and individual values, as an acute comment by Anthony Giddens (1976) suggests: "Just as there is no room here for the creative capacity of the subject on the level of the actor, so there is a major source of difficulty in explaining the origins of transformations of institutionalized value-standards themselves" (p. 96; Alford & Friedland, 1985; cf. Giddens, 1979). Students of Marx take a quite different risk: explaining away action as overly determined, being so structurally rooted that a Marxist theory of social action or interaction may hardly be possible. Students of Durkheim, too, risk reducing action to a functional, norm-conformative response to the needs and imperatives of encompassing social systems.

Vickers suggests another approach: a communications theory of action that far surpasses an information theory to become a social and ethical theory too (cf. Habermas, 1984). Vickers does not just argue that our conception of deliberate, value-guided rational action is central to our understanding of planning, policy-making, and regulation. He goes still further to show us how such a theory of action must be explicitly ethical and political, accounting not only for variations in performance but for variations in actors' evaluations—their valuing—as well.

So, when Vickers suggests that the role of planners and policy advisors is to inform decision makers and the affected public regarding policy choices, we know full well that he means that advisors must not only communicate facts but refine and educate the public's and decision makers' evaluations as well, to *cultivate their appreciation of the situations and possibilities they face.*

A SCIENCE OF VALUATION?

But how ought planners and policy advisors to influence others' evaluations—their processes of valuing? Writing about information sciences, schools of systems theory, and their implications for policy-making and action, Vickers was keenly aware that the very success of these information-centered fields could ironically serve not to clarify but rather to obscure fundamental social problems. In a particularly insightful essay, "Science is Human," Vickers (1970b) wrote:

> So far the emergence of the computer as a human partner has not merely speeded the solution of the kind of problems that computers can solve but has begun to push *still further into the background the more important problems which at present they cannot solve, notably the evolution of criteria for making multi-valued choices.* . . . This constitutes (another) area of inquiry in which communication theory does not yet help us. To describe the process by which interests are generated and standards evolved as mediated by dialogue and reflection asserts nothing but the not yet accepted fact that the process involves more than the reactions of responsiveness. (p. 214)

How, then, are we to understand processes of valuing, of learning to value? In part, we know that one's value judgments may be influenced by where one lives or works, by institutional position and political pressures, in addition to basic biologically rooted stresses such as hunger, exhaustion, or exposure. Yet rather than quarrel with arguments suggesting that value judgments are exclusively products of political influence, Vickers points instead to a deeper problem. Given multiple options and multiple values (and an awareness of political forces and ideological influences), what are we to want? What should we want (Elster, 1983; March, 1988)?

Vickers refuses both to leave this question to the whims of fancy or to go to the other extreme and pretend that an experimental science of values or ethics is at hand. "Learning what to want," he wrote in *Freedom in a Rocking Boat,* "is the most radical, the most painful, and the most creative art of life" (Vickers, 1970a, p. 76; Wiggins, 1978).

Pointing to the limits of a social science rooted in the traditions and canons of physical science, Vickers (1970b) also wrote sharply:

> The only peculiarity of science as human activity is that its values—its interests and standards of success—are those of the map-maker, not the map user. The observation, so often repeated, that our age is richer in know-how than in know-what is only another way of saying that a map is no substitute for a journey. An age which does not know where it wants to go concentrates on the making of maps, just as, not knowing what it wants to buy, it concentrates on the making of money. "Money," wrote an economist, "is dope, a tranquillizer against the effects of not knowing what to do." Science, similarly, is a tranquillizer against the effects of not knowing where to go. It would be silly to blame science for this and tragic to expect to get the whole answer from the map. (p. 214)

This problem lies at the heart of the policy sciences, for they cannot help but be sources of evaluative judgments. Policy-making and political action inherently affect others. They change social relations, weakening some and strengthening others. They take sides. They inevitably accept or reject, complement or contradict, existing structures of authority and power, whether these are formally institutionalized into official positions, represented in concentrations of economic capital, or embodied in the leadership of social movements. Rooted in a contentious and ambiguous political world, policy scientists can hardly speak or write without dignifying certain options and not others, without honoring certain concerns and not others (Seeley, 1963). But by misleadingly casting decisions as technically derived, as if freed from the responsibilities of human judgment, scientific justifications for unpopular actions might mitigate popular opposition.

Indeed, the promise of modern science has now been appropriated by all segments of the political spectrum. Whether they understand action to obey the laws of history or those of the market, advocates of left, right, and center present much contemporary political action and policy-making as scientifically based. But notice what would no longer be necessary if moral and political choices could be scientifically decided, either by experts or ideologically by keepers of the appropriate faith: an informed public, citizens who were active members of a political community, political obligations of citizens to one another, popular political mandate, democratic processes of argument, discourse, and accountability. How convenient for opponents of democratic political systems if scientific decision making could render accountability obsolete! How very simple, innocent, and autocratic a scientistic politics might be.

This problem, of course, is not a new one. Today in the public policy fields, we face the prospect less of a democratic polity wrestling with decisions or the effective rule of the wise than of the centrality of the administrative expert, the crucial scientific advisor, the technocrat knowing intricately either the dynamics of the market, the shifting conjuncture of political-economic forces, or the imperatives of history (Fischer, 1990; Nussbaum, 1986). Of course the problems of markets, political-economic conjunctures, and historical understanding are crucial ones. But we fool ourselves if we allow their problem solvers to obscure the challenge Vickers finds at the heart of all action and policy-making: the development of judgment and practical appreciation; knowing the relevant facts and learning what to want; learning how to value and evaluate possibilities of public action (Nussbaum, 1991).

THE PLANNER'S ROLE

Recognizing the limits of the policy sciences, Vickers suggests a role for those who wish to inform and improve policy-making and political action. Such work, which we may call *planning* more generally, should cultivate actors' appreciations; it should educate both the public and the policymaker. Planners should elaborate, refine, and expose assumptions about relevant factual conditions no more or less than assumptions about relevant value and interest implications. Planners should set forth innovations and possible routes of action so, as Vickers (1965) wrote,

> facilitating rather than blocking or misdirecting the dialogue on which institutional regulation depends. This is the most the planner can do. It is also the least that the policy maker should require him to do, for this dialogue is critically important and at present critically inadequate. (p. 92)

This formulation of planners' and policy analysts' roles is fully consistent with a democratic political tradition, but it also begs questions that need, as Vickers suggests, immediate attention. Let us grant that science, instrumentally conceived, can give us a road map but not tell us where to go. And let us grant that the planner, wishing to inform politically and ethically decent policy and action, knows full well that he or she must not only bring to bear instrumental, know-how knowledge but also refined and elaborated judgments of value, relevance, interest, and significance as well. What sort of planning and policy dialogue, then, can the planner inform? *What vision and skill are necessary to facilitate that "critically important and at present critically inadequate" dialogue on which institutional policy-making and regulation depends?*

Vickers's work poses this fundamental question, but it does not address it in detail. Hardly a last word on policy formulation, his work does not teach us how policy dialogue is vulnerable, for example, to needless manipulations stemming from radical inequalities of power, information, wealth, status, and resources; from organized lobbies, bureaucratic language, organizational rivalries, and prestructured interests rooted no more in status incentives at times than in class structure.

Sir Geoffrey Vickers never pretended that his analyses could be the last word. Rather, the remarkable freshness, insight, and productive and hopeful character of his writing lies precisely in its clear sense that here he is posing pressing questions for others to refine and pursue to enable further planning dialogue and the democratization of policy-making.

This formulation of planning practice—to encourage rather than to preempt the critical dialogue on which informed policy-making depends—can now be still further developed, strengthened, and effectively and ethically put into practice (Fischer & Forester, 1993). Vickers's notion of planning and policy-making activity as fundamentally communicative can be developed in far greater detail by appropriating recent related work in fields of sociology and communications (Deetz, 1992; Habermas, 1984). In addition, planners who wish to facilitate actual policy-relevant dialogue and debate can learn to anticipate and counteract certain regular institutional sources of misinformation: organized conflict, bureaucratic self-protection, biased testimony, poorly written or obfuscating reports, incomplete or deliberately withheld information, overstatements of needs or costs, and so on (Benhabib, 1988; Forester, 1989, 1993a).

So we can take Vickers's notion of appreciation to encompass our reading not just of the relevant facts of alternative policy options but of the political and organizational process of planning and policy-making itself (Bryson & Crosby, 1993; Forester, 1992, 1994a; Healey, 1993; Reich, 1990). Eyes open to the political world staging their work, planners can appreciate how, concretely, genuine policy-making dialogues can be needlessly threatened, slanted, obscured, blocked, or misdirected. Such appreciation calls for organizational and political skills too often slighted in schools of planning and policy-making (Baum, 1990; Reardon, Welsh, Kreiswirth, & Forester, 1993). A crucial element of planning practice, accordingly, is the anticipation and subsequent countering of bureaucratic, political, or economic pressures that can unjustly structure agendas of policy-making debate, exclude affected parties or their representatives, and so have the promise of legitimate debate mask the continued domination of already established power.

What actually constitutes legitimate domination or policy-making debate in the modern polity or political economy is yet another fundamental issue to which Vickers's work points us but does not address in detail. What are more or less legitimate ways to structure decision-making processes (of information flow, consultation, debate, and so forth) in a local community action group, a union, a political party, a government agency? How much should the leadership's advisors consult others, and which others, and how?

Vickers's work is all the more important because it teaches us how basic questions of political and social theory are perpetually posed and resolved in the ongoing work of planners and policymakers. Like the question of legitimate representation, these issues are never solved once and for all. Yet Vickers makes quite clear that planners and policymakers, inevitably political communicators, have a particular opportunity and responsibility: to shape the appreciation, the understanding of fact and value, the recognition of real possibility and genuine significance, of the polity at large (Forester, 1992, 1994b; Reich, 1990). As he wrote about innovation in policy-making,

> Innovations occur in the appreciative field and spread from their originators to others. Potentialities, formerly ignored, are noticed and become potent as norms; and often the proximate cause can be traced to the individual who first saw what might be and prized it as what should be, and cried, "Look!" and caused his fellows to see and to value, and in time to realize, what he first saw. History has its dramatic examples but we need not look further than the Buchanan committee, allowing this creative vision to disturb the lucid waters of their official prose, "Of this there can be no doubt, that there are potentialities for enriching the lives of millions of people who have to live in towns beyond anything most of them have yet dreamed of." (Vickers, 1965, p. 112)

Planning and policy-making must not only inform decision makers' choices but educate participants' imaginations, not only report evaluations but cultivate appreciation and good judgment, not only exercise power responsibly but empower others to act responsibly, to do justice, as well. This challenge, to learn about and discern value no less than to seek it, is the legacy of Sir Geoffrey Vickers's work, and it virtually defines the vocation of planning and policy analysis.

REFERENCES

Alford, R., & Friedland, R. (1985). *Powers of theory*. Cambridge: Cambridge University Press.

Baum, H. (1990). *Organizational membership*. Albany: State University of New York Press.

Benhabib, S. (1988). Judgment and the moral foundations of politics in Arendt's thought. *Political Theory, 16*(1), 29-51.

Bryson, J. M., & Crosby, B. C. (1993). Policy planning and the design and use of forums, arenas, and courts. *Environment and Planning B: Planning and Design, 20*, 175-194.

Deetz, D. (1992). *Democracy in an age of corporate colonization*. Albany: State University of New York Press.

Elster, J. (1983). *Sour grapes*. Cambridge: Cambridge University Press.

Fischer, F. (1990). *Technocracy and the politics of expertise*. Newbury Park, CA: Sage.

Fischer, F., & Forester, J. (Eds.). (1993). *The argumentative turn in policy analysis and planning*. Durham, NC: Duke University Press.

Forester, J. (1989). *Planning in the face of power*. Berkeley: University of California Press.

Forester, J. (1992). Envisioning the politics of public dispute resolution. In A. Sarat & S. Sibley (Eds.), *Studies in law, politics, and society* (Vol. 12). San Francisco, CA: JAI.

Forester, J. (1993a). *Critical theory, public policy, and planning practice*. Albany: State University of New York Press.

Forester, J. (1993b). Learning from practice stories: The priority of practical judgment. In F. Fischer & J. Forester (Eds.), *The argumentative turn in policy analysis and planning*. Durham, NC: Duke University Press.

Forester, J. (1994a). *Activist mediation and public disputes: A profile of Larry Susskind.* In D. M. Kolb and Associates (Eds.), *When talk works.* San Francisco, CA: Jossey-Bass.

Forester, J. (1994b). *Politics, pragmatism, and vision: Political judgment in planning practice.* Unpublished manuscript.

Giddens, A. (1976). *New rules for sociological method.* London: Hutchinson.

Giddens, A. (1979). *Central problems in social theory.* Berkeley: University of California Press.

Habermas, J. (1984). *The theory of communicative action.* Boston, MA: Beacon.

Healey, P. (1993). The communicative work of development plans. *Environment and Planning B: Planning and Design, 20,* 83-104.

Levin, M. (1994). Action research and critical systems thinking: Two icons carved out of the same log? *Systems Practice, 7*(1), 25-41.

Lovibond, S. (1983). *Realism and imagination in ethics.* Minneapolis: University of Minnesota Press.

Majone, G. (1989). *Evidence, argument, and persuasion in the policy process.* New Haven, CT: Yale University Press.

March, J. (1988). *Organizations and decisions.* New York: Blackwell.

Nussbaum, M. (1986). *The fragility of goodness.* Cambridge: Cambridge University Press.

Nussbaum, M. (1991). *Love's knowledge.* Oxford: Oxford University Press.

Reardon, K., Welsh, J., Kreiswirth, B., & Forester, J. (1993). Participatory action research from the inside: A profile of Ken Reardon's community development practice in East St. Louis. *American Sociologist, 24*(1), 69-91.

Reich, R. (1990). Policy making in a democracy. In R. Reich (Eds.), *The power of public ideas.* Cambridge, MA: Harvard University Press.

Richardson, H. (1990). Specifying norms as a way to resolve concrete ethical problems. *Philosophy and Public Affairs, 19,* 279-310.

Seeley, J. (1963). Social science: Some probative problems. In A. Vidich & M. Stein (Eds.), *Sociology on trial* (pp. 53-65). Englewood Cliffs, NJ: Prentice-Hall.

Throgmorton, J. (1993). Survey research as rhetorical trope: Electric power planning arguments in Chicago. In F. Fischer & J. Forester (Eds.), *The argumentative turn in policy analysis and planning* (pp. 117-144). Durham, NC: Duke University Press.

Vickers, G. (1965). *The art of judgment.* New York: Basic Books.

Vickers, G. (1970a). *Freedom in a rocking boat.* London: Penguin.

Vickers, G. (1970b). Science is human. In G. Vickers, *Value systems and social process* (p. 198). London: Penguin.

Vickers, G. (1973). Communication and ethical judgment. In L. Thayer (Ed.), *Communication: Ethical and moral issues* (pp. 325-336). London: Gordon and Breach Science.

Wiggins, D. (1978). Deliberation and practical reason. In J. Raz (Ed.), *Practical reasoning* (pp. 144-152). Oxford: Oxford University Press.

5

Systems Theory and Management Thinking

PETER CHECKLAND

Two inquiring systems developed since the 1960s—Vickers's concept of the appreciative system and the soft systems methodology, are highly relevant to the problems of the 21st century. Both assume that organizations are more than rational goal-seeking machines and address the relationship-maintaining and Gemeinschaft aspects of organizations, characteristically obscured by functionalist and goal-seeking models of organization and management. Appreciative systems theory and soft systems methodology enrich rather than replace these approaches.

Two rich metaphors provide a useful frame within which any consideration of the problems facing us in the late 20th century can, with advantage, be placed. As a result of the first industrial revolution, based on energy, and the current second one, based on information, the world is increasingly Marshall McLuhan's "global village." More and more problems need to be examined in a global rather than a local context and, as we do so, we need to remember that we are all of us, in Buckminster Fuller's great phrase, "the crew of Spaceship Earth."

Thanks to the material successes of the two industrial revolutions we are a crew with rising expectations of high living standards. But we are increasingly aware that the wealth-generating machine may not be able to meet those expectations without doing unacceptable damage to Spaceship Earth, which, together with the free supply of energy from our sun, is the only given resource we have.

This triangle—of expectations, wealth generation, and protection of the planet—will have to be managed with great care at many different levels as we enter the 21st century if major disasters are to be avoided. Unfortunately, our current ideas on *management* are rather primitive and are probably not up to the task. They stem from the technologically oriented thinking of the 1960s, and they now need to be enlarged and enriched. This may well be possible from the systems thinking of the 1970s and 1980s, which has placed that body of thought more firmly within the arena of human affairs.

This article will examine the legacy of thinking about management and organizations that we get from the 1960s and develop a richer view that stems from more recent systems thinking, especially Vickers's work on the theory of *appreciative systems* and work on soft systems methodology, which can be seen as a way of making practical use of Vickers's concepts. This, it is argued, is more relevant than the current conventional wisdom to managing the problems of the new century.

MANAGEMENT AND ORGANIZATION

In spite of a huge literature—some of it serious, much of it at the level of airport paperbacks—and courses in colleges and universities worldwide, the role of the manager and the nature of the process of managing remain problematic, whether we are concerned with trying to manage global, institutional, or personal affairs. Anyone who has been a professional manager in an organization knows that it is a complex role, one that engages the whole person. It requires not only the ability to analyze problems and work out rational responses but also, if the mysterious quality of leadership is to be provided, the ability to respond to situations on the basis of feelings and emotion.

One of the reasons the manager's role remains obstinately problematic stems from our less-than-adequate thinking about the context in which managers perform, namely the organization. Some basic systems thinking indicates that if we adopt a limited view of organization then the conceptualization of the manager's role will inevitably also be rather threadbare. Thus a manager at any level occupies a role within a structure of roles that constitutes an organization. The activity undertaken by managers can be seen as a system of activity that serves and supports and makes its contribution to the overall aims of the organization as a purposeful whole. Now, if one system serves another, it is a basic tenet of systems thinking that the system that serves can be conceptualized only after prior conceptualization of the system served (Checkland, 1981, p. 237). This is so because the form of a serving system, if it is truly to serve, will be dictated by the nature of the system served: That will dictate the necessary form of any system that aspires to serve and support it.

Now there is a conventional wisdom about the nature of organization that persists in spite of the fact that anyone who has worked within an organization knows that this image conveys only part of the story. The conventional model is that an organization is a social collectivity that arranges itself so that it can pursue declared aims and objectives that individuals could not achieve on their own. Given this view of organization, the manager's role is to help achieve the corporate goals, and it follows that the manager's activity is essentially rational decision making in pursuit of declared aims. This is the conventional wisdom even though intuitively we all have a rich sense that organizations in which we have worked are more than rational goal-seeking machines. The experienced day-to-day reality of organizations is that they have some of the characteristics of the tribe and the family as well as the characteristics necessary if they are to order what they do rationally so as to achieve desired objectives such as, in the case of industrial companies, survival and growth. In spite of this folk knowledge, the orthodoxy has been very strong, and we can see this both in the literature of organization theory and in that of management science.

ORGANIZATION THEORY

This is not the place to discuss the development of organization theory in any detail, but it is useful for present purposes to mark the general shape of this field as it emerges in such wide-ranging studies as Reed's (1985) *Redirections in Organisational Analysis*. The general shape is that of the establishment of an orthodoxy (the systems/contingency model that held sway from the 1930s to the 1960s) and the challenge to that orthodoxy since then, with no single dominant alternative. Nevertheless, the challenging models do, in general, have in common the fact that they see organizations not as reified objects independent of organizational members, as in the orthodox systems model, but as the continually changing product of a human process in which social reality is socially constructed: the title of Berger and Luckmann's (1966) well-known book — *The Social Construction of Reality*—neatly captures this alternative strand of thinking.

At a broad level of generalization, we can see the two major approaches as reflecting the two main categories of thinking about organizations on which a pioneering sociologist, Ferdinand Tönnies, built his account. In his major work *Gemeinschaft und Gesellschaft* (1887) (translated as *Community and Association* by Loomis, 1955), Tönnies constructed models of two types of society or organization. There is the natural living community into which a person is born, the family or the tribe (Gemeinschaft), and there are the formally created groupings (Gesellschaft) that a person joins in some contractual sense, as when he or she becomes an employee of a company or joins a climbing club.

In general, the orthodox view of organizations emphasizes their Gesellschaft nature, that they are created to do things collectively (*achieve goals* is the usual language) that would be beyond the reach of individuals. The alternatives emphasize rather that all social groupings take on some flavor of Gemeinschaft: Being in an organization is something like being part of a family. Intuitively, the lived experience of organizations that we all gradually acquire gives us the folk knowledge that organizations exhibit some of the characteristics of both models.

That the orthodox view has been dominant can be seen by perusing college textbooks, which present students with the conventional wisdom. For example, in Khandwalla's (1979) *The Design of Organizations*, the view of organizations as open systems devoted to achieving corporate objectives is described as "the most powerful orientation in organization theory today" (p. 251). Much attention is paid to well-known work aimed at correlating an organization's structure with its core tasks carried out in an environment with which it interacts (Lawrence &

Lorsch, 1967; Pugh & Hickson, 1976; Woodward, 1965; etc.). Reed's (1985) survey argues that "systems theorists . . . had dominated organizational analysis since the 1930s" (p. 35) but that by the 1960s there was no common history or intellectual heritage. By the 1970s, a systems-derived approach was "struggling to retain its grip on organizational studies" (p. 106). This does not mean that the orthodoxy has lost its adherents, however. In the same year that Reed's book was published, Donaldson (1985) brought out his *In Defence of Organization Theory*, the defense being of the "relatively accepted contingency-systems paradigm" (p. ix).

Both Reed and Donaldson make much reference to a book that marks as much as any other the challenge to the orthodox systems view: Silverman's (1970) *The Theory of Organizations*. Silverman contrasts the systems view from the 1950s and 1960s with what he calls "the Action frame of reference" in which action results from the meanings that members of organizations attribute to their own and each other's acts. Organizational life becomes a collective process of meaning attribution; attention is displaced away from the apparently impersonal processes by means of which, in the conventional model, a reified organization as an open system responds to a changing environment. Some of Silverman's subheadings convey the nature of his argument: Action not behaviour, Action arises from meanings, Meanings as social facts, Meanings are socially sustained, Meanings are socially changed.

This important work opens the way to various alternatives to the systems orthodoxy. Donaldson's discussion, for example, includes social action theory, the sociology of organizations, and the strategic choice thesis. Just as the orthodoxy draws on a positivist philosophy and a functionalist sociology, the alternatives are underpinned philosophically by phenomenology, and sociologically by an interpretive approach derived from Weber and Schutz.

It has to be said that the orthodox view provides a much clearer model of organization, and hence the manager's role, than is provided by the alternatives. Concentrating on the Gesellschaft aspects of an organization, the conventional view sees it as an open system seeking to achieve corporate objectives in an environment to which it has to adapt. Its tasks are analyzed and assigned to groups within a functionalist structure, and the managers' role is essentially that of decision making in pursuit of corporate aims that also provide the standards against which progress will be judged. No similarly clear picture is provided by the alternatives, beyond the notion that organizations are characterized essentially by discourse that establishes the meanings that will underpin action by individuals and groups.

It is not at all surprising that that section of the management literature most concerned with intervening in, in order to influence and shape, real-world situations, namely management science, should itself focus on the orthodox systems model.

MANAGEMENT SCIENCE

In examining briefly the state of thinking in management science, it is useful to focus on the work of Herbert Simon. There are two reasons for this. First, it has been a dominating contribution in the field; second, in developing an approach based on the work of Vickers, we find that he explicitly contrasted his approach with that of Simon, drawing attention to the reliance of Simon on a goal-seeking model of human action that he himself was deliberately trying to transcend.

In the period after the Second World War, strenuous efforts were made to apply the lessons from wartime operations research to industrial companies and government agencies. In doing this, a powerful strand of systems thinking was developed—it would now be thought of as "hard" systems thinking—concerned broadly with engineering a system to achieve its objectives. Systems were here assumed to exist in the world; it was assumed that they could be defined as goal seeking; and ideas of system control were generalized in cybernetics. These ideas mapped the orthodox stance of organization theory discussed in the previous section, and they conceptualized the manager's task as being to solve problems and take decisions in pursuit of declared goals. Indeed, this paradigm is succinctly expressed in Ackoff's (1957) assumption that problems ultimately reduce to the evaluation of the efficiency of alternative means for a designated set of objectives.

This is the field to which Simon has made such a significant and influential contribution, the flavor of which is captured in the title of his 1960 book: *The New Science of Management Decision.*

At a round table devoted to his work, Zannetos (1984) summarized Simon's legacy as "a theory of problem solving, programs and processes for developing intelligent machines, and approaches to the design of organizational structures for managing complex systems" (p. 75).

Overall, Simon sought a science of administrative behavior and executive decision making. In an intellectually shrewd move that has no doubt helped to make this body of work so influential, Simon wisely abandoned the notion that managers and administrators seek to *optimize*, replacing it with the idea of *satisficing*: the idea that the search is for solutions that are *good enough* in the perceived circumstances, rather than optimal (March & Simon, 1958). Nevertheless, the flavor of hard systems thinking is retained in the claim that the search is "motivated by the existence of problems as indicated by gaps between performance and goals" (p. 73).

Similarly in another of Simon's major contributions, the development with Newall of GPS (general problem solver), a heuristic computer program that seeks to simulate human problem solving, the whole work is built on the concept of problem solving as a search for a means to an end that is already declared to be desirable (Newall & Simon, 1972). Simon (1960) stated,

Problem solving proceeds by erecting goals, detecting differences between present situation and goal, finding in memory or by search tools or processes that are relevant to reducing differences of these particular kinds, and applying these tools or processes. Each problem generates subproblems until we find a subproblem we can solve—for which we have a program stored in memory. We proceed until, by successive solution of such subproblems, we eventually achieve our overall goal—or give up. (p. 27)

This is an especially clear statement of the thinking, derived from the systems theory of the 1950s, that has dominated management science and that underlies organization theory's orthodox model of what an organization is.

It is the argument here that this goal-seeking model, largely adequate though it was in the management science that contributed to post-Second World War industrial development, is not rich enough to support and sustain the management thinking now needed by the crew of Spaceship Earth, that spaceship having become akin to a global village.

An alternative, richer perspective is provided by the systems thinking of the 1970s and 1980s, and in particular by Vickers's development of appreciative systems theory and by an approach to intervention in human affairs that can be seen as making practical use of that theory, namely, soft systems methodology.

These are discussed in the next section, but it may be useful to point out at once that these are developments in what is now known as "soft" systems thinking, as opposed to the hard systems thinking of the 1950s and 1960s that permeates both orthodox organization theory and Simonian management science. The usual distinction made between the two is that the hard systems thinking tackles well-defined problems (such as optimizing the output of a chemical plant), whereas the soft approach is more suitable for ill-defined, messy, or wicked problems (such as deciding on health care policy in a resource-constrained situation). This is not untrue, but it fails to make an intellectual distinction between the two. The real distinction lies in the attribution of systemicity (having the property of system-like characteristics). Hard systems thinking assumes that the world is a set of systems (i.e., is *systemic*) and that these can be *systematically* engineered to achieve objectives. In the soft tradition, the world is assumed to be problematic, but it is also assumed that *the process of inquiry* into the problematic situations that make up the world can be organized as a system. In other words, assumed systemicity is shifted: from taking the world to be systemic to taking the process of inquiry to be systemic (Checkland, 1983, 1985b).

Thus in the following section both appreciative systems theory and soft systems methodology describe inquiring processes—the former with a view to understanding, the latter with a view to taking action to improve real-world problem situations.

Finally, we may note that soft systems thinking can be seen as representing the introduction of systems thinking into Silverman's action frame of reference, although the organization theory literature is apparently at present innocent of any knowledge of post-1960s developments in systems thinking (Checkland, 1994).

APPRECIATIVE SYSTEMS THEORY

THE NATURE OF AN APPRECIATIVE SYSTEM

The task that Vickers set himself in his "retirement" after 40 years in the world of affairs was to make sense of that experience. In the books and articles that he then wrote he constructed

> an epistemology which will account for what we manifestly do when we sit round board tables or in committee rooms (and equally though less explicitly when we try, personally, for example, to decide whether or not to accept the offer of a new job). (G. Vickers, personal communication, July 1974)

In his thinking as this project developed, Vickers first rejected the ubiquitous goal-seeking model of human activity; then he found systems thinking relevant to his task; but he also rejected the cybernetic model of the steersman (whose course is defined from outside the system), replacing it by his more subtle notion of "appreciation" (Vickers, 1965, is the basic reference). He expressed his intellectual history in the following terms in a letter to the present writer in 1974:

> It seems to me in retrospect that for the last twenty years I have been contributing to the general debate the following neglected ideas:
> (1) In describing human activity, institutional or personal, the goal-seeking paradigm is inadequate. Regulatory activity, in government, management or private life consists in attaining or maintaining desired relationships through time or in changing and eluding undesired ones.
> (2) But the cybernetic paradigm is equally inadequate, because the helmsman has a single course given from outside the system, whilst the human regulator, personal or collective, controls a system which generates multiple and mutually inconsistent courses. The function of the regulator is to choose and realise one of many possible mixes, none fully attainable. In doing so it also becomes a major influence in the process of generating courses.
> (3) From 1 and 2 flows a body of analysis which examines the "course-generating" function, distinguishes between "metabolic" and functional relations, the first being those which serve the stability of the system (e.g. budgeting to preserve solvency and liquidity), the second being those which serve to bring the achievements of the system into line with its multiple and changing standards of success. This leads me to explore the nature and origin of these standards of success and thus to distinguish between norms or standards, usually tacit and known by the mismatch signals which they generate in specific situations, and values, those explicit general concepts of what is humanly good and bad which we invoke in the debate about standards, a debate which changes both. (G. Vickers, personal communication, 1974)

In developing the theory of appreciative systems and relating it to real-world experience, Vickers never expressed the ideas pictorially, in the form of a model, although this seems a desirable form in which to express a system. (His explanation for this lack was disarming: "You must remember," he said, "that I am the product of an English classical education" [G. Vickers, personal communication, 1979]). What follows is an account of the model of an appreciative system developed by Checkland and Casar (1986) from the whole corpus of Vickers's writings.

From those writings we may highlight some major themes that recur:

- 'A rich concept of day-to-day experienced life (compare Schutz's [1967] *Lebenswelt*)
- A separation of judgments about what is the case, *reality judgments*, and judgments about what is humanly good or bad, *value judgments*
- An insistence on *relationship maintaining* as a richer concept of human action than the popular but poverty-stricken notion of goal seeking
- A concept of action judgments stemming from reality and value judgments
- A notion that the cycle of judgments and actions is organized as a system

The starting point for the model is the Lebenswelt, the interacting flux of events and ideas unfolding through time. This is Vickers's "two-stranded rope," the strands inseparable and continuously affecting each other. Appreciation is occasioned by our ability to select, to choose. Appreciation perceives (some of) reality, makes judgments about it, contributes to the ideas stream, and leads to actions that become part of the events stream. Thus the basic form of the model is that shown in Figure 1. There is a recursive loop in which the flux of events and ideas generates appreciation, and appreciation itself contributes to the flux. Appreciation also leads to action that itself contributes to the flux.

It is now necessary to unpack the process of appreciation. From Vickers's writings we take the notion of perceiving reality selectively and making judgments about it. The epistemology of the judgment making will be one of relationship managing rather than goal seeking, the latter being an occasional special case of the former. And both reality and value judgments stem from standards of both fact and value: standards of what *is*, and standards of what is good or bad, acceptable or unacceptable. The very act of using the standards may itself modify them.

These activities lead to a view on how to act to maintain, to modify, or to elude certain forms of relevant relationships. Action follows from this, as in Figure 2.

The model also tries to capture Vickers's most important point and greatest insight, namely, that there is normally no ultimate source for the standards by means of which what is noticed is deemed good or bad, important or unimportant, relevant or irrelevant, and so on. The source of the standards is *the previous history of the system itself*. In addition, the present operation of the system may modify its present and future operation through its effect on the standards. These considerations, together with those already discussed, yield Figure 2 as a model of an appreciative system. The most difficult aspect to model is the dynamic one, but it should be clear from Figure 2 that the dynamics of the system will be as shown in Figure 3. The form of the appreciative system remains the same, whereas its contents (its *setting*) continually (but not necessarily continuously) change. An appreciative *system* is a process whose products—cultural manifes-

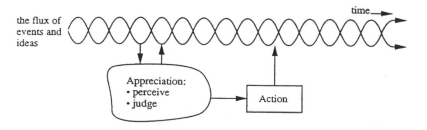

Figure 1:   The Structure of an Appreciative System
SOURCE: Checkland and Casar (1986).

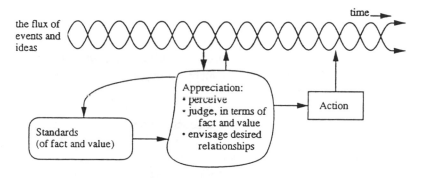

Figure 2:   The Structure of an Appreciative System Expanded
SOURCE: Checkland and Casar (1986).

tations—condition the process itself. But the system is not operationally closed in a conventional sense. It is operationally closed via a structural component (the flux of events and ideas) that ensures that it does not, through its actions, reproduce exactly itself. It reproduces a continually changed self, by a process that Varela (1984) called the "natural drift" of "autopoietic systems" (Maturana & Varela, 1980), systems whose component elements create the system itself. Through its (changing) filters the appreciative system is always open to new inputs from the flux of events and ideas, a characteristic that seems essential if the model is to map our everyday experience of the shifting perceptions, judgments, and structures of the world of culture.

Vickers's claim was that he had constructed an epistemology that can provide convincing accounts of the process by which human beings and human groups deliberate and act. The model in Figures 2 and 3 is a systemic version of the epistemology.

Checkland and Casar (1986) used it to give an account of the learning in a systems study of the Information and Library Services Department of what was

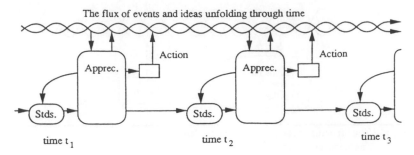

Figure 3:   The Dynamics of an Appreciative System
SOURCE: Checkland and Casar (1986).

then ICI Organics (a manufacturer of fine chemicals within the ICI Group), a study that has been described in detail elsewhere (Checkland, 1985a; Checkland & Scholes, 1990). This study was carried out by a group of managers in the function with some outside help in the use of soft systems methodology (SSM), which was the methodology used. It is a way of making practical use of the notion of an appreciative system, and it will be discussed briefly in the next section. It entails structuring a debate about change by building models of purposeful activity systems and comparing them against perceptions of the real world as a means of examining what the appreciative settings are in the situation in question and how they and the norms or standards are changing. In the study in question, there were three cycles of this learning process.

In the first cycle, the study team's interest and concern was to rethink the role of their function in a changing situation. They perceived many facts relevant to this, which resulted in 26 relevant systems. They selected and judged these facts in terms of a conception of a particular relationship and standards relevant to it: They accepted the relevance of a simple model that took as given that their function was a support to the wealth-generating operations of their company, and they implicitly made use of standards according to which a good version of this relationship would be to make efficient, effective, and timely provision of information to other parts of the company.

These considerations contributed to the ideas stream of the Lebenswelt and led to the action of exploring several perceptions of the relationship between the function and the rest of the company in greater depth. In this second methodological cycle, the focus was still on the relationship between function and company but the appreciative settings began to change. This can be expressed as a change in standards resulting from the first cycle of appreciation. The shift was in the concept of what would constitute a good relationship:

The focus shifted from ILSD (Information and Library Services Department) as a reactive function responding quickly and competently to user requests and having the expertise to do it, to ILSD as a proactive function, one which could on occasion tell actual and potential users what they *ought* to know. (Checkland, 1985a, p. 826)

In the third cycle, the new concept of ILSD was developed and, in the language of Figure 2, several hypothetical forms of relevant relationships were considered. This led to attention being given both to internal relationships within the function (How different would they have to be to sustain a proactive role?) and to the relationship between the function and the company. These considerations led to decisions on actions necessary to broaden the appreciative process. The actions taken were to make both internal (within ILSD) and external presentations of the results of the study. These events entered the company's Lebenswelt and had the effect of starting to bring about the change in the company's appreciative system, as evidenced by the remark made by the research manager at the external presentation, namely, that "I have known and worked with ILSD for 20 years and I came along this morning out of a sense of duty. To my amazement I find I now have a new perception of ILSD" (Checkland, 1985a, p. 830).

Finally, the company's subsequent allocation of significant new resources to ILSD can be described as illustrating its implicit adoption of new standards with respect to the Information and Library Services function, standards whose change stems from the recent history of the company's appreciative system, involving input of ideas and events from the systems study itself.

THE APPRECIATIVE PROCESS IN ACTION: SOFT SYSTEMS METHODOLOGY

It is not appropriate here to give a detailed account of SSM, which is described in numerous books and articles since the early 1970s. (The basic books describing its development are Checkland, 1981; Checkland & Scholes, 1990; and Wilson, 1984; a burgeoning secondary literature may be sampled via, for example, Avison & Wood-Harper, 1990; Davies & Ledington, 1991; Hicks, 1991; Patching, 1990; and Waring, 1989.)

SSM was not an attempt to operationalize the concept of an appreciative system; rather, after SSM had emerged in an action research program at Lancaster University, it was discovered that its process mapped to a remarkable degree the ideas Vickers had been developing in his books and articles (Checkland, 1981, chap. 8).

The Lancaster program began by setting out to explore whether or not, in real-world managerial rather than technical problem situations, it was possible to use the approach of systems engineering. It was found to be too naive in its questions (What is the system? What are its objectives? etc.) to cope with managerial complexity, which, we could now say, was always characterized by conflicting appreciative settings and norms. Systems engineering as developed for technical (well-defined) problem situations had to be abandoned, and SSM emerged in its place.

The development of SSM has been characterized by four points in time at which what can now be seen, with hindsight, as crucial ideas moved the project forward (Checkland & Haynes, 1994). The first was the realization that all real-world problem situations are characterized by the fact that they reveal human beings seeking or wishing to take *purposeful action*. This led to purposeful action being treated seriously as a systems concept. Ways of building models of human activity systems were developed. Then it was realized that there can never be a single account of purposeful activity, because one observer's terrorism is another's freedom fighting. Models of purposeful activity could only be built on the basis of a declared Weltanschauung. This meant that such models were never models *of* real-world action; they were models *relevant to* discourse and argument about real-world action; they were epistemological devices that could be used in such discourse and debate; they were best thought of as *holons*, using Koestler's (1967) useful neologism, which could structure debate about different ways of seeing the situation. This led to the third crucial idea, that the problem-solving process that was emerging would inevitably consist of a learning cycle in which models of human activity systems could be used to structure a debate about change. The structure was provided by carrying out an organized comparison between models and perceived real situations in which accommodations between conflicting perspectives could be sought, enabling action to be taken that was both arguably desirable—in terms of the comparisons between models and perceived situation—and culturally feasible for a particular group of people in a particular situation with its own particular history. (The fourth crucial idea, not relevant here, was the realization that models of human activity systems could be used to explore issues concerning what information systems would best be created to support real-world action—which took SSM into the field of information systems and information strategy.)

Given these considerations, SSM emerged as the process summarized in Figure 4. This is a picture of a *learning system* in which the appreciative settings of people in a problem situation—and the standards according to which they make judgments—are teased out and debated. Finally, the influence of Vickers on those who developed SSM means that the action to improve the problem situation is always thought about in terms of managing relationships—of which the simple case of seeking a defined goal is the occasional special case.

CONCLUSION: THE RELEVANCE OF APPRECIATIVE SYSTEMS THEORY AND SSM TO MODERN MANAGEMENT

It is not difficult to envisage the situations in both industry and the public sector in which the thinking about problems and problem solving would be significantly helped by the models underpinned by hard systems thinking, namely the models that see organizations as coordinated functional task systems seeking to achieve declared goals and that see the task of management as decision making in support of goal seeking. These models would be useful in

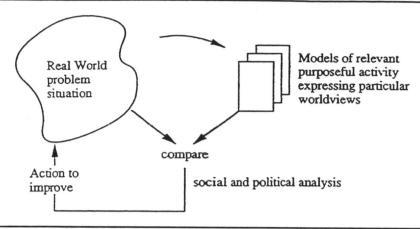

Figure 4:   Soft Systems Methodology as a Learning System
SOURCE: Checkland and Scholes (1990).

situations in which goals and measures of performance were clear-cut, communications between people were limited and prescribed, and in which the people
in question were deferential toward the authority that laid down the goals and
the ways in which they were to be achieved. But this image has never accurately
described life in most organizations as most people experience it, and it has
become less and less true since the end of the Second World War. Since that time
the trends have been toward much increased capacity for communication,
greater complexity of goals as economic interdependence has increased, much
reduced deference toward authority of any kind, and the dismantling of mono-
lithic institutionalized power structures. The dethronement of the mainframe
computer by the now ubiquitous personal computer is at once both a metaphor
for these changes and one of the catalysts for their occurrence.

   In such a situation richer models of organization and management will be
helpful, and it has been argued that those based on Vickers's appreciative
systems theory and SSM have a role to play here. More important, they do not
replace the older models but rather subsume and enhance them. In SSM,
focusing on a unitary goal is the occasional special case of debating multiple
perceptions and proceeding on the basis of *accommodations* between different
interests. For Vickers, managing relationships is the general case of human
action, the pursuit of a goal the occasional special case.

   Vickers himself has usefully differentiated his stance from that of Simon in
remarks that relate to the latter's *Administrative Behaviour* (Simon, 1957):

   The most interesting differences between the classic analyses of this book and my
   own seem to be the following:
      (1) I adopt a more explicitly dynamic conceptual model of an organisation and
   of the relations, internal and external, of which it consists, a model which applies
   equally to all its constituent sub-systems and to the larger systems of which it is
   itself a part.

(2) This model enables me to represent its "policy makers" as regulators, setting and resetting courses or standards, rather than objectives, and thus in my view to simplify some of the difficulties inherent in descriptions in terms of "means" and "ends."

(3) I lay more emphasis on the necessary mutual inconsistency of the norms seeking realisation in *every* deliberation and at *every* level of organisation and hence on the ubiquitous interaction of priority, value and cost.

(4) In my psychological analysis linking judgments of fact and value by the concept of appreciation, I stress the importance of the underlying appreciative *system* in determining how situations will be seen and valued. I therefore reject "weighing" (an energy concept) as an adequate description of the way criteria are compared and insist on the reality of a prior and equally important process of "matching" (an information concept).

(5) I am particularly concerned with the reciprocal process by which the setting of the appreciative system is itself changed by every exercise of appreciative judgment. (Vickers, 1965, p. 22)

As an example of the relevance of SSM to current problems of managing complexity, we offer recent work done within the National Health Service (NHS) in the United Kingdom. (Some of this is described in Checkland & Holwell, 1993; Checkland & Poulter, 1994; and Checkland & Scholes, 1990, chap. 4.)

In recent years the NHS has been subjected to several waves of government-imposed change. First there was the imposition of a system of accountable management, replacing the previous consensus management of teams of professionals. This had hardly settled down before it was replaced by an internal quasi-market. In this development the old district health authorities (into which the previous change had introduced district general managers) became purchasers of health care for a defined population, whereas hospitals and some general practitioners became providers of health care, the two being linked by contracts (although not legally binding ones) for particular services at a negotiated price. All these changes have entailed a considerable shift in appreciative settings for health professionals, and the NHS has been experiencing a period of considerable turmoil.

In the study described in Checkland and Scholes (1990), the problem was addressed of how a Department of Community Medicine in what was then a district health authority could evaluate its performance. Clearly the evaluation standards would depend completely on this department's image of itself and its role within the district. This is not a casual consideration, because concepts of community medicine range from *providing epidemiological data* to *managing the delivery of health care*. In this work, SSM-type models of purposeful activity relating to concepts of community medicine were built, with participation of members of the department, and eventually an evaluation methodology was developed. This was based on a structured set of questions derived from models that members of the department felt expressed their shared appreciative settings with regard to their image of the role of community medicine, which in their case was a very proactive interventionist one.

More recently, much work has been done in NHS hospitals and purchasing authorities as they assimilate and adapt to the purchaser-provider split (Checkland & Holwell, 1993). The new appreciative settings have been explored with participants via models of notional systems to enact the purchaser and provider roles. These have served to structure coherent debate concerning the requirements of the new roles.

In a recent study in a large teaching hospital, the work was part of a project to re-create an information strategy for the hospital suitable to cope with the new arrangements (Checkland & Poulter, 1994). In this work half a dozen teams of hospital workers representing the different professions were set up; members included clinicians, nurses, professionals from the finance and estates offices, and so on. Over a period of about 6 months, with a plenary meeting of team leaders every month, the teams discussed their activity and its contribution to meeting the requirements of the contracts for providing particular health care services that the hospital would in future negotiate with purchasers. Activity models were built and then used to structure analysis of required information support. This was related to existing information systems, and the information gaps identified helped in the formulation of the new information strategy.

One incident that occurred during this process may be recounted. It illustrates, in microcosm, the change of appreciative settings that can occur in the process of using SSM. It concerns a working group made up of nurses in the teaching hospital, led by a senior nurse. The group was building activity models relevant to providing nursing care, before using them to examine required information support.

Within SSM, when would-be relevant activity models are built, careful concise accounts of them as transformation processes are formulated (so-called Root Definitions). Various questions are asked in clarifying these definitions, one of which is "If this notional system were to exist, who would be its victims or beneficiaries?" Nurses asking this question naturally wish to answer, "The patients." That is what their whole ethos, education, and professionalism tell them. That illustrates why they are in the profession. It was therefore something of a shock to this group—brought to their attention by the structured requirements of the SSM process—to realize in discussion that under the new arrangements the *technically* correct answer is nearer to being "The hospital contracts manager." This is because, under the so-called internal market, each contract for a health care service that involves nursing care ought technically to include the cost of providing a certain level (and quality) of nursing care. The nurses' task is then to provide what the contract calls for. Beyond this, of course, there is a theory according to which the interests of patients will, in fact, best be met by the new purchaser-provider contracts.

But it is not easy for nurses to accept this. The senior nurse who described this incident at one of the plenary discussions said that this question, and the issue it exposed, occupied the team for much of one of their meetings. It gave her insight into the NHS changes and helped her to understand her own misgivings about a supposed internal market in health care. Geoffrey Vickers would have appreciated this story.

Given our self-consciousness and the degree of mental autonomy that we seem to possess as human beings, that part of our thinking that is beyond the unreflecting stream-of-consciousness involvement in everyday life can itself be thought about. This can be done by examining the mental models that we use to make sense of our worlds. It is entirely plausible that our perceptions will be colored by those mental models. And it follows that they need both to be better than primitive and to change as our human and social world changes.

It has been argued here that the models of organization and management that have been useful since the 1950s need to be enriched. It has then been argued that appreciative systems theory and SSM can help to provide such enrichment. They do not replace the earlier functionalist and goal-seeking models: They enclose and enhance them in ways more appropriate to institutional life at the end of the century.

REFERENCES

Ackoff, R. L. (1957). Towards a behavioural theory of communication. In W. Buckley (Ed.), *Modern systems research for the behavioural scientist* (pp. 209-218). Chicago, IL: Aldine.

Avison, D. E., & Wood-Harper, A. T. (1990). *Multiview: An exploration in information systems development*. Oxford: Blackwell.

Berger, P., & Luckmann, T. (1966). *The social construction of reality*. Harmondsworth: Penguin.

Checkland, P. (1981). *Systems thinking, systems practice*. Chichester: Wiley.

Checkland, P. (1983). OR and the systems movement. *Journal of the Operational Research Society, 34*, 661-675.

Checkland, P. (1985a). Achieving desirable and feasible change: An application of soft systems methodology. *Journal of the Operational Research Society, 36*, 821-831.

Checkland, P. (1985b). From optimizing to learning: A development of systems thinking for the 1990s. *Journal of the Operational Research Society, 36*, 757-767.

Checkland, P. (1994). Conventional wisdom and conventional ignorance: The revolution organization theory missed. *Organization, 1*(1), 29-34.

Checkland, P., & Casar, A. (1986). Vickers' concept of an appreciative system: A systemic account. *Journal of Applied Systems Analysis, 13*, 3-17.

Checkland, P., & Haynes, M. G. (1994). Varieties of systems thinking: The case of soft systems methodology. *System Dynamics Review, 10*, 189-197.

Checkland, P., & Holwell, S. (1993). Information management and organizational processes: An approach through soft systems methodology. *Journal of Information Systems, 3*, 3-16.

Checkland, P., & Poulter, J. (1994). *Application of soft systems methodology to the production of a hospital information and systems strategy*. United Kingdom: HISS Central Team of the NHS Management Executive.

Checkland, P., & Scholes, J. (1990). *Soft systems methodology in action*. Chichester: Wiley.

Davies, L., & Ledington, P. (1991). *Information in action: Soft systems methodology*. London: Macmillan.

Donaldson, L. (1985). *In defence of organization theory*. Cambridge: Cambridge University Press.

Hicks, M. J. (1991). *Problem solving in business and management*. London: Chapman & Hall.

Khandwalla, P. N. (1979). *The design of organizations*. New York: Harcourt Brace.

Koestler, A. (1967). *The ghost in the machine*. London: Hutchinson.

Lawrence, P. R., & Lorsch, J. W. (1967). *Organization and environment*. Cambridge, MA: Harvard University Press.

March, J. G., & Simon, H. A. (1958). *Organizations*. New York: Wiley.

Maturana, H. R., & Varela, F. J. (1980). *Autopoiesis and cognition*. Dordrecht: Reidel.

Newall, A., & Simon, H. A. (1972). *Human problem solving*. Englewood Cliffs, NJ: Prentice-Hall.

Patching, D. (1990). *Practical soft systems analysis*. London: Pitman.

Pugh, D. S., & Hickson, D. J. (1976). *Organization structure in its context*. Farnborough: Saxon House.

Reed, M. I. (1985). *Redirections in organisational analysis*. London: Tavistock.

Schutz, A. (1967). *The phenomenology of the social world*. Evanston, IL: Northwestern University.

Silverman, D. (1970). *The theory of organizations*. London: Heinemann.

Simon, H. A. (1957). *Administrative behaviour* (2nd ed.). New York: Macmillan.

Simon, H. A. (1960). *The new science of management decision*. New York: Harper & Row.

Tönnies, F. (1955). *Community and association [Gemeinschaft und Gesellschaft]* (C. P. Loomis, Trans.). London: Routledge & Kegan Paul. (Original work published 1887)

Varela, F. J. (1984). Two principles of self-organization. In H. Ulrich & G. J. Probst (Eds.), *Self-organisation and management of social systems* (pp. 25-32). Berlin: Springer-Verlag.

Vickers, G. (1965). *The art of judgment*. London: Chapman & Hall.

Waring, A. (1989). *Systems methods for managers*. Oxford: Blackwell.

Wilson, B. (1984). *Systems: Concepts, methodologies and applications*. Chichester: Wiley.

Woodward, J. (1965). *Industrial organization: Theory and practice*. London: Oxford University Press.

Zannetos, Z. S. (1984). Decision sciences and management expectations. In J. P. Brans (Ed.), *Operational research '84* (pp. 69-76). Amsterdam: North Holland.

6

Health, Health Care Reform, and the Care of Health

NANCY MILIO

This article explores the pressures bearing on health care systems in advanced industrialized countries, particularly the United States, drawing on Geoffrey Vickers's concepts that direct attention to systemic interactions between individual health and the "health-supporting milieus" and between health and other aspects of public policy. It argues that more coordinated policies over a broad front, the management of expectations, and the development of a less technically oriented, more caring health system will all be necessary if a healthy longevity and greater equality of health are to be achieved.

A historically new situation in health and health care services compelled policymakers in Western industrial countries to address new policy issues during the 1980s and 1990s. Different streams of social and economic change came together, requiring new thinking and action by governments and other major players. Aging populations were rapidly growing, economic growth stagnated or was in recession, health care costs accelerated, and government budgets incurred large deficits. The United States, without a national health care program, experienced these problems on a large scale. But similar issues faced countries with a national health care system, including the United Kingdom, the Netherlands, France, Germany, and Canada, where health and health care held a prominent place in political debate.

The insights of Sir Geoffrey Vickers continue to be relevant to such a debate. This article, based on the experience in Western affluent countries, as documented mainly in the United States, will sketch out the conditions for sustainable health, the role and shape of the health care services needed to support health, and the leadership required to move toward more equitable health-supporting social conditions, and will draw, as appropriate, on Vickers's conceptual framework.

HEALTH

In his "What Sets the Goals of Public Health?" Geoffrey Vickers (1958/1984e) conceived of health as a norm—a tacit standard of what is socially and individually acceptable—a "relationship ever to be renewed" if it is to be sustained. In the Vickers vision, physical health could not be separated from mental health, nor individual from environmental health in its broadest sense. Ultimately, it was the society and its cultural tenor that would support or erode the health of its members. The rapid and accelerating changes brought on by industrialization and its technological tools not only strained the health reserves of individuals as they tried to adjust but also made the search for, and acceptance of, health-supporting social solutions more difficult. Leadership for this task belonged to those concerned with public health.

Geoffrey Vickers anticipated what many countries are today experiencing: As work became progressively more automated, industry would be an acceptable producer of goods and services, but no longer of jobs, and the resulting displaced workers would become a growing health problem, as contemporary studies, noted below, indicate.

This perspective contrasts with the conventional view, as mirrored in current health care systems, where health means the absence or control of medically diagnosed problems, at the individual level. This conventional view now fits uncomfortably with changes in demographic and epidemiological patterns and economic realities, as "disabled longevity" and inequalities in health become more starkly apparent (Milio, 1991).

Assisted living for older and disabled people has become a major concern in affluent countries. With the enlarging share of elderly people ranging from at least 12% to almost 20% of the population, and the numbers of old-old (over 80 years of age) growing rapidly, there will be an increasing need to provide more health and long-term care simply due to the loss of biological reserve that accompanies aging (General Accounting Office [GAO], 1991a). Beyond that, however, there is growing evidence that Americans and others are becoming increasingly disabled by chronic and other illnesses, independent of normal aging, with an increasing share of longer life burdened by compromised living, and so imposing additional demands on health care delivery (Olshansky et al., 1991; Secretary of State for Health, 1992).

Dutch researchers have shown, for heart disease, how the small drop in new cases of heart disease was more than matched by a greater decline in death rates, producing postponement of the onset of heart disease to the later years of life and increasing its severity and prevalence as people lived longer lives (Bonneux et al., 1994). This meant more years of disabled life, a "trade-off of mortality for morbidity," thus contradicting the view of some forecasters that aging populations would be healthier until their later years, when they would have a short period of illness before death (Fries, 1980). The difference in projections here is that high technology medicine, such as invasive coronary revascularization techniques, prolongs life with illness, thus auguring an increase in the use of high-cost medical care and long-term assisted care for a greater period of time.

Viewed from a societal perspective, this poses problems both in high costs in medical investment that might otherwise find different uses, and in high social costs from the inability of increasingly well-educated elder populations to contribute to the social good. An alternative scenario—a healthy longevity, instead of a disabled longevity—is possible and is experienced by a small segment of elders who have known lifelong social and economic security that supported healthy living (Guralnik & Kaplan, 1989). In other words, their living conditions prevented much chronic illness.

To know Geoffrey Vickers in his last years was to appreciate the reservoir of social wealth that resides in the experience of older people and that can be a shared treasure among people of all ages, offered by those who are healthy in their last decades of life.

Another basic dimension of the end-of-the-century health issue in both affluent and poor countries is that the burden of disability from illness and injury falls most heavily on the groups that are already disadvantaged by their social and economic condition. This situation is perhaps most stark in the United States, relative to its wealth. Here, the official poverty level that determines eligibility for government programs is set too low to sustain average mortality (Keeney, 1980).

The impact of poverty on the health of poor people has compounding effects. For example, partly as a result of deficit-reduction cutbacks in public support services for more than a decade, the health of poor children in the United States (especially Black children) declined over the past 15 years (GAO, 1992g; Montgomery, 1992). Without adequate prenatal and other services in maternal nutrition and shelter, babies are likely to be born with low birth weights and so to incur more illness as children, predisposing them to lower educational achievement, poorer jobs, and lower incomes than they might otherwise have had (Williams, 1990).

People with low incomes are at greater risk of life-threatening acute and chronic disease, of disabling diseases, of injuries, and of death, especially in infancy, childhood, and young adulthood (GAO, 1992a). Their average life expectancy is thus shorter (Rogers, 1992). In the United States, they are also likely to get inadequate medical care and often no preventive services such as public health vaccines, especially when they are Black (Hutchins, Gindler, Atkinson, et al., 1993).

Race discrimination further contributes to inequalities in health and in health services as it interferes with doctor-patient relations (Escarce, Epstein, Colby, & Schwartz, 1993), clinic and cancer care (Howard, Hankey, Greenberg, et al., 1992; Lieu, Newacheck, & McManus, 1993), and other types of treatment (Elickson, Bell, & McGuigan, 1993; Hogue & Hargraves, 1993). What is more, when disadvantaged people receive care, they recover less fully and less quickly (Office of Technology Assessment, 1992).

Although the health of disadvantaged groups has improved over the decades, it has done so less rapidly than that of more advantaged people. Inequalities in health between advantaged and disadvantaged groups have increased, especially during the last decade (Rogers, 1992). The difference in death rates between the highest and lowest paid workers in the United Kingdom, for example, almost doubled in recent years. In those countries where income distribution is least unequal, average life expectancy is highest, as in Sweden, the Netherlands, and Norway, where there are generous retirement, disability, unemployment, and family allowance programs (Marmot & McDonnell, 1986; Susser, 1993; Whitehead, 1987). Yet, even in these more equitable nations, inequalities in access to services and uneven health status between comparable age/sex groups remain, albeit with narrower gaps than elsewhere (Fox, 1989; Kohler & Martin, 1985).

By contrast, in the former Communist system, as economic constraints began to affect all civilian services and living conditions, health problems increased; these ranged from acute and chronic conditions to actual increases in infant mortality (e.g., Hungary, Romania, Union of Soviet Socialist Republics [USSR]) and a decline in life expectancy at birth and at subsequent ages (e.g., Hungary, USSR) by the late 1980s (Wnuk-Lipinski & Illsley, 1990a, 1990b).

BEGINNINGS OF THE POLICY DEBATE

Although disability and the care of older people and of the poor have been recognized as health services problems for decades, what began to change in the late 1970s was that, as the numbers in these groups and the reliance on expensive technology grew, the incremental costs of care rose faster than economic growth, government revenues, and employer profits in an international and ever more competitive global economy. This, in turn, brought new and powerful voices to the political arena that called for major change, in addition to the less influential social and health groups of the past. As a result, the focus of debate began to shift from people's need for, and access to, health services to the costs of services, from the service system to the industry; the traditional language of care changed to that of the economic marketplace.

One of the first approaches to the cost issue in the 1970s and early 1980s was the attempt to reduce disability from chronic disease and injury by holding individuals responsible for their own health. The issue was defined as that of lifestyle behaviors that needed to be changed, by means of information campaigns and other health education techniques.

Geoffrey Vickers also stressed individual responsibility, but he did so always in the larger societal context that took account of the forces that encouraged individuals to both take on and carry out the commitments they accepted. In *Responsibility—Its Sources and Limits*, Vickers (1980) pointed out that individuals must have the ability and the cultural and social support to enable them reliably and consistently to meet their chosen or required obligations. Support must come from organizations, preeminently governmental ones, as they themselves accept their responsibility to respond to ever-changing environments. The new environment, not controllable by individual action, was complex and changing fast: It was characterized by limited natural resources, changes in work patterns and income distribution, interdependent economies, and rising expectations. The basis for individual responsibility, in other words, is public and community responsibility.

In the 1980s, the rubric of individual responsibility for health came to mean two things. In the most pragmatic sense, it meant financial responsibility; people simply paid more out of their pockets for health care, more so in the United States than in other countries where smaller fees were the norm. Second, and more widely observed, it meant following certain healthy habits such as eating low-fat, low-cholesterol, high-fiber foods, not using tobacco or abusing alcohol, exercising regularly, and managing stress (Louis Harris & Associates, 1993). The adequacy of living and working conditions or the distress arising from them was not within the conceptual scope of healthy lifestyles.

As is well-known, there have been measurable improvements over the past 20 years in some aspects of diet, tobacco and alcohol use, and exercise patterns—primarily among the more affluent sections of the population. These groups not only had easiest access to new options in food, exercise, and leisure time activities; they also operated in settings in which attractiveness in physical and other elements of presence were necessary for advancement, and this gave them strong incentives to change.

Even so, although beef consumption declined, the eating of high-fat cheeses, desserts, and processed convenience foods increased, whereas exercise habits have shown no increase over the past 10 years—all consistent with the time constraints, work life, and social requisites of affluent people. Further, only half of younger people could meet nutritional and exercise standards, and overall, people in the United States, the United Kingdom, and Western Europe were becoming more overweight and obese, that is, gaining more than 20% of their recommended weight—placing them at high risk of chronic, disabling disease (Louis Harris & Associates, 1993; Secretary of State for Health, 1992).

Notably, the largest improvements in health habits involved the use of vehicle seatbelts and reduced drunk driving and cigarette consumption at a time when these changes were required by governmental and workplace policy; that is, individual behavior grounded in public policy showed some responsiveness to societal change (Louis Harris & Associates, 1993). In effect, healthy lifestyles were followed because nonvoluntary, explicit norms encouraged more consistent and sustainable improvements in the public health; this was more effective than simple public admonitions that left the burden of reliable change on the individual.

Individuals may not be able to make the healthy choices they might wish to make when immediate constraints push them toward other choices, such as lower cost but less nutritious food at the local supermarket, unavailable exercise sites, or nonsupportive attitudes among their peers. Individuals have little or no control over their surroundings and so are dependent on their communities to maintain healthful conditions and choices.

In *The Undirected Society*, Vickers (1959) discussed the social conditions for health and well-being and how accelerating changes brought on by technological advances make those conditions difficult to maintain. He went far beyond the obvious need for medical attention and care for physical and mental illness to the milieus in which these occur. He identified as fundamental needs adequate income, housing and food, as well as education for participation in social and democratic life, and he pointed to the related social and political need to constrain expectations so that, within limited natural and public resources, basic needs for all could be met.

He identified a major challenge to modern industrialized societies in the fact that they had ever more new choices generated by their technologies than they could actualize or tolerate socially, and he argued that the key to well-being lay more in dampening aspirations than in satisfying them. This restraint was a prerequisite to meeting the needs of health in the broadest sense, in an organized and sustainable way. The leadership for this ongoing and never-attainable, but essential, task of managing expectations lay with public policymakers, especially leaders in public health.

In the decades since Vickers was writing, much has been learned about how social conditions, invariably shaped by public policy, affect people's health. Living conditions, which might be called the health-supporting milieus of people's lives, have declined in recent years for many social groups in affluent nations, making such groups vulnerable to disabled longevity and widening the gap between their health and that of their more advantaged counterparts.

During the 1980s, for example, for every 1% increase in unemployment, there was more than a 3% to 5% increase in heart disease and stroke mortality and a more than 6% increase in homicides (Catalano, 1991). Evidence from Britain and the United States shows that the impact of added economic strains poses larger health risks to disadvantaged people (Smith, 1987). Yet, in the United States, less than 30% of unemployed people received jobless insurance benefits compared with more than half in the 1950s (GAO, 1992b), and budget-tightening restrictions on unemployment insurance tipped the balance into poverty for over 250,000 people in 1990 (GAO, 1993).

The impact of an unhealthy environment falls disproportionately on disadvantaged groups: lead poisoning and incineration, for instance, primarily affect inner-city dwellers (GAO, 1992c), an important and neglected issue. In the United States, 3 to 4 million preschoolers have blood lead levels high enough to cause permanent impairment of nervous system and psychological functioning (Landrigan, 1992). Not all pregnant women who are eligible for women-infant food benefits have access to them, in spite of the fact that food benefits can reduce low birth weight by 25% and are cost-effective (GAO, 1992a). Poor children have least access to preschool programs; 5 million children are ill prepared to begin school because of poverty, often having related nutritional, health, and language problems. Retarded growth from undernutrition affects as many as one in seven preschoolers in some low-income groups (GAO, 1992f). All of this builds disability into the American future.

The private housing market supplies less affordable, low-income housing but the need continues to grow: One in two low-income families will not be able to find affordable rental housing in the next 10 years (GAO, 1992d). The grim irony here is that federal investment in housing and other inner-city needs were being displaced in the federal budget during the 1980s and early 1990s by the relentless growth of health care costs (GAO, 1992e).

In spite of the evidence pointing to deficiencies in health-supporting milieus, resulting in damage that had to be remedied by health care, by the 1990s the health policy debate—in the United States and other countries—had moved to an almost exclusively economic argument about health care services, as though these considerations alone were pertinent to better health (Report by the Government Committee, 1992; Secretaries of State, 1989; Susser, 1994).

The Vickers framework makes clear the systemic interdependence between housing and environmental and health policies; in practice, however, little policy attention has been paid to these linkages and some public policies have themselves eroded lifestyles and created health risks. Health problems then feed into problems in financing health care. It is these cost and financing issues that are the focus of today's debate about health care, now a trillion dollar industry in the United States.

The accelerating cost of health care that has typified the U.S. system during the last quarter century has its roots in part in these inequities in living and working conditions and in levels of health. The litany of these and other causes of the high cost is long and, to a degree, familiar in many countries:

- Better educated and aging populations, who tend to equate quality of care with high technology (Pew Commission, 1991) and can afford to buy increasing amounts of care, are "overserved" (GAO, 1991b).
- Health care organizations, responding to rising costs and the necessity to compete (i.e., attract patients and physicians) in an environment where health care is economically (demand) based rather than need based, increase their income by "unbundling" services to charge separate fees for each; they conduct costly advertising and promotion programs, engage in "product differentiation," and buy unneeded amounts of high technology, fueling a "medical arms race" that becomes an incentive for overuse of technology (Congressional Budget Office, 1991; GAO, 1991b; Millar, 1993).
- A growing number of uninsured and underserved individuals are increasingly children (one third); as a result of cuts and restrictions in Medicaid public financing, and because of increases in part-time, low-wage jobs and cuts in employee-paid insurance during the 1980s, most of the uninsured (85%) are in working families (Ahuja & Mueller, 1991). This situation produces deferred care, sicker patients requiring more costly care, and the shifting of those excess costs by hospitals to other payers, which, in turn, raises insurance premiums.
- Overhead costs of insurance administration among 1,500 companies (5.2% of health spending) in the United States are twice as high as those of systems in Canada and the United Kingdom (Congressional Budget Office, 1991).
- Other countries provide universal access to health services at lower costs to society, to government, and to individuals than the United States—about 7% to 9% of gross domestic product (GDP) compared with more than 14% in the United States—and do so with healthier outcomes (Rowland, 1991; Schreiber, Poullier, & Greenwald, 1991; Vall-Spinosa, 1991).

THE VICKERS VISION OF THE CARE OF HEALTH

Geoffrey Vickers's conception of public health was far wider than the delivery of health services, "wider than commonly accepted in the field of public health," as he wrote in *Industry, Human Relations, and Mental Health* (Vickers, 1964a). His conception was similar to that of the great leaders of the early public health movement who saw its tasks of preventing disease, prolonging life, and promoting health as requiring not only health services but also the "development of social machinery which will ensure to every individual in the community a standard of living adequate for the maintenance of health" (Winslow, 1926).

More recently, the Institute of Medicine in the United States called on the public health community to collaborate with the policy sectors of education, social services, housing, and income maintenance, explicitly recognizing that the origins of health and illness are too complex to leave individuals solely responsible for their own health (Institute of Medicine, 1988). This same view was acknowledged in the recent U.K. Ministry of Health policy statement on "The Health of the Nation," which noted the importance to health of adequate living and working conditions, education, economic well-being, safe water and sewerage, and sound nutrition, as well as health services (Secretary of State, 1992). Actual policy debate, however, focuses attention on system efficiencies, not on ways to improve health (Holland & Graham, 1994; Susser, 1994).

Nonetheless, it is the responsibility of the public health institutions to draw attention to the need to eliminate, and protect people from, environmental hazards, to ensure medical services throughout their extensions into Vickers's "world of the well," and to stimulate private and public bodies, including policymakers, to create living and working conditions and foster public attitudes that are supportive of health and well-being. Immunity for individuals, as Vickers recognized, was more than the specific resistance that could be built up through vaccines; it was also bolstered, as studies show, by adequate nutrition and living standards. But medicine was increasingly concerned with building individual immunity rather than preventing risk (Vickers, 1958/1984e).

Geoffrey Vickers recognized the growing difficulties of financing a health care system dominated by hospital-based, sickness-focused technologies, and the fact that the medical procedures that were technically possible would always exceed resources, thus "making avoidable trouble" for the future as resource-allocation decisions would "grow harder with the passage of time." What he advocated more than 25 years ago was commensurate attention to care in the community and the soft technologies—the commitment of interorganizational and political skills—to make such arrangements possible (Vickers, 1958/1984e, 1967/1984b).

The increasing technical and bureaucratic emphasis within many professional roles in the health care field was also problematic, in Vickers's view. In "The Changing Nature of the Professions," Vickers (1974/1984a) pointed out that, although professionals were valuable as advisors and educators of, and doers on behalf of, their clients, their most valued asset was their capacity for judgment in their field of competence: acting in partnership with clients and public. He cautioned that, if professionals (and clients) became obsessed with technologies—whether of machines or economics or other numeracies—and so less skilled in forging effective partnerships to address personal and public problems, the outlook was "as bleak for the public polity as for the professions."

His concern always moved from the individual in health and illness, and the care and support for the families of the ill, to the consequences for communities that must also be affected by their members' problems. Effective community support involved aid from a variety of health and other organizations, private and public, and the development of the public understanding that would make this possible. The instruments that could reshape environments, mold ideas and standards of acceptability, and design new structures for action were mainly organizations, the means to act collectively. Vickers (1958/1984e, 1967/1984b) elaborated these ideas in "What Set the Goals of Public Health?" and in "Community Medicine," where he first coined that term, which has since been used in several variations in different countries.

HEALTH CARE POLICY-MAKING

Geoffrey Vickers allowed no illusions about the complexity and difficulties involved in the task of bringing about effective action in the interests of the public's health. The ongoing process of policy change was a kind of impossible necessity, at best a temporary resolution of priority issues, never a once-and-for-all achievement, never a reachable goal. It is rather a goal-setting process, an attempt to find an acceptable, if not optimal, relationship between new realities and standards of acceptability, each of which change with changing societal conditions, events, and perceptions, each at its own pace. This "appreciative" process—that of judging the gap between what is and what ought to be among a limited number of issues that rise to public attention—then triggers the "regulative" side of policy-making, that of deciding what, if anything, ought to be done (Vickers, 1963).

The developments in health policy in the 1990s, as experienced in the United States, can be illuminated in the light of the Vickers framework that can perhaps suggest strategic insights into how those processes may approach their stated goal of providing comprehensive health benefits to all Americans that can never be taken away, and perhaps move toward the still larger, longer term task of finding better ways to promote health and prevent disease, as well as prolonging life among all social groups.

The facts that tens of millions of Americans have no health insurance, that the United States spends more on health care than any other industrial nation, and that the rate of rising costs is three times that of inflation have been true for decades, as noted earlier. Why then did reform of the system become a high policy priority in the early 1990s? Why did "reality judgments," to use Vickers's term, define system reform as a problem demanding action? The answer is that other aspects of the environment were changing, other significant events were taking place, and with them perceptions of what was important enough to require policy attention shifted.

Vickers was interested in the highly selective process by which people choose selected aspects of reality to notice. During the 1980s, it was the rising costs of health care that many people were predisposed to notice, and important political players began to demand action to contain them. The high costs of health insurance to large businesses, at $3,200 per worker, began to erode wages of unionized workers during this decade and health benefits became an issue in the vast majority of labor disputes (Congressional Budget Office, 1991).

State governments, most of which cannot constitutionally incur budget deficits, saw health care crowding out other state priorities as the cost of public health care increased by more than half over the decade. Federal health spending in the same period rose by 40% to make up 14.4% of the federal budget and health care costs became the sole predicted cause of the massive federal deficit to the end of the century (GAO, 1991b).

Even lower cost preventive services, which could obviate the need for more costly services later, were not being used as people lost their insurance coverage—the single most important influence affecting middle-aged people's (45-64 years) uptake of those services (Woolhandler & Himmelstein, 1988).

Not surprisingly, public opinion polls showed that 9 out of 10 Americans were dissatisfied with the health care system and the vast majority, along with corporate and labor leaders, favored major changes (Blendon, Leitman, Morrison, & Donelan, 1990; Holland & Graham, 1994). This kind of social climate then made the political risk of making major changes in health care less daunting, if not actually a requirement for elected policymakers.

Legislators read polls and election results showing that voters, especially middle-class constituents, were worried about paying for health care, particularly the long-term care of chronically ill elders, and all of this was compounded by a stagnant economy and only narrow public support for incumbent office-holders.

In effect, current health care arrangements were no longer acceptable, no longer affordable economically or politically. The slogan of universal, comprehensive health insurance, developed in ways that could encompass a range of political ideologies, had a prominent place in the 1992 Democratic presidential platform. It served many political and economic interests among party funders and voting supporters, both liberals and centrists. It also could accommodate the interests of the poor and other excluded groups, as well as the social justice aspirations of some liberals, especially the public health community that had pressed for universal health care for decades.

Thus, for the first time in history, a new administration took office in the United States in 1992 with national health care reform high on its agenda. It

proposed a system of universal health insurance covering comprehensive benefits, regulated and implemented by the states under national standards. It also,
for the first time, proposed mechanisms to link the system of health care delivery
to the separate state-based, governmental public health system that traditionally
provided a variety of environmental, occupational, food quality, housing safety,
infectious disease control, and community health information services (Health
Security Act, 1993).

During this same period many industrialized countries, impelled by accelerating health care costs in the face of stagnant economies and threatening national
budget deficits, were moving toward a kind of controlled competition in their
national health care programs: the United Kingdom, the Netherlands, France,
Germany, Australia, New Zealand, and Canada ("Diagnosis Critical," 1993;
Holland & Graham, 1994; Hurst, 1991; Report by the Government Committee,
1992; Vall-Spinosa, 1991; Wilson, 1993). To a significant although far lesser
degree than in the United States, health services became conceived of as an
industry, in which providers of services were more like entrepreneurs who must
be able to balance their budgets and therefore use their resources, ideally, where
and when they were appropriate and necessary, or reap the fiscal consequences.
However, the regulatory mechanisms of the market would not necessarily
deliver appropriate services to patients under less than ideal conditions.

If the goal-setting process during the 1980s marked the appreciative phase
of health care policy-making, the election of a new administration in the early
1990s signaled the beginning of the regulatory phase, the consensus that there
was a disparity between the current health care system and what was needed and
possible. Even at this point, however, the opposition, for tactical reasons,
declared there was no crisis—and thus no need for major change (Shalit, 1994).
Nonetheless, policy action had to meld sufficient agreement to enact a workable,
specific policy.

In a political world of large and powerful players—financial corporations in
the insurance industry, profit-making interstate health care systems, medical
organizations, world-scale manufacturers of technology and drugs—the task of
consensus building is almost overwhelming. The health interests of the public,
the economic interests of an industry, and the political interests of officials are
all at stake.

Geoffrey Vickers often pointed out that constraints were inherent in policy-
making: in his earlier writing in *The Undirected Society* (Vickers, 1959), in
"Values, Norms, and Policies" (Vickers, 1973/1984d), and elsewhere. These
include the fact that limitations on resources will mean that a new choice will
rule out or minimize resources for other choices—someone's ox will be gored
in a world of tight budgets.

A major decision, such as reform of health care, is also a "multivalued choice"
(Vickers, 1968). It has many aims and consequences at many levels—economic,
social, and health-related—and some may be slighted or damaged if not given
due weight, notably for those with least voice. The means available to reshape

the system—such as organizational infrastructures for community-based services, electronic networks to improve and link administrative and information tasks, or the capacity to operate new systems—may not be at hand.

Vickers also discussed the press of time, a crucial element often omitted by policy analysts: time to negotiate and educate, time to phase in changes at a tolerable social and individual pace, time to view the effects and reformulate decisions on the basis of experience. Simultaneously, the problems may grow at a faster pace, and new problems requiring priority attention may arise such as the foreign policy issues that constantly demand the president's attention in spite of his commitment to health care reform.

Despite the seeming impossibility of the policy-making task, Vickers insisted on the need for responsible governments to take decisive action when situations warranted. He offered a number of ways of improving the political skills needed to reduce conflict and to arrive at sufficient agreement for action.

TOWARD A NEW APPRECIATION OF BETTERING HEALTH

To move toward sustainable health—toward a healthy longevity and equity in health—is a political and economic, a social and cultural task, a long-term project that will span decades. Only by strengthening the health reserves of people and preventing disease before it begins, rather than controlling it afterward, can societies reap the benefits embodied in their enlarging groups of elders whose experience, skills, commitment, and time can help to rebind and rebuild communities that seem to be losing their cohesion in a world of competition. The care of health among all social groups throughout the life span by health-supporting environments and supportive health services when necessary may well contain medical costs within socially affordable bounds.

But this shift in priorities from medical care to health support will require, in the Vickers framework, new reality judgments and new standards for judging what ought to be; new views of how to close the gap between today's disabling direction and what is desired in a future of better health. The leadership to propose this new future can only be, as in the past, from those who now perceive the problem and the possibilities, indeed the necessity to change course.

At best, even a less technologically oriented, more caring health care system has only limited means to provide primary prevention—in the form of immunizations, birth control, some anti-infectants, and health advice—which is only effective if it can be followed. Otherwise, prevention is secondary prevention: screening for disease that already exists through prenatal and other examinations, laboratory and other tests, and attempting to contain or cure newly found problems (Milio, 1983).

As currently organized in most countries, health care systems do not have the interorganizational linkages or the policy mandate to influence, by reallocation of budgeted priorities, the conditions under which people live, except in very circumscribed, albeit important, areas such as food safety, environmental protection, and building codes. Only a few countries, influenced by the vision of public health officials, have moved to broaden the compass of health authority—with difficulty, persistence, and skill (Milio, 1990).

A major barrier to re-cognizing health and health support is the very condition that damages health: the growing economic, social, and political fissures that divide the haves from the have-nots, the growing legacy of competitive economies. These fissures cause differing interests, making common perspectives and commonly held priorities for change increasingly difficult.

Nonetheless, for Geoffrey Vickers, the task of public leadership is to shape appreciative processes, to inform, to educate, to help public and organizational interests, including other political and bureaucratic interests, to re-cognize these contentious issues and the options available for change. Public health leaders, for example, could critique the current directions in the care of health, pointing out the social, economic, and health consequences of increasing disability and inequalities in health, as well as new ways to configure a system that can support health, one that, for example, would also monitor the health impacts on populations of social and economic policies and practices (Milio, 1981).

The first step, of reshaping reality judgments through education and advocacy, might well require new skills by proponents, access to new kinds of information, to new media, and to high-level policymakers. Use of the new information technologies could be not only a new channel to inform and communicate but also a means to build coalitions and multiply support in ways that earlier public health leaders could not do. Technology, however, cannot replace face-to-face negotiations, the bedrock of political change.

Vickers proposed that negotiators, in addition to being ready to compromise within limits, could engage in "mutual persuasion" where the sides reveal the constraints under which they operate, the costs of change to them, and the possibilities for change that they envision. Proponents would also suggest what the actions in question may mean for future relations between the parties. This forces other parties to think about the longer term consequences of new approaches by weighing the benefits relative to the costs of future cooperation in an increasingly uncertain and interdependent world (Vickers, 1972/1984c).

For proponents of healthy change, the task of reaching a new appreciation of health and its care may seem a Sisyphean effort, an impossible necessity. Geoffrey Vickers offered some encouragement, however, in his "The Psychology of Policymaking and Social Change" (Vickers, 1964b). He said that the attempt to help governors and governed recognize situations, even when the effort fails to result in timely policy action, nonetheless results in a degree of resetting of the appreciative system. It will never be as it was before, and so it becomes a basis for further refocusing. This task then can be seen, as he expressed it in *Freedom in a Rocking Boat*, as part of "our search for our humanity" (Vickers, 1972).

REFERENCES

Ahuja, S., & Mueller, K. (1991). Synopsis of health insurance proposals. *Center for Health Services Research Quarterly Report, 1*(3), 1-7.

Blendon, R., Leitman, R., Morrison, I., & Donelan, K. (1990). Satisfaction with health systems in ten nations. *Health Affairs, 9*(2), 185-192.

Bonneux, L., et al. (1994). Estimating clinical morbidity due to ischemic heart disease and congestive heart failure: The future rise of heart failure. *American Journal of Public Health, 84*, 20-28.

Catalano, R. (1991). The health effects of economic insecurity. *American Journal of Public Health, 81*, 1148-1152.

Congressional Budget Office. (1991). *Universal health insurance coverage using Medicare's payment rates.* Washington, DC: U.S. Government Printing Office.

Diagnosis critical. (1993, October 9). *The Economist,* pp. 57-58.

Elickson, P., Bell, R., & McGuigan, K. (1993). Preventing adolescent drug use: Long-term results of junior high program. *American Journal of Public Health, 83*, 856-861.

Escarce, J., Epstein, K., Colby, D., & Schwarz, J. (1993). Racial differences in the elderly's use of medical procedures and diagnostic tests. *American Journal of Public Health, 83*, 948-954.

Fox, J. (Ed.). (1989). *Health inequalities in European countries.* Aldershot: Gower.

Fries, J. (1980). Natural death and the compression of morbidity. *New England Journal of Medicine, 303*, 130-135.

General Accounting Office. (1991a). *Long-term care for the baby boomers.* Washington, DC: Author.

General Accounting Office. (1991b). *US health care spending.* Washington, DC: Author.

General Accounting Office. (1992a). *Early intervention.* Washington, DC: Author.

General Accounting Office. (1992b). *Education issues.* Washington, DC: Author.

General Accounting Office. (1992c). *Environmental protection issues.* Washington, DC: Author.

General Accounting Office. (1992d). *Housing issues.* Washington, DC: Author.

General Accounting Office. (1992e). *Investment issues.* Washington, DC: Author.

General Accounting Office. (1992f). *Labor issues.* Washington, DC: Author.

General Accounting Office. (1992g). *Poverty trends, 1980-88: Changes in family composition and income sources among the poor.* Washington, DC: Author. (Testimony before the Subcommittee on Human Resources, Committee on Ways and Means, House of Representatives)

General Accounting Office. (1993). *Decline in UI beneficiaries.* Washington, DC: Author.

Guralnik, J. M., & Kaplan, G. A. (1989). Predictors of healthy aging: Prospective evidence from the Alameda County study. *American Journal of Public Health, 79*, 703-708.

Health Security Act of 1993, H. R. 175 § 1757 (1993).

Hogue, C., & Hargraves, M. (1993). Class, race, and infant mortality in the United States. *American Journal of Public Health, 83*, 9-12.

Holland, W., & Graham, C. (1994). Commentary: Recent reforms in the British National Health Service. *American Journal of Public Health, 84*, 186-189.

Howard, J., Hankey, B., Greenberg, R., et al. (1992). A collaborative study of differences in the survival rates of Black patients and White patients with cancer. *Cancer, 69*, 2349-2360.

Hurst, J. W. (1991). Reforming health care in seven European nations. *Health Affairs, 10*(3), 7-21.

Hutchins, S., Gindler, J., Atkinson, W., et al. (1993). Preschool children at high risk for measles: Opportunities to vaccinate. *American Journal of Public Health, 83*, 862-867.

Institute of Medicine. (1988). *The future of public health.* Washington, DC: National Academy Press.

Keeney, R. (1980). Mortality rates induced by economic expenditures. *Risk Analysis, 10*(1), 150-154.

Kohler, L., & Martin, J., (Eds.). (1985). *Inequalities in health and health care.* Gotenburg: Nordic School of Public Health.

Landrigan, P. (1992). Environmental disease—Preventable epidemic. *American Journal of Public Health, 82*, 941-943.

Lieu, T., Newacheck, P., & McManus, M. (1993). Race, ethnicity, and access to ambulatory care among US adolescents. *American Journal of Public Health, 83,* 960-965.

Louis Harris & Associates. (1993). *The 1992 Baxter survey of American health habits.* New York: Author.

Marmot, M., & McDonnell, M. (1986). Mortality decline and widening social inequalities. *The Lancet, 2,* 274-276.

Milio, N. (1981). *Promoting health through public policy.* Philadelphia: F. A. Davis.

Milio, N. (1983). *Primary care and the public's health.* Lexington, MA: D. C. Heath.

Milio, N. (1990). *Nutrition policy for food-rich countries.* Baltimore: Johns Hopkins University Press.

Milio, N. (1991). Toward healthy longevity: Lessons in food and nutrition policy development from Finland and Norway. *Scandinavian Journal of Social Medicine, 19,* 210-217.

Millar, B. (1993). Is management top heavy again? *Healthcare Management, 1,* 12-16.

Montgomery, L. (1992, November). *Increased effects of poverty on the health of U.S. children and young people since 1976.* Paper presented at the annual meeting of the American Public Health Association, Washington, DC.

Office of Technology Assessment. (1992). *Does health insurance make a difference?* Washington, DC: Author.

Olshansky, S., Radberg, H., Carnes, B., Cassel, C., & Brody, J. (1991). Trading off longer life for worsening health: The expansion of morbidity hypothesis. *Journal of Aging and Health, 3*(2), 194-216.

Pew Commission. (1991). *Healthy America: Practitioners for 2005.* New York: Pew Memorial Trust.

Report by the Government Committee. (1992). *Choices in health care.* The Hague, the Netherlands: Ministry of Welfare, Health and Cultural Affairs.

Rogers, R. (1992). Living and dying in the U.S.A.: Sociodemographic determinants of death among Blacks and Whites. *Demography, 29*(2), 287-303.

Rowland, D. (1991). Health status in East European countries. *Health Affairs, 10,* 202-215.

Schreiber, G., Poullier, J., & Greenwald, L. (1991). Health care systems in twenty-four countries. *Health Affairs, 10,* 22-38.

Secretaries of State for Health, Wales, Northern Ireland and Scotland. (1989). *Working for patients.* London: HMSO.

Secretary of State for Health. (1992). *The health of the nation.* London: HMSO.

Shalit, R. (1994, February 14). Republicans and health care. *New Republic,* pp. 19-22.

Smith, R. (1987). *Unemployment and health.* London: Oxford University Press.

Susser, M. (1993). Health as a human right. *American Journal of Public Health, 83,* 418-436.

Susser, M. (1994). Health care reform and public health. *American Journal of Public Health, 84,* 173-175.

Vall-Spinosa, A. (1991). Lessons from London: The British are reforming their national health service. *American Journal of Public Health, 81,* 1566-1570.

Vickers, G. (1959). *The undirected society.* Toronto: University of Toronto Press.

Vickers, G. (1963). Appreciative behaviour. *Acta Psychologica, 21,* 3.

Vickers, G. (1964a). *Industry, human relations, and mental health* (Tavistock Pamphlet No. 9). London: Tavistock.

Vickers, G. (1964b). The psychology of policy making and social change. *British Journal of Psychiatry, 110,* 467.

Vickers, G. (1968). *Value systems and social process.* London: Tavistock.

Vickers, G. (1972). *Freedom in a rocking boat.* New York: Penguin.

Vickers, G. (1980). *Responsibility—its sources and limits.* Seaside, CA: Intersystems.

Vickers, G. (1984a). The changing nature of the professions. In Open Systems Group (Eds.), *The Vickers papers.* London: Harper & Row. (Original work published 1974)

Vickers, G. (1984b). Community medicine. In Open Systems Group (Eds.), *The Vickers papers.* London: Harper & Row. (Original work published April 29, 1967)

Vickers, G. (1984c). The management of conflict. In Open Systems Group (Eds.), *The Vickers papers*. London: Harper & Row. (Original work published 1972)

Vickers, G. (1984d). Values, norms, and policies. In Open Systems Group (Eds.), *The Vickers papers*. London: Harper & Row. (Original work published 1973)

Vickers, G. (1984e). What sets the goals of public health? In Open Systems Group (Eds.), *The Vickers papers*. London: Harper & Row. (Original work published March 22, 1958)

Whitehead, M. (1987). *The health divide: Inequalities in health in the 1980s*. London: Health Education Council.

Williams, D. (1990). Socioeconomic differentials in health: A review and redirection. *Social Psychology Quarterly, 53*(2), 81-99.

Wilson, D. (1993, September 9). Success of pact with B.C. doctors hinges on big cuts. *Globe and Mail*, p. A7.

Winslow, C.E.A. (1926). *The evolution and significance of the modern public health campaign*. New Haven, CT: Yale University Press.

Wnuk-Lipinski, E., & Illsley, R. (1990a). International comparative analysis: Main findings and conclusions. *Social Science & Medicine, 31*(8), 879-889.

Wnuk-Lipinski, E., & Illsley, R. (1990b). Social equality and health in non-market economies. *Social Science & Medicine, 31*(8), 833-836.

Woolhandler, S., & Himmelstein, D. (1988). Reverse targeting of preventive care due to lack of health insurance. *Journal of the American Medical Association, 259*, 2872-2874.

7

Community Medicine and the World of the Well

PATRICK C. PIETRONI

This article explores the systemic roots of the concept of community care as developed by Geoffrey Vickers in the 1960s and its subsequent elaboration in theory and in practice. It analyzes the radical 1990 reforms in the U.K. National Health Service in terms of an attempted shift to automatic market regulators to carry the gross burdens of choice that colliding expectations and relatively fixed resources are generating in health care, and it explores the changing role and possible changing training of practitioners in health and social care delivery.

I am afraid of those who look for a tendency between the lines and who insist on seeing me as necessarily either a liberal or a conservative. I am not a liberal, not a conservative, not a gradualist, not a monk and not an indifferentist.

—Anton Chekov
Letter to Alexey N. Pleshcheyev

Geoffrey Vickers and Anton Chekov both broke out of the constraints of their original discipline, background, and culture. Vickers—lawyer, civil servant, public sector manager, and holder, for 16 years, of the honorary position of chairman of the Research Committee of the Mental Health Research Fund—published extensively on medical matters and helped point the way toward many of the current issues and debates in health care today. Chekov, the qualified doctor, left the practice of medicine, but in his writings was able to signal, with an artistry that will outlast most academic publications, the dilemmas and pitfalls that face politicians, practitioners, and patients alike.

Vickers was able to escape from the rigidity of his Victorian upper-middle-class background, embrace systems theory, and address the limitations of a science-based epistemology bound by a 17th-century worldview. His challenge to the direction of professionalism in medicine was based on his own abiding concern for the importance of human rather than technological values and of ethical judgments. What is the relevance of Vickers's thinking to the current issues of health care delivery? This article will explore how the systems approach began to influence the intellectual debate in medicine; what the 1990 policy reforms of the U.K. National Health Service mean in terms of a change in the mechanisms of regulation, an abiding concern of Vickers; whether the move toward community-oriented primary health care meets the needs of what Vickers called "the world of the well," that is, the community outside the hospital where the overwhelming majority of patients are treated; and it asks how professionalism would need to change to accommodate Vickers's favorite definition of the doctor's function, "to cure sometimes, to relieve often, to support always" (Vickers, 1967/1984c, p. 169).

MEDICINE AND SYSTEMS THEORY

Vickers was increasingly uncomfortable with the notion of causality as it is expressed in the traditional scientific method—how to connect elements known to be associated with one another in the correct way, when that correct way involves looking for a logical sequence of cause and effect. The billiard ball notion of causality, and the associated neglect of the impossibility of continuous linear development, has dominated Western scientific thought for the past 300 years and has influenced the progress of medicine to the point where cries of "enough!" are being heard. Vickers was critical of the dominant Western conception of man as goal seeking rather than relationship maintaining:

> The concept of goal-seeking, apt enough as a model of behaviour in those situations in which effort leads through successful achievement to rest, was generalised as the standard model of human "rational" behaviour, although most human regulative behaviour, as I shall try to show, is norm-seeking and, as such, cannot be resolved into goal-seeking, despite the common opinion to the contrary. (Vickers, 1963/1984a, p. 152)

Vickers's starting point that human beings are norm seeking, and his emphasis on relationships rather than outputs, led naturally to his interest not in hospital but in community medicine, which, at the time of the 1967 article of that title published in *The Lancet*, did not have a name. Vickers defined it as managing illness "in the world of the well" (Vickers, 1967/1984c, p. 168). The objective of hospital medicine was to cure patients, isolated from their social and family context, using the latest technological means available. What he termed *community medicine* focuses attention on care rather than cure and on what is meant by health as much as what is meant by illness.

Health, Vickers argued, was as important a concept as illness for the medical profession and one much more difficult to define, and it was "clearly a norm, not a goal . . . a relationship not to be attained once for all but ever to be renewed" (Vickers, 1958/1984f, p. 125). It was obvious to Vickers that health had a social as well as a biological dimension and that the community physicians would need to work with epidemiologists and social scientists "to disentangle more clearly the nature of the dynamic balance which we should recognize as health and the conditions which favour or threaten it" (Vickers, 1958/1984f, p. 130). These ideas, originating in an address at Harvard School of Public Health in 1957, were radical ones, with uncomfortable implications for an elitist profession, jealous of its status and ever watchful to maintain its boundaries.

> Since the concept of health is now thus extended from the individual to society and from the biological norm to all kinds of other norms, we should be careful not to suppose that anything to do with health is necessarily something on which doctors can speak with authority. (Vickers, 1968, p. 390)

The challenge that Vickers posed for future doctors is a formidable one and we shall return to it again. Vickers was clear that medicine would have to respond to the insights derived from the work of Weiss and von Bertalanffy, and his writings predated the classic work of George Engel by some years. In the article "What to Expect of a Doctor," he wrote,

> The massive change in our conceptual system has made it possible to relate the psycho-social and the biological sciences, not by resolving the first into the second but by showing how they relate to and take from the second. How far this will carry us it is too early to say. (Vickers, 1968, p. 389)

Nearly 10 years later, George Engel (1977) wrote,

> I contend that all medicine is in crisis and, further, that medicine's crisis derives from the same basic fault as psychiatry's, namely, adherence to a model of disease no longer adequate for the scientific tasks and social responsibilities of either medicine or psychiatry. (p. 129)

Engel has labeled his approach to medicine biopsycho-social, and contrasted this with the biomedical model that he sees as the predominant "folk medicine" of Western society. Like Vickers, Engel draws heavily on systems theory to expand and explain his concept of the biopsycho-social approach. Nature is ordered both as a hierarchy and a continuum. Each level of system in the hierarchy possesses distinct characteristics of its own: A cell, for example, operates very differently from a person. Each system can operate as a dynamic whole but at the same time is a component of a higher system: A cell is part of a tissue, tissues form organs, and so on. Thus each system is both a whole and at the same time forms a part of a greater whole. It is by exploring the nature of the part and the whole that the natural scientist operates.

HOLISM AND FAMILY THERAPY

Engel has elaborated on his original article, both within the field of clinical practice and medical education, and has carried much of the approach that Vickers pioneered deep into the medical establishment, as evidenced by the special 10th anniversary issue of *Family Systems Medicine* entitled "The Behavioural Scientist in Primary Care Medicine" (Engel, 1992).

At the same time as systems thinking was beginning to influence medical thinking and practice, the concept of holism and holistic medicine was also finding its voice. Smuts, the South African historian, explorer, and military leader, first coined the term *holism* in his book *Holism and Evolution* (Smuts, 1926). There is no direct reference by Vickers to Smuts's work, but the implications of holistic thinking in medicine pointed in much the same direction as Vickers's approach, that is, to consider the medical practitioner as one part of a varied team of professionals concerned with the well-being of the patient, and to consider the patient not as an isolated individual but as part of a network of relationships. Both preceded and predicated the major policy reforms that have occurred in the United Kingdom in the past 5 years.

COMMUNITY CARE

Not only was Vickers the first to publicize the term *community medicine* but his vision of what this meant is even more relevant today than when he first delivered his lecture entitled "Community Medicine" in 1966. Vickers identified the community as the "world of the well" and described it as "a complex system of human relationships, organised in countless, interlocking sub-systems. Every illness stresses one or more of these systems, notably the home where the sick person lives and the place where he works" (Vickers, 1967/1984c, p. 170). Vickers contrasted the world of the well with the 1% of the population who resided in "another world—the world of the hospital." He was aware how doctors, invariably trained in the world of the hospital, were ill prepared for the task of working in the world of the well. In 1961, White had published an article in the *New England Journal of Medicine*, identifying a pattern of symptom presentation that supported the need to look outside the hospital system if a true picture of human pathology was to be obtained. White discovered that every month, of 1,000 adults, 750 developed a symptom of some kind. Of those 750, 250 went to their general practitioner and, of those, 10 to 15 were referred to a hospital and, of the 10 to 15, 1 to 2 were seen at a teaching hospital (White, Kerr, Williams, Franklin, & Greenberg, 1961). White, like Vickers, inferred that if medical students received their education only in hospital settings, their understanding and ability to respond to patients and their problems as presented to them in the community was likely to be limited. Vickers identified the purpose of community medicine as follows:

> It is responsible for managing, in the world of the well, the human estate of sickness, and mortality. I include in this the management of the non-pathological crises of life, birth, growth, senescence—death also . . . and the management of all illnesses, whether curable or not. . . . I include the relief of suffering, aid in living with disability, whether transient or permanent, limitation of disturbance in all the social systems which an illness disturbs, notably the household in which it is to be contained, and partnership with the layman or, more often, laywoman who is primarily charged with the care of the sick individual in the community and chiefly stressed by that responsibility. (Vickers, 1967/1984c, p. 169)

It is difficult to imagine being able to better this last definition of community medicine or community care and it is a sign of Vickers's vision that he was able to outline so succinctly this area of medical care that has been neglected for so long. He recognized the powerful resistance that the idea of community medicine faced: "Both layman and doctor should reject the idea, the novel and mischievous idea, that 'inpatient' medicine is the only 'real' medicine" (Vickers, 1967/1984c, p. 169). Vickers then set out, in one of his most provocative statements, to suggest that these "two streams of medicine may require" two separate streams of undergraduate education. That is, Vickers, who had himself no formal medical status of any kind, ventured to question the basic assumption underlying the time-honored practice of medical schools, still largely intact to this day, that doctors are trained in hospital. We shall return to this theme later.

Some of the concepts of community medicine propounded by Vickers were being simultaneously explored and implemented by a small handful of health care workers in the United Kingdom. A comparison of three very different U.K. examples (the Peckham Experiment, 1935-1950; Glyncorrwg Community Practice, 1966-1989; and the Marylebone Health Centre, 1986-) nevertheless illustrate how one or two exceptional doctors were feeling their way toward the ideas that Vickers so clearly laid out.

THE PECKHAM EXPERIMENT

The pilot phase of this extraordinary experiment began in 1926. By the time it closed, it was attracting over 10,000 visitors a year and its founders, Dr. George Scott Williamson and Dr. Innes Pearse, were in great demand as speakers and lecturers all over the world. The hypothesis they set up to test was that "health is more infectious than disease." They believed that, if they provided an environment where individuals could come and participate in "healthy activities," during which time they could be provided with "periodic healthy examination," including information on how to promote their health, their quality of life would improve.

The experiment initially began in a small health center in South London. It operated as a form of club, and 30 families came together to organize it. It rapidly outgrew its accommodation, and a new intentionally built construction, the pioneer of health centers, was designed and built in 1935.

It was hoped that, with the onset of the National Health Service (NHS), some of the principles embodied by the Peckham Experiment would be incorporated within the planning of the new health centers due to be built. However, neither the importance of design of building nor the participatory nature of the experiment or, more important, the focus on health, was seen as important by those who influenced the framework of the NHS. The health centers built within the NHS were managed and organized by doctors; the service offered was a reactive, disease-based model, and the preventive and promotional focus was minimized. With the death of the pioneers of the Peckham Experiment, much of the impetus for their method of work was lost and attempts to keep the model alive have proved difficult and problematic (Pearse, 1989).

Vickers emphasized the need for the concepts of "personal doctoring" (general practice) and "social medicine" (public health) to come together to enable the new field of community medicine to flourish. He nevertheless acknowledged that "the rate of change of mental habits is reckoned in generations." One general practitioner whose mental habits were ahead of his generation and who pursued the ideas propounded by Vickers, Dr. Julian Tudor-Hart, has recorded his own pioneering work in the medical literature.

GLYNCORRWG COMMUNITY PRACTICE

The community in Glyncorrwg, a South Wales village, was very closely involved with the mining industry but suffered, like many industrial communities, from the loss of its main source of employment. In 1966, 92% of men 16 to 64 years old were fully employed but by 1986, this percentage had dropped to 48. It was in this context that Tudor-Hart has emphasized the importance of social organizational cohesion on the health of a community and the need to foster a new kind of doctor to meet the demands of the next few decades. He drew attention to the importance of the family group and community involvement in helping to sustain the health of individuals and suggested that doctors needed to move away from a reactive, individually based, clinically oriented practice of medicine to one that was proactive, family and community based, and that accepted the social, cultural, economic, and political factors that influence health and disease (Tudor-Hart, 1988).

Like the pioneers at Peckham, Tudor-Hart highlighted the importance of architecture and the built environment: He described the impact of a swimming pool on the health and well-being of his patients. Likewise, Vickers held the view that "the most enduring signature that a man can inscribe on the world is a building" and that "the whole physical milieu is increasingly a human artefact; and this artefact is a commitment ever more permanent and ever more potent for multiple good or ill" (Vickers, 1974/1984b, p. 272). The importance of architecture to community care is no better illustrated than in the third experiment where Vickers's ideas are being explored.

MARYLEBONE HEALTH CENTRE

The Marylebone Health Centre is an ordinary general practice offering a traditional orthodox medical service to over 5,500 patients. It is situated in central London and in 1987 began to experiment with different models of delivering community care. These experiments included the following:

1. the use of complementary therapies—osteopathy, massage, herbal medicine, homeopathy, available as appropriate to patients;

2. a counseling and psychotherapy unit enabling many of the emotional and psychological concerns to be dealt with directly;
3. a social care unit with outreach workers to ensure that the more vulnerable members of the community (elderly, homeless, single parents) receive direct access to a range of services that impact directly on their level of well-being;
4. a health promotion and health education unit providing a range of self-care and self-help activities encouraging patients to learn about, and take more control of, their own health; and
5. a patient-participation program, run and staffed by the patients themselves, ensuring that a number of volunteer activities (befriending, practical support, crèche, telephone advice service, practice newsletter) is available to the community living around the health center.

The site of the health center, in the crypt of a church, provides an architectural site that is not only beautiful and aesthetically pleasing but that symbolizes the holistic nature of the project, paying attention to the whole person—psychologically, spiritually, and socially—not just physically.

The experiment in delivering community care was accompanied by a rigorous research study, that is, the synthesis of physicians and social scientists that Vickers had argued for. Within the first 3 years it became apparent that outcome measures of prescribing, investigative procedures, and referral on to specialists were substantially different from other practices with similar populations: Prescribing costs were about 50% below the U.K. average for a similar practice, and referrals to hospital were almost 30% below. Another of the research studies has shown that the crucial element at Marylebone was not just the addition of new services and facilities but the way these were put together in an integrated service and the way in which the practitioners worked together (Pietroni, 1990, pp. 191-195).

In comparing these three examples of community care, some of the basic principles enunciated by Vickers appear to be common to all of them (see Table 1).

REVIEW AND REFORM OF THE
U.K. NATIONAL HEALTH SERVICE, 1990

For many in the United Kingdom, the establishment of the NHS in 1948, with its commitment to universal health care from cradle to grave and its egalitarian financial underpinning, free at the point of need, represented the acme of civilized political principles. The socialist belief that by providing free and universal care the demand for medical attention would gradually reduce as the population's standard of health improved, that is, that the system would prove self-limiting, was soon recognized to be unfounded. Indeed, the opposite situation developed where increased demand, resulting from a growing elderly population, an increase in what was technologically possible, and above all ever-increasing expectations, began to collide with fixed budgeting and resource allocation. Vickers recognized the acuteness of the approaching dilemmas as early as his 1957 Harvard address:

TABLE 1: A Comparison of the Peckham, Marylebone, and Glyncorrwg Experiments

Peckham Experiment	Marylebone Experiment	Glyncorrwg Community Practice
1. Our concept (is) that health is a mutual synthesis of organism and environment.	1. There is an interconnectedness between human beings and their environment.	1. We must accept the full implications of both groups and individuals practicing an open style of medicine.
2. In this new field there was as yet no existing knowledge of well-defined entities, relationships, dynamics, and regularities that the bionomist might encounter.	2. Tolerating uncertainty, taking risks, and making mistakes are part of the stepping stones in the search for wholeness.	2. We need to admit to ourselves, to our colleagues, and to our patients what we do not yet know and what we have not yet done.
3. Approaching conventionally as a scientist, how then is he or she to fulfil the technological requirements of assessment; how is he or she to measure his or her material?	3. Research studies should pay due cognizance to the moral, ethical, and financial consequences of their outcome. This does not mean that we discard science, rather that we respond imaginatively and creatively as scientists to discover the construction of health and disease as a social process.	3. We must learn to apply scientific principles imaginatively to the health care of the millions of people as they actually live and work.
4. It is essential to grasp that the processes that sustain and develop an individual's health care are other than the processes that underlie and govern his or her disease.	4. Health and disease lie along a continuum and represent the organic-intrinsic state of harmony with the universe.	4. We must learn to deal with measurable continuously distributed variables in which disease (requiring active remedial intervention) is difficult or even impossible to separate from health (requiring active conservation).
5. Supper is an important time of meeting for all members of the staff. At times these lead to discussions that may run deep.	5. It will not be possible for doctors to address the health problems of the 21st century unless we learn how to share our power, not only among our colleagues in the health team but also with our patients.	5. We must accept that effective medical care, and even more the effective conservation of health, requires an enormous range of skills other than those of doctors, including skills of other medical, nursing, and health professionals who have been systematically subordinated to, and exploited by, us and our predecessors, and that our own skills will survive only if they can be shown to be useful.
6. Health, of which we were in search, demanded that the family should shoulder the responsibility for its own actions—this was basic to the hypothesis on which the work was conceived.	6. Users of health care services need to be offered knowledge, skills, and support to enable them to take an active interest in their health and emotional well-being. They can also share the responsibility for helping to maintain the organization designed to promote health and community care.	6. We must accept patients as colleagues in a jointly designed and performed production in which they will nearly always have to do most of the work. We must look to a more dependable alliance with the ordinary people we serve.

115

The amount of effort which can plausibly be devoted to the health of the individual and the community increases with every scientific development and will, I think, increase indefinitely. Thus the services which might be provided may well continue to exceed, perhaps by an ever-increasing margin, the services which can in fact be provided, since the total will be limited by the amount of resources available, having regard to conflicting demands. (Vickers, 1958/1984f, p. 129)

Successive governments, operating a system of delegated decision making to the medical profession, found themselves unable to control expenditure, let alone meet the increasing demand for health care from professionals, health unions, and the public alike. The reorganization into a three-tiered service (regional, area, district) in the early 1970s failed to curb expenditure or indeed to provide better planning. It was not until the publication of *Priorities for Health and Personal Social Services in England* (Department of Health and Social Services, 1976) and the *National Health Service Management Inquiry* (Griffiths Report, 1983) that the idea of centrally controlled and managed health and social services operating within fixed budgets and cash limits was promoted. This led to a series of policy statements and working documents that finally culminated in the National Health Service and Community Care Act of 1990, which has introduced the most fundamental reorganization of the health and social services since 1948. All areas of activity—hospitals, general practice, community nursing, and personal social services—have been completely reorganized, and several fundamental changes will ensure that professional working patterns will alter substantially.

These changes include the following:

1. centrally and politically controlled NHS executive planning with clear strategic policy plans as set out in *The Health of the Nation* (Department of Health, 1991);
2. the introduction of the internal market, with the separation of purchasers and providers across both secondary and primary care;
3. the creation of independent hospital trusts, general practice fund-holders, and community trusts, each responsible for working within fixed and possibly diminishing budgets;
4. the introduction of the patient as consumer, with rights to be enshrined in a *Patients' Charter* (Department of Health, 1992);
5. the transfer of responsibility for the provision of community care from Social Security, Housing and Health to Social Services and local authorities—the delivery of such services to be through social workers under the new title of care managers;
6. the legislative requirement for packages of care to be allocated to the private sector and away from the public sector; and
7. the closure of long-stay hospital facilities for the elderly, the chronic sick, and the mentally ill, and the encouragement of such patients to be cared for in the community.

The rhetoric that underpinned many of the policy reforms, although superficially attractive—it spoke of a "user-centred seamless service," of "care in the community," of "putting the patient first"—failed to convince the medical, nursing, and social care professions that the basis of the reforms was anything other than the fundamental dismantling of the public financing of health and welfare services. The introduction of the internal market, with its emphasis on financial rectitude and balanced budgeting, together with the encouragement of a mixed economy of care (private, voluntary, public, and statutory), has meant that many of the cherished professional freedoms have now been eroded.

The introduction of market mechanisms into the NHS was an attempt to introduce an automatic regulator into the system. A market in health care, like the free market in the economy at large, assumed that the aggregated actions of the countless actors in the system would automatically, without external interference, serve the best interests of the whole population. The appeal of such an automatic regulation of the mounting burden of health care demands to any government unable to meet them is entirely understandable. It promised to remove the odium of thankless difficult choices from the political process to a nonpolitical self-regulating system. This is a classic example of what Peter Senge calls "shifting the burden" (Senge, 1992, p. 107). The shifting-of-the-burden structure explains a wide range of behaviors where well-intended "solutions" actually make matters worse over the long term. Opting for symptomatic solutions is enticing. Apparent improvement is achieved. Pressures, either external or internal, to *do something* about a vexing problem are relieved. But easing a problem symptom also reduces any perceived need to find more fundamental solutions. Meanwhile, the underlying problem remains unaddressed and may worsen, and the side effects of the symptomatic solution make it still harder to apply the fundamental solution. Senge regards such strategies, whether in management or personal life, as flawed and ultimately self-defeating.

The assumptions underpinning the 1990 NHS health care reforms appear to be that the automatic regulators of the market can substitute for the excruciatingly difficult choices, posed by an ever-increasing demand pushing ever more strongly against a fixed resource, which would otherwise fall to deliberate human agency. The tendency for Western societies to believe that automatic regulators can substitute for deliberate human regulation based on ethical principles derived largely, Vickers believed, from a change in what he called the appreciative setting associated with the Enlightenment. It lay at the heart of what he believed to be the weakness of Western culture.

Deliberate human regulation is at its most difficult in the health area, where the choices between who should and who should not have priority for treatment pose ethical issues of the most complex kind. Choices become ever more difficult with every advance in medical technology, given deeply held beliefs that, once something is possible, everyone is equally entitled to benefit from it, and that it should be free at the point of delivery. Vickers's general observation about the consequences of acts of God increasingly becoming acts of man is nowhere more telling than in the health area: "Increasing power over the natural environment focuses human expectations on what man should do rather than on what nature will do and thus hugely expands the ethical dimension" (Vickers, 1973/1984e, p. 198). And what is within the compass of acts of man poses choices and adds a further burden to the political process. No wonder that governments should be tempted to shift the burden.

Vickers, however, argued persuasively that one cannot use the market as a regulator in matters affecting life and death. "A resource that is inexpansible, indispensable and overscarce can no more be distributed through the machinery of the market than can the places in too few lifeboats on a sinking ship" (Blunden, 1984, p. 33). Such issues must rest on the deliberate exercise of human judgment and the exercise of what Vickers called "balancing through time a host of disparate criteria, not all of which—usually not one of which—can be fully satisfied" (Vickers, 1972/1984d, p. 180). If this is not done, linear developments will ultimately breed, at huge costs, their own reversals.

IMPLICATIONS FOR PROFESSIONALISM

Where does all this leave the practitioners? The NHS reforms have felt, to many doctors, nurses, and social workers, like the loss of professional autonomy and independence to a management takeover. Doctors had previously assumed and insisted that they, and they alone, could determine standards of medical and surgical care that patients received. Clinical freedom meant that they could prescribe whatever drug they chose and perform whatever operation or procedure they felt appropriate. Accountability was informal and patients had access to the courts if gross errors occurred. Nurses and social workers have never possessed the autonomy that doctors have traditionally had, but they too have seen the new reforms as an erosion of their professional independence. The 1990 reforms have struck some as ironical: A radical right-wing government has introduced reforms that have eroded the independence of the professional, in contrast to the radical socialist government of 1948 whose major reform setting up the NHS preserved, and indeed enhanced, the professionals' control of the health and welfare services.

It is the erosion of professional freedom and autonomy that has dominated the response to many reforms introduced in 1990. Vickers's analysis, which defined systems in terms of their regulatory mechanisms, would suggest that that erosion, in one form or another, was likely to occur as escalating demands bore down on fixed resources. The relative freedom of the doctor during the period up to 1990 was possible because of relative abundance in medical goods and services. There are, however, other dimensions to the changing role of professionals within this field and Vickers's article of 1974, entitled "The Changing Nature of the Professions," provided a useful framework for considering these. Vickers identified "five great changes" that he predicted would alter the relationship between the professional and his patient/client. These five changes included the following:

1.   Members of many professions were now tending to operate mainly as functionaries, whole-time officials in governmental or business organizations.

2. Many professionals were also becoming technologists, and this technological expertise bred "a score of specialities" in the medical professions; in particular it helped to degrade the concept of medical care as distinct from cure.
3. The rising level of education among laymen muted the distinction that once gave prestige to the "learned professions" as such.
4. The area of professionalism widened hugely in at least four directions. Vickers gave as examples of these new professions probation officers, personnel managers, computer programmers, and business managers.
5. What he called multiprofessional professions emerged.

Vickers believed that much of the value of the professional consisted in the ability to give independent advice based on the exercise of dispassionate judgment, because the professional was "dependent on the good will of no single client, however large, and setting his own definition of the way in which his skills should be used" (Vickers, 1974/1984b, p. 280).

Vickers's analysis of professionalism anticipated some of the issues raised by Donald Schön. Schön's seminal article, "The Crisis of Professional Knowledge," attracted much attention to his concept of the "reflective practitioner," applicable in every area of professional activity (Schön, 1992, p. 49). In calling for the liberation of the professions from the tyranny of the university-based professional schools, Schön, like Vickers before him, is attacking the influence of misplaced scientific methodologies. In Schön's view, the university-based professional schools have succumbed to the erroneous view that good professional practice is dependent on the use of "describable, testable, replicable techniques derived from scientific research based on knowledge that is objective, consensual, cumulative and convergent." His different perspective that involves practitioners "making judgments of quality for which they cannot state adequate criteria, display skills for which they cannot describe procedures or rules" evokes, as Vickers did, the importance of tacit knowledge. Schön argues that tacit areas of knowledge or skill form some of the most important aspects of competent practice. He terms the differing approaches to the professional task as those of "rigour or relevance."

Schön and his colleagues describe four professional roles they perceive within health care. The *practical* professional is pragmatic, problem-solving, arrives at solutions by trial and error, and is involved with the everyday clinical problems. The *expert* professional claims expert knowledge, which may result in being distanced from everyday problems. He or she calls on a body of expertise that he or she alone has and that can often be difficult to share with others. The *managerial* professional is familiar from the field of social work and social services. The two-tiered model applies where an experienced practitioner will become a manager responsible for personnel, planning strategies, and the management of resources. Experienced practitioners may also provide a supervisory backup to less experienced practitioners. The fourth professional role, the *reflective* practitioner, is the ideal. He or she "recognises that others have important and relevant knowledge to contribute and that allowing this to emerge is a course of learning for everyone. Reflective practitioners look for a sense of freedom and real connection with, rather than distance from, clients" (Schön, 1983, pp. 49-63).

Schön's concept of the reflective practitioner could well describe Vickers's own lifework. The logic of both men's approaches calls into question both the traditional role and the traditional training of medical practitioners. Vickers approached this question by exploring the changing boundaries of medical practice:

> In the last fifty years the field of the psycho-social sciences has widened almost as much as that of the physio-biological sciences. Further and no less important, the studies of ecology and ethology have prepared our minds to think ecologically and ethologically about our own species. So in seeking to define the field of a doctor's authority we have to ask, as we should not have had to ask fifty years ago, "Where does medicine stop?" (Vickers, 1968, p. 389)

Vickers expected much more from the future doctor than medical education currently prepares medical students to possibly provide. He wrote, for instance,

> I would prophesy the planning and design of the urban environment will absorb an ever greater share of our attention, our wealth and our best brains. It will be the major variable in the quality of life, not only for the poor but for everyone. And in its design the doctor has an important word which he alone can speak. (Vickers, 1968, p. 388)

Vickers was aware that the expansion of the doctor's role could not be encompassed within the traditional medical curriculum and he proposed a provocative and novel solution to the problem. He suggested that in future the "two streams of medicine," hospital and community medicine, should have separate educational pathways: "The medical profession would divide into two main streams by an option which would usually be exercised early and which though not irrevocable would seldom be reversed" (Vickers, 1968, p. 390). This proposal received a critical response from the medical profession when it was first propounded and would still be regarded as radical. Another, equally controversial, contribution that Vickers made was to suggest that medicine needed to tread the path from a single profession to a multiprofessional service. Although the path is rough, it leads out of an impasse of professional rivalry among medical, paramedical, and associated social care professionals to an alternative that at its best would unite the professions in a common service loyalty, without diluting their individual professional expertise.

The commitment to collaborative care, teamwork, and multidisciplinary educational activities is one of the strongest themes that emerges from Vickers's writings on health. What distinguishes his contribution is the systemic quality and range of his thinking, which led him to rare insights into the work of an area of professional practice of which he was never formally part. The concepts of community practice and of interprofessional working are now commonplace. Nevertheless, if one surveys the ever-increasing literature on interprofessional work, one is faced with what Kilcoyne (1991) described as "the litany of disappointment and frustration at the patchiness or absence of fruitful and democratic communication between professionals" (p. 34).

As Vickers himself perceived, however, the rate of change in mental habits "is reckoned in generations" (Vickers, 1967/1984c, p. 173).

REFERENCES

Blunden, M. (1984). Geoffrey Vickers—An intellectual journey. In Open Systems Group (Eds.), *The Vickers papers* (pp. 3-42). London: Harper & Row.

Department of Health (1991). *The health of the nation*. London: HMSO.

Department of Health (1992). *The patients' charter*. London: HMSO.

Department of Health and Social Services (1976). *Priorities for health and personal social services in England*. London: HMSO.

Engel, G. (1977). The need for a new medical mode. *Science, 196*(8), 129.

Engel, G. (1992). The behavioural scientist in primary care medicine. *Family Systems Medicine, 10*, 317-331.

Griffiths Report (1983). *The National Health Service management inquiry*. London: HMSO.

Kilcoyne, A. (1991). Post Griffiths: The art of communication and collaboration in the primary health care team. *Marylebone Monographs, 1*, 34.

Pearse, H. I (1989). *The quality of life*. Edinburgh: Scottish Academic Press.

Pietroni, P. C. (1990). *The greening of medicine*. London: Gollancz.

Schön, D. (1983). *The reflective practitioner*. London: Temple Smith.

Schön, D. (1992). The crisis of professional knowledge. *Journal of Interprofessional Care, 6*(1), 49-63.

Senge, P. M. (1992). *The fifth discipline: The art and practice of the learning organisation*. London: Century Business.

Smuts, J. C. (1926). *Holism and evolution*. London: Macmillan.

Tudor-Hart, J. (1988). *A new kind of doctor*. London: Merlin.

Vickers, G. (1968, March 7). What to expect of a doctor. *British Hospital Journal and Social Service Review*, pp. 388-390.

Vickers, G. (1984a). Appreciative behaviour. In Open Systems Group (Eds.), *The Vickers papers* (pp. 152-167). London: Harper & Row. (Original work published 1963)

Vickers, G. (1984b). The changing nature of the professions. In Open Systems Group (Eds.), *The Vickers papers*. London: Harper & Row. (Original work published 1974)

Vickers, G. (1984c). Community medicine. In Open Systems Group (Eds.), *The Vickers papers*. London: Harper & Row. (Original work published April 29, 1967)

Vickers, G. (1984d). The management of conflict. In Open Systems Group (Eds.), *The Vickers papers*. London: Harper & Row. (Original work published June, 1972)

Vickers, G. (1984e). Values, norms and policies. In Open Systems Group (Eds.), *The Vickers papers*. London: Harper & Row. (Original work published 1973)

Vickers, G. (1984f). What sets the goals of public health? In Open Systems Group (Eds.), *The Vickers papers* (pp. 122-134). London: Harper & Row. (Original work published March 22, 1958)

White, E., Kerr, Williams, Franklin, & Greenberg. (1961). The ecology of medical care. *New England Journal of Medicine, 256*, 585-892.

8

The Process of Education

ALVIN M. WHITE

Geoffrey Vickers advocated and illustrated the efficacy of informal education. Children and older students can and do learn within the contexts of tasks and questions that are meaningful to them. This article is about surprisingly successful learning in informal settings. Informal learning has often been encouraged because of the failure of more traditional approaches. Mathematics has been assumed to be certain and the model of describing truth. The certainty of mathematics and the formal mode of discussing mathematics are being reconsidered. Connections between mathematics and humanistic disciplines are the bases of a worldwide movement of mathematically minded scholars.

Students and teachers often confuse information and knowledge. Students view their task as memorizing facts. Teachers encourage such a view by presenting their messages with no hint of history or evolution. Addition and multiplication facts are presented to be memorized; rapid response is rewarded. Particular problems are to be solved by particular methods. Teachers deal with the expanding curriculum by talking faster. There is no time for reflective thinking. A student remarks to a classmate, "There are five reasons why Hamlet is a great play, but I can remember only three."

Much of our knowledge is contextual. Our behavior shows that we are aware of the law, even if we have not formally studied it. We also have a working knowledge of natural science as it impinges on the environment. Our knowledge was acquired outside of formal education.[1]

INFORMAL EDUCATION

California children were recently (1994) assessed using standardized tests. The results were discouraging. Most children were seriously deficient in reading and in mathematics, although there were some exceptions. Earlier tests found similar conclusions. The responses ranged from denial to despair. Some called for "back to basics" as a solution again, although that idea has led to failure.

There are, however, happier stories. A fifth-grade teacher in a small district in Southern California was enrolled by others in a mathematics problem-solving workshop. On her arrival she was dismayed. Mathematics was not her interest. Her interest was literature and art; mathematics was given very little attention.

The promise of help and support persuaded her to stay. She learned about problem solving for fifth graders and was inspired by the workshop leaders. Her students were enrolled in the international Mathematical Olympiads for Elementary Schools (MOES).[2] About five years after the workshop there were 72,000 contestants in the MOES. Seventeen children had perfect scores, and three of those perfect scores were from this teacher's class!

A local TV station sent a crew to interview the students and their teacher. All of the children were working on problems and talking. Very few were sitting. When a student solved a problem, the teacher checked it, and the student moved to help those still working. Before the workshop the teacher lectured or talked to the students from the front of the classroom. After the children experienced interesting mathematics in an active way, they demanded more of the same. Passivity for the teacher and her students was rejected. The children were having too much fun. Another example is of a seventh-grade teacher who had a personal computer in her classroom. One morning she showed a new computer procedure to one of her students. By the afternoon 200 students had learned that procedure!

Contrary to popular opinion, intrinsic motivation is crucial to learning:

> The chief impediments to learning are not cognitive. It is not that students cannot learn; it is that they do not wish to. If educators invested a fraction of the energy they now spend trying to transmit information in trying to stimulate the students' enjoyment of learning, we could achieve much better results.[3]

Csikszentmihalyi has studied artists, chess players, rock climbers, surgeons, and others who are caught up in their tasks, when their sense of self is not separate from what they are doing, when their concentration is like breathing. He calls this complete absorption in the task *Flow: The Psychology of Optimal Experience*.[4] The activity is done for intrinsic rewards. Such activity can include studying, writing poetry, and solving mathematical problems. There is evidence that extrinsic rewards, compared to intrinsic rewards, are counterproductive.

AN INFLUENTIAL STUDY

Hassler Whitney, a member of the Institute for Advanced Study at Princeton until he died recently, devoted the last several years of his life as an active advocate for elementary school children as they encountered arithmetic and mathematics. His discovery of a series of articles published in 1935 ("The Teaching of Arithmetic: The Story of an Experiment"[5]) had a profound effect on him. He distributed copies of these articles to all of his friends for several years and influenced many mathematicians and educators. As a memorial to Hassler Whitney, the *Humanistic Mathematics Network Journal*[6] reprinted the articles in the May 1991 issue. The articles strongly support the idea of informal learning and intrinsic motivation.

L. P. Benezet was the superintendent of schools in Manchester, New Hampshire, when the experiment occurred:

> I was distressed at the inability of the average child in our grades to use the English language. If the children had original ideas, they were helpless about translating them into English which could be understood. I went into a certain eighth grade room one day and was accompanied by a stenographer who took down, verbatim, the answers given me by the children. I was trying to get the children to tell me, in their own words, that if you have two fractions with the same numerator, the one with the smaller denominator is the larger. I quote typical answers:
> The smaller number in fractions is always the largest. If the numerators are both the same, and the denominators one is smaller than the one, the one that the smaller is the larger. The denominator that is smallest is the largest. . . . The trouble was not with the children or with the teacher. It was the curriculum. . . . For some years I had noted that the effect of the early introduction of arithmetic had been to dull and almost chloroform the child's reasoning faculties.

In 1929, Benezet proposed an experiment of abandoning all formal instruction in arithmetic below the seventh grade and concentrating on teaching the children to read, to reason, and to recite. The children in the experimental rooms were encouraged to do a great deal of oral composition. They reported on books that they had read, on incidents that they had seen, on visits that they had made. They told the stories of movies that they had attended and made up romances on the spur of the moment. A happy and joyous spirit pervaded the experimental rooms. The children were no longer under the restraint of learning multiplication tables or struggling with long division. They were thoroughly enjoying their hours in school. The children were given practice in estimating heights, lengths, areas, and so on and became acquainted with numbers through their reading and play.

In comparisons of the traditional seventh-grade classrooms with the experimental classrooms on writing about a painted scene, the experimentally taught children were judged to be about two years ahead of the traditionally taught children in maturity of expression. The parents of the children of the traditional classroom all spoke English, whereas most of the children of the experimental groups came from homes in which English was not spoken.

By the fall of 1932, about one half of the third-, fourth-, and fifth-grade rooms in the city were working under the new curriculum. Four schools began teaching arithmetic in the sixth grade. A professor at Boston University tested 200 sixth-grade children on arithmetic, half from the traditional classes and half from the experimental classes. By the middle of April, all the classes were practically on a par and when the last test was given in June, it was one of the experimental classes that led the city.

> In other words these children, by avoiding the early drill on combinations, tables . . . had been able in one year, to attain the level of accomplishment which the traditionally taught children had reached after three and one-half years of arithmetical drill.

In the fall of 1933, the experimental program was extended to the whole city. There would be no formal instruction in arithmetic until Grade 6, although the children would acquire a sense of number through telling time, birthdays, and other informal ways. When the processes of arithmetic were discussed, the children would be informed of the reasons for those processes.

Despite the success of the experimental program, a motion to abandon the new program was only defeated in the school board by a vote of nine to four. A committee of three was appointed to study the problem carefully. Superintendent Benezet took two members of the committee and a stenographer with him to visit four schools in his city of Manchester and three in a city about 30 miles away. In each advanced fifth-grade class he presented the following puzzle:

> A wooden pole is stuck in the mud at the bottom of a pond. There is some water above the mud and part of the pole sticks up into the air. One-half of the pole is in the mud; 2/3 of the rest is in the water; and one foot is sticking out into the air. How long is the pole?

The traditional class students answered with gibberish. The children in the experimental class gave elegant explanations and solutions. The committee reported to the board and the board accepted their report, saying that the superintendent was on the right track. They merely suggested that, to quiet the outcry of some of the parents, the teaching of the tables should begin a little earlier in the course.

These informal approaches are consistent with contemporary views of mathematics and education.

TRADITIONAL THINKING IN MATHEMATICS

Mathematics was for 2,000 years an example of truth and certainty, and geometry as presented by Euclid was the model. Plato wished not merely to understand nature through mathematics but to substitute mathematics for nature herself.[7]

Descartes wrote that he counted as the most certain truths numbers and other matters that pertain to arithmetic, geometry, and to pure and abstract mathematics.[8] Spinoza treated human vice and folly geometrically. Human actions and desires are considered as Euclid considered lines and planes.[9] Although Hume introduced doubt and skepticism about truth and certainty, Kant in his *Prolegomena* reaffirmed confidence in mathematics: "We can say with confidence that certain pure *a priori* synthetical cognitions, pure mathematics and pure physics are actual and given; for both contain propositions which are thoroughly recognized as absolutely certain . . . and yet are independent of experience."[10]

Although Euclid's geometry was the epitome of truth and certainty for 2,000 years, there was some concern about the independence of the fifth postulate about parallel lines. In the 18th century several mathematicians were actively considering the fifth postulate. Many attempted to prove the parallel postulate to be a consequence of the other postulates. In the 19th century the audacious idea was not to prove the parallel postulate but to deny it. Johann Bolyai and Nikolai Lobatchevsky carried out the details of this idea and are honored for the creation-discovery of non-Euclidean geometry. This new creation carried with it the destruction of the faith that mathematics was the model of truth and certainty. The intellectual pillars of the temple of truth crumbled.[11]

The relationship of mathematics to the physical world was expressed by Einstein in 1921: "Insofar as the propositions of mathematics give an account of reality they are not certain; and insofar as they are certain they do not describe reality."[12] Mathematics did not end with the crisis of non-Euclidean geometry. There were many later crises as well as many triumphs. Mathematics continues to develop internally as a subject and externally as applied to many fields, and the possibility of applications to new fields creates new mathematics.

CONTEMPORARY VIEWS OF MATHEMATICS

In the early years of the 20th century, philosophers and philosophically minded mathematicians were concerned with establishing a proper foundation for mathematics. Three notable movements were Logicism, Intuitionism, and Formalism.[13] The actual practice of mathematics was barely affected by the philosophical discussions, although tastes and standards of rigor evolved somewhat. Teaching of mathematics in schools and colleges was essentially unchanged. During the sixties, there was a strong movement in the United States and in much of the rest of the world to revolutionize the school curriculum. The common theme of all philosophical camps was that mathematics should be presented as a formal system.[14] The curriculum was known as the New Math.

The New Math lasted about one generation. In 1986, three-inch headlines in African newspapers proclaimed the end of New Math. In the past two decades, several mathematicians and mathematics educators have challenged the view that the most significant aspect of mathematics is reasoning by deduction culminating in formal proofs. In their view there is much more to mathematics than formal systems. Many agree that when a proof is valid because of its form only, without regard to its content, it is likely to add very little to understanding and may not even be very convincing. Proof has become more informal and may depend for its validity on social practice.[15]

In mathematical practice, in the real life of mathematicians, proof is convincing argument as judged by qualified people. The passage from an informal theory to a formalized theory entails some loss of meaning. The informal has connotations and alternative interpretations that are not in the formalized theory. Thus any result that is proved formally may be challenged: "How faithful are this statement and proof to the informal concepts we are actually interested in?" Also, full formalization and complete formal proof even if possible in principle may be impossible in practice. More than *whether* a conjecture is correct, mathematicians want to know *why* it is correct.[16]

To a student, the essence of mathematical truth may be a formal proof. The crucial element, however, is not the deductive scheme but the mathematical ideas whose relationships are illuminated by the proof in a new way. It is the intuitive bridging of the gaps in logic that forms the essential component of understanding.[17]

The new standards for teaching published by the National Council of Teachers of Mathematics in 1990 advocate active learning, preferable in cooperative groups.[18] Teachers should be concerned with students' intuitive understanding and their ability to create their own meanings. Intuitive understanding and personal meaning are encouraged by conversations within cooperative groups.

The U.S. National Science Foundation (NSF) and other funding agencies are encouraging states and school districts to educate or reeducate teachers and administrators about how children learn and the teacher's role in that process. The new view of how mathematical knowledge is created and understood is a strong motivation for the national effort. The national need and the availability of money from the NSF have brought forth many focused efforts to write new books and to create new curricula for college and precollege students. A less focused, more informal movement is the humanistic mathematics network. The idea that mathematics is one of the humanities, and that the teaching, learning, and creating of mathematics issue from the same psyche as literature, art, and music has attracted a worldwide network of people who share that idea. The existence of the network has encouraged individuals to try new approaches that might have been considered radical a few years ago.

HUMANISTIC MATHEMATICS

In 1986, with support from the Exxon Education Foundation, a three-day conference to "examine mathematics as a humanistic discipline" was convened. Thirty-six mathematicians from all the regions of the United States participated. There was no definition and no set agenda—just a willingness to exchange views. A common response of the participants was "I was startled to see so many who shared my feelings."

Two related themes that emerged from the conference were (a) teaching mathematics humanistically and (b) teaching humanistic mathematics. The first theme sought to place the student more centrally in the position of inquirer than is generally the case, while at the same time acknowledging the emotional climate of the activity of learning mathematics. What students could learn from each other and how they might better come to understand mathematics as a meaningful rather than an arbitrary discipline were among the ideas of the first theme.

The second theme was focused less on the nature of the teaching and learning environment and more on the need to reconstruct the curriculum and the discipline of mathematics itself. The reconstruction would relate mathematical discoveries to personal courage, discovery to verification, mathematics to science, truth to utility, and, in general, it would relate mathematics to the culture in which it is embedded.

Humanistic dimensions of mathematics discussed included the following:

1. An appreciation of the role of intuition, not only in understanding but in creating concepts that appear in their finished versions to be "merely technical."

2. An appreciation of the human dimensions that motivate discovery: competition, cooperation, the urge for holistic pictures.
3. An understanding of the value judgments implied in the growth of any discipline. Logic alone never completely accounts for *what* is investigated, *how* it is investigated, and *why* it is investigated.
4. There is a need for new teaching, learning formats that will help wean our students from a view of knowledge as certain, to be "received."

In the following year a newsletter was circulated to the conference participants. Now, in 1994, the newsletter is a journal and is sent to over 1,100 people all over the world. The movement, which began as the personal vision of a few, has become a major part of mathematical culture. What was viewed with skepticism is now accepted and expected. Humanistic mathematics is not a new discovery. It is a recent rediscovery of ideas that go back to Plato and later to D'Alembert, Condorcet, Bacon, and more recently to Whitehead, Cassirer, Wilder, and Bronowski. It has provided a vocabulary for previously unarticulated concepts and approaches.

Several conferences on the subject have been independently organized. There are sessions on humanistic mathematics at every annual meeting of the Mathematical Association. Early on, in the spirit of mathematics, there were questions and discussions as to the precise meaning of humanistic mathematics. Now there is a growing recognition that even the definitions of mathematics must be negotiated, and informal proofs are more usual and successful than rigorous formalistic proofs.[19] The presenters at the contributed paper sessions of the annual meetings, the authors whose essays appear in the journal,[20] in the recent book on humanistic mathematics,[21] and the readers are not searching outside of themselves for a definition. The personal meanings that everyone finds seem to fit together and to be mutually supportive.

Those who have seen the journal for the first time write with the shock of recognition, asking to receive copies of their own. An essay is often included with the letter. The humanistic mathematics network affords mathematicians, teachers, and others the opportunity of having colleagues who also consider mathematics to be one of the humanities; who understand mathematics to have much in common with literature, philosophy, art, music, and criticism; who eschew dogmatic teaching styles that expect students to parrot the lecturer.[22]

Pure mathematics is ultimately one of the humanities because it is an intellectual discipline with a human perspective and a history that matters. Humanistic mathematics is not just "friendly math." It is mathematics with a human face.[23] Mathematics, along with literature and music, is a language of the imagination. The essence of science is the right to repeat an experiment, whereas the essence of mathematics is the right to understand. The structures with which mathematics deals are like lace, the leaves of trees, and the play of light and shadow on a meadow.[24]

Mathematics consists of eternal truths about eternal objects. This was surely Plato's view. The mystery is how we could come to know such truths. We learn mathematics by doing computations—and by being surprised by the results. When we describe a physical situation mathematically, where does the vagueness go? It cannot just disappear—the answer is that the vagueness goes into the word *approximately*.[25]

The public image of mathematics as an elegant, polished, finished product obscures its human roots. It has a private life of human joy, challenge, reflection, puzzlement, intuition, struggle, and excitement. Mathematics is a humanistic discipline, but the humanistic dimension is often limited to its private world.[26]

Many mathematicians, teachers, government officials, and others are concerned with improving the learning of mathematics from elementary school through college. The ideas and spirit of the humanistic mathematics movement make contact with the actual processes of teaching, learning, understanding, and creating mathematics. Students, teachers, and professors can join in appreciating the common human spirit in the humanities and in mathematics. Intuition and imagination are encouraged. The importance of history and the personal voice is increased. Human relationships and values enter the classrooms and conversations.

Kenneth Boulding commented that the criteria of acceptance of mathematical arguments include elegance, beauty, and simplicity. There are no such things as *facts*; there are only messages filtered through a changeable value system.[27]

The creative process was surveyed by Brewster Ghiselin.[28] The excerpts from artists, poets, mathematicians, and other creative people all tell of the same experience. "It is evident that in both art and science the inventor is to some degree incited and guided by a sense of value in the end sought, something . . . like an intimation of usefulness." William Blake and A. E. Housman tell of the necessary period of gestation. Bertrand Russell remarked on the fruitless effort he used to expend in trying to push his creative work to completion by sheer force of will before he discovered the necessity of waiting for it to find its own subconscious development. Henri Poincaré describes mathematical creation as choosing the most useful combinations. The mathematician relies on intimations of fruitfulness.

Donald Schön quotes Chris Alexander on the knowing involved in design. He believes that we can often recognize and correct the "bad fit" of a form to its content, but that we usually cannot describe the rules by which we find a fit bad or recognize the corrected form to be good.[29] Geoffrey Vickers comments on Alexander's remark that it is not only artistic judgments that are based on a sense of form that cannot be fully articulated:

> Artists, so far from being alone in this, exhibit most clearly an oddity which is present in all such judgements. We can recognize and describe deviations from a norm very much more clearly than we can describe the norm itself.[30]

For Vickers, it is through such tacit norms that all of us make the judgments, the qualitative appreciations of situations, on which our practical competence depends.[31]

Writing about education, Vickers asks some interesting questions:

How *little* skill and knowledge need we acquire in this field in order to further our understanding . . . might not even specialties be better taught if teachers saw the subject matter in the context of all the other specialties to which they contribute and which contribute to them? . . . Academics should become primarily teachers, absorbed by the excitement of passing on what they know and engaging interest, especially in what they do not know, but long to know, and believe to be knowable. . . . The way we arrange and expound some understanding that we have achieved is seldom the way in which we acquired it. . . . Teaching can only be a guide to learning; it cannot be a substitute. Perhaps we would do better to speak of all educational establishments, not as places of teaching, but as places of learning. Viewed thus, it seems less improbable that less structured and less specialized teaching might result in quicker learning, even in the specialties.[32]

TACIT KNOWING

Michael Polanyi introduced the idea of tacit knowledge: that we know more than we can tell.[33] In the preface to *Personal Knowledge*,[34] he asserts that he rejects the ideal of scientific detachment: "In the exact sciences, this false ideal is perhaps harmless, for it is in fact disregarded there by scientists." But it exercises a destructive influence in other areas and falsifies our whole outlook far beyond the domain of science.

Polanyi comments, "To form part of science, a statement must be not only true, but also interesting, and, more particularly, interesting to science. Reliability, exactitude, does count as a factor contributing to scientific merit, but it is not enough."[35]

Whitehead asserts, "It is more important that a proposition be interesting than that it be true. This statement is almost a tautology. . . . But of course a true proposition is more apt to be interesting than a false one."[36]

The humanistic mathematics movement seeks to return to the educational process the excitement and wonderment of the moments of discovery and creation.

The discoveries of science, the works of art are explorations—more, are explosions, of a hidden likeness. The discoverer or the artist presents in them two aspects of nature and fuses them into one. This is the act of creation, in which an original thought is born, and it is the same act in original science and original art. . . . The poem or the discovery exists in two moments of vision: the moment of appreciation as much as that of creation. . . . We re-enact the creative act, and we ourselves make the discovery again. At bottom, there is no unifying likeness there until we too have seized it, we too have made it for ourselves.[37]

The process of learning, if it is encouraged, has much in common with the process of creating. The mystery of how one acquires new knowledge and how one is transformed by that new knowledge has been a concern at least since Plato. A passage in the *Phaedrus* (pp. 251 ff.) says,

The soul is awe-stricken and shudders at the sight of the beautiful, for it feels that something is evoked in it that was not imparted from without by the senses but has always been laid down there in a deeply unconscious region.[38]

In an echo of Blake, Housman, Russell, Poincaré, and others quoted by Ghiselin about gestation and revelation, Heisenberg, writing about the role of beauty in the exact sciences, asks:

What is it that shines forth here? How comes it that with this shining forth of the beautiful into exact science the great connection becomes recognizable, even before it is understood in detail and before it can be rationally understood. In what does the power of illumination consist and what effect does it have on the onward progress of science?[39]

The humanistic mathematics movement seeks to restore to the contemporary classroom the contact with the humanities and with human affairs that have sustained and strengthened mathematics at least since the Babylonians. Polanyi describes the transition from the excitement of the pioneer to the routine classroom:

As we pursue scientific discoveries through their consecutive publications . . . we observe that the intellectual passions aroused by them appear gradually toned down to a faint echo of their discoverer's first excitement at the moment of Illumination. . . . A transition takes place here from a heuristic act to the routine teaching and learning of its results. . . . The impulse which in the original heuristic act was a violent irreversible self-conversion of the investigator and may have been followed by an almost equally tempestuous process of converting others, is first repeated as a milder version of itself . . . and will thus assume finally a form in which all dynamic quality is lost.[40]

The exhilaration that Polanyi describes for the discoverer or investigator is often absent from the classroom, although it was present in the fifth-grade class that competed in the MOES. It was also present in the seventh-grade classes through which the knowledge of the new computer procedure diffused. Those learning situations were characterized by strong student interdependence and support. The teachers were guides. The students found the intrinsic motivation that Csikszentmihalyi described.

Many reformers look to technology to improve education. If the technology reduces the opportunity for interaction among students and between teachers and students, then some of the essential ingredients of successful education and transformation are also reduced. When the inner life and personal meanings that we share as a species are awakened, the dynamic quality of learning can emerge.

NOTES

1. Vickers, G. (1981). Three needs, two buckets, one well. In Alvin M. White (Ed.), *Interdisciplinary teaching* (pp. 11-18). San Francisco, CA: Jossey-Bass.

2. Mathematical Olympiads for Elementary Schools, P.O. Box 190, Old Westbury, NY 11568.

3. Csikszentmihalyi, M. (1990). Literacy and intrinsic motivation. *Daedalus, 119*(2), 115-140.

4. Csikszentmihalyi, M. (1990). *Flow: The psychology of optimal experience.* New York: Harper & Row.

5. Benezet, L. P. (1935, 1936). The teaching of arithmetic, I,II,III. *Journal of the National Education Association,* Nov. 1935, Dec. 1935, Jan. 1936.

6. *Humanistic Mathematics Network Journal,* May 1991, Harvey Mudd College, Claremont, CA 91711.

7. Kline, M. (1982). *Mathematics, the loss of certainty* (p. 16). New York: Oxford University Press.

8. Ibid., p. 42.

9. Spinoza, B. (1976). *Ethics* (pp. 24-25). Citadel.

10. Kline, op. cit., p. 75.

11. Ibid., chap. 4; see also Richards, J. L. (1988). *Mathematical visions.* London: Academic Press.

12. Ibid., p. 97.

13. Korner, S. (1962). *The philosophy of mathematics.* New York: Harper & Row.

14. Hanna, G., & Jahnke, H. (1993). Proof and application. *Educational Studies in Mathematics, 24*(4), 421-438.

15. Ibid.

16. Hersh, R. (1993). Proving is convincing and explaining. *Educational Studies in Mathematics, 24*(4), 389-399.

17. Ibid.

18. National Council of Teachers of Mathematics. (1991). *Professional standards for teaching mathematics* (pp. 151-159). Reston, VA: Author.

19. Hanna & Jahnke, op. cit.

20. Humanistic Mathematics Network Journal.

21. White, A. (Ed.). (1993). *Essays in humanistic mathematics.* Washington, DC: The Mathematical Association of America.

22. Ibid., p. 15.

23. Tymoczko, T. (1993). Humanistic and utilitarian aspects of mathematics. In A. White (Ed.), *Essays in humanistic mathematics* (p. 13). Washington, DC: The Mathematical Association of America.

24. Buchanan, S. (1993). Poetry and mathematics. Quoted by Jack Wales, in A. White (Ed.), *Essays in humanistic mathematics.* Washington, DC: The Mathematical Association of America.

25. Goodman, N. D. (1993). Modernizing the philosophy of mathematics. In A. White (Ed.), *Essays in humanistic mathematics.* Washington, DC: The Mathematical Association of America.

26. Buerk, D., & Szablewski, J. (1993). Getting beneath the mask, moving out of silence. In A. White (Ed.), *Essays in humanistic mathematics.* Washington, DC: The Mathematical Association of America.

27. Boulding, K. (1961). *The image* (p. 13). Ann Arbor, MI: Ann Arbor Paperback.

28. Ghiselin, B. (1952). *The creative process* (pp. 20, 26). University of California.

29. Schön, D. (1983). *The reflective practitioner* (p. 52). New York: Basic Books.

30. Ibid., p. 53.

31. Ibid., p. 53.

32. Vickers, op. cit., p. 17.

33. Polanyi, M. (1966). *The tacit dimension* (p. 4). New York: Doubleday.

34. Polanyi, M. (1964). *Personal knowledge.* New York: Harper & Row.

35. Polanyi, M. (1966). *The tacit dimension* (p. 66). New York: Doubleday.

36. Whitehead, A. N. (1967). *Adventures of ideas* (p. 244). New York: Free Press.

37. Bronowski, J. (1965). *Science and human values* (p. 19). New York: Harper & Row.

38. Plato, quoted in Heisenberg, W. (1975). *Across the frontiers* (p. 171). New York: Harper & Row.

39. Heisenberg, op. cit., p.175.

40. Polanyi, M. (1964). *Personal knowledge* (p. 172). New York: Harper & Row.

9

The Management of International Conflict

MALCOLM DANDO

This article begins by discussing why there was a period of relative peace in the conflict-prone international system following the Second World War. It then asks why events have proceeded so disastrously in Yugoslavia since the end of the Cold War. It is argued that Sir Geoffrey Vickers's views on conflict processes and their management, in particular his stress on the stabilizing forces of trust and bonds of membership, can help us understand what has gone wrong in Yugoslavia. The final section returns to the question of the state of the international system in the current transitional period, and it is suggested that the building of a sense of solidarity vital for coping with our massive global problems could be enhanced by a wider understanding of Vickers's views.

John Lewis Gaddis's major article (1986) on the "long peace" that followed the Second World War has generated a considerable literature concerned with analyzing the factors that allowed for this period of relative stability in the conflict-prone international system (Kegley, 1991b). We will return to the wider question of the generation and maintenance of peace in the international system later, but we need to begin by understanding Gaddis's view of the nature of the international system itself. Gaddis (1986) argued that systems theory provides a useful means by which to begin thinking about international relations and suggested that political scientists believe an international system exists under two conditions:

> First, interconnections exist between units within the system, so that changes in some parts of it produce changes in other parts as well; and, second, the collective behaviour of the system as a whole differs from the expectations and priorities of the individual units that make it up. (p. 102)

Gaddis then went on to propose that systems theory was particularly useful because it helped us to differentiate between stable and unstable political structures, and, in this regard, he referred to Deutsch and Singer's definition of stability as "the probability that the system retains all of its essential characteristics: that no single nation becomes dominant; that most of its members continue to survive; and that large-scale war does not occur" (p. 103). He concluded, however, by warning of the difficulty in predicting how long the period of post-Second World War stability would last.

Indeed, Gaddis appeared to anticipate what was to happen in the years between the publication of "The Long Peace" and our situation today. In examining the various possibilities he asked: "But what about a substantial decline in the overall influence of either great power that did not immediately result in war?" (p. 141). Unfortunately, the leaders of the Western world proved to be much less perceptive in understanding and reacting to the breakup of the Soviet Union in the second half of the 1980s.

At the close of a recent interview, the very experienced British statesman Lord Healey was asked if there were any shadows on his obvious personal happiness. He replied, in stark terms (Attallah, 1994, p. 45), that we are returning to times that could be as disastrous as the period following the French Revolution. Lord Healey's perception is strongly reinforced by the view expressed in the 15th edition of *World Military and Social Expenditures*: that an all-time record number of 29 major wars were under way in 1992, and that war deaths were the highest recorded for 17 years (Sivard, 1993, p. 20).

If Western policy throughout the Cold War period had any real justification, it was that "containment" of the Soviet Union would eventually lead to a moderation of its behavior, which would then permit an accommodation between the two blocs. It therefore has to be asked why, when the hoped-for change in Soviet behavior occurred, Western reaction was so slow that disorder rather than a smooth move to a new world order was the result? Certainly by 1990 even such a formerly strong opponent as the British Prime Minister Margaret Thatcher could state that

> we do not see this new Soviet Union as an enemy, but as a country groping its way towards freedom. We no longer have to view the world through a prism of East-West relations. The Cold War is over. (Thatcher, 1990, p. 11)

Unfortunately, shortly afterward, the period in power of the remarkable Mikhail Gorbachev—with whom Mrs. Thatcher thought she could do business—was also over.

It is easy now to consult the prestigious annual reviews of the International Institute of Strategic Studies' *Strategic Survey* and to follow how analyses of the "threat" from the Soviet Union evolved in the West during the late 1980s. The problem for Western elites was, in part, the well-known difficulty of psychologically surmounting long-embedded hostile images of an adversary (Jervis, 1979, p. 309). Against a background of elite distrust it was probably inevitable that Gorbachev's attempts to convince us of his good intentions would fail (Dando, 1991). Thus our help was too limited and too late to help prevent the dangerous disintegration not only of the Soviet empire but increasingly now of the Russian heartlands. For most West Europeans, however, events on the border of the empire—in Yugoslavia—have been the most difficult to comprehend in the 1990s.

A standard mid-1970s account described Yugoslavia as a country with a population of 20 million, a relatively low population growth rate, and an expanding industrial base (Jones, 1974, p. 112). It also emphasized the diversity of the people. Although "South Slavs" made up 80% of the population, they comprised five nationalities (Croats, Slovenes, Macedonians, Montenegrins, and the most numerous—Serbs); they practiced three religions (Greek Orthodox, Roman Catholic, and Muslim); and they even used two different alphabets (Latin and Cyrillic).

Yugoslavia was only created this century. Its peoples experienced vicious fighting both against German forces and between various internal groups during the Second World War. Yet, under Marshal Tito, it had come to be seen as a progressive state by many West Europeans. Fears of what might happen after his death did increase during the 1980s but nothing had prepared most Europeans for what happened after Slovenia, Croatia, and then Bosnia-Herzegovina declared independence in 1991 and 1992. The international community as a whole seemed powerless to stop the spiral of violence between various groups that included the establishment of concentration camps, organized rape, and "ethnic cleansing." Nothing like this had been seen in Europe for 50 years, and the violence grew to such an extent that a United Nations War Crimes Commission was set up to prosecute those involved (Lewer, Milisic, Gillard, & Beckett, 1994).

Only this year, after yet another major atrocity involving scores of deaths in Sarajevo market and under the threat of international air strikes, did it appear that the violence might actually be starting to wind down. Many observers believed that very strong international action taken much earlier might have prevented much of the violence that occurred. Unfortunately, it is a fact that the intervention that did take place was inadequate and, despite having lived together in one country since 1945, the people involved lacked the resources to prevent the degeneration of the conflict themselves.

CONFLICT PROCESSES

It could, of course, be argued that by setting up a totalitarian state Tito did not allow the skills ultimately needed to cope with the post-Cold War situation to be developed in the Yugoslavian population. Indeed, given the widespread military training for guerrilla warfare that was provided to defend the state of Yugoslavia, it might be argued that the only skills made available were precisely those for the kind of civil warfare we have witnessed. Yet we cannot avoid this question: Are the skills that would have been needed to effect a peaceful transition actually available anywhere? Do we actually know, and can we teach, the skills necessary to manage difficult and dangerous potential conflicts?

Within the academic community involved in the study of peace, two dimensions of that concept are recognized. As O'Connell (1994) stated in his recent analysis of the question "Can peace be studied?": "Positively, the idea of peace involves free co-operation among persons and groups for aims that include security, justice and freedom; and negatively, it seeks to eliminate force and violence" (p. 3). The events in Yugoslavia were a terrible shock for West

Europeans, in part because of their success in creating the European Union over the last half century. As O'Connell noted, this involved moving from a concentration on the negative aspect of peace—avoiding another European civil war—to the positive cooperation and friendship that exist today. Peace then is something that comes about because we wish to secure other things. As O'Connell (1994) argued:

> First, we want society to function so as to fulfil our needs, not least needs of security, welfare, and freedom; second, we want it to form a social whole within whose boundaries we can identify with others; and third, we want social living and habits to be agreeable/aesthetic/congenial to our tastes. (p. 2)

Necessarily, to achieve these goals, we seek to exercise some control over our behavior, that of others, and the environment within which we coexist. Necessarily also, we accept that others exert some control over us. Out of such reciprocity and coordination comes a sense of order and predictability. Crucially, O'Connell concluded that

> out of predictability in society comes trust. *Trust is a reliance on others to do what we expect of them. The heart of social living is knowing what to expect* [italics added]. Desired ends, community and agreeableness converge within the easefulness of predictability and together add up to the existence of peace. (p. 2)

This understanding of peace, as Augustine's "tranquillity of order," has a long tradition. The question remains of what can be done to help restore such peace when it is manifestly falling apart as in Yugoslavia. What is to be done when former neighbors turn to murder and pillage?

Largely through the recognition that parties involved in a conflict that is degenerating often lack the resources necessary to restore peaceful relations themselves, many scholars have, in recent years, concentrated on developing means of effective, active mediation. Mediation can be defined as "the voluntary acceptance by disputants of third party assistance in seeking a mutually acceptable solution to their conflict" (Woodhouse, 1992, p. 2). Official and unofficial mediation at the state and nonstate levels can be complementary in a situation such as Yugoslavia. Nevertheless, we still have to ask if there is any more coherent overall standpoint from which to view these kinds of insights to understand conflict and its management better in the next century.

THE MANAGEMENT OF CONFLICT

The obvious discipline within which to seek such an overview is systems theory. As we have seen, Gaddis (1986) referred in his article on the long peace to the work of Deutsch and Singer in stressing the insights that systems theory gives into the nature of self-regulation (p. 103). He noted the difference between negative and positive feedback loops, leading to regulation or aggravation of processes (in the latter case, for example, to all-out war). But does the study of systems allow for a more detailed insight than that?

One systems theorist who greatly admired the work of Karl Deutsch was Sir Geoffrey Vickers (Vickers, 1991, p. 70). For Vickers also the concept of order was central. As he stressed in the foreword to his last major study, *Human Systems Are Different* (Vickers, 1983):

> The essence of systems thinking, as I understand it, is the concept of form or order, sustained through time by a self-correcting process, that notices deviations from the standards which define order and responds with actions which sustain or restore it. (p. vii)

As we shall see later, although Vickers was far from certain that the human species would be able to cope with the problems it was creating for the next century, he saw time as almost as important a concept as order:

> To a mind accustomed to systems thinking, time is an ever present dimension, and *the preservation of order through time is the basic problem both in understanding the past and in influencing the future* [italics added]. Stability, even more than change, demands to be explained, aspired to and regulated. (p. viii)

Against that general background, we can examine Vickers's specific thinking on our present concerns over conflict management. Vickers's (1972/1984) article, "The Management of Conflict," was first published in the influential journal *Futures* in the early 1970s. It is probably best summarized here under its original subheadings (Vickers, 1972/1984).

THE AMBIGUITY OF CONFLICT

The article opens by boldly stating that "human societies survive only so long as they can resolve or contain the conflicts which they generate" (Open Systems Group, 1984, p. 177). Vickers stressed the importance of this point because, in his view, the level of conflicts created by human beings was increasing and the means available to deal with such conflicts were manifestly under strain. He suggested that part of the problem was caused by the inadequate ideas that history had left us and put forward the simple, but startling, idea that

> *we use the word conflict in two very different senses.* We use it of any situation in which the parties involved are constrained to decide between alternatives none of which is wholly acceptable to them all. . . . We use it also of the hostilities which erupt when such conflicts can be neither resolved by "acceptable" means nor contained within "acceptable" limits. (Open Systems Group, 1984, p. 177, italics added)

The paper then seeks to explain how conflicts degenerate from the first form—which Vickers clearly saw as inevitable in human societies—into the second—which he thought was extremely dangerous. He pressed this view strongly:

> Once a conflict passes this critical point, it becomes a threat to the system as such, not merely to its present state; and thereupon it changes both its nature and its parties. . . . Those who become thus divided are almost bound to redefine each other as aliens or enemies. (Open Systems Group, 1984, p. 178)

Vickers cited international and civil wars as well-known examples of such crossings of the threshold between the two types of conflict. For the student of systems the important point is this concept of a threshold because thresholds "are a common feature of systems of all kinds. They mark the point, not always predictable, at which the system's capacity for sustaining itself is overwhelmed" (p. 179). Vickers said that his purpose in writing the article was to attempt to provide a more precise meaning to the idea of a threshold between the two types of conflict in regard to political societies.

THE SOURCES OF CONFLICT

In a section that has many similarities to the views derived from the study of peace by O'Connell (1994), Vickers argued that the constraints that lead us into conflicts are of three quite distinct types:

> The three kinds of constraint which I have described are reflected in three familiar verbs. *What we can and cannot do, must and must not do, ought and ought not to do* [italics added] are defined by the constraints imposed on us by circumstances, by other people and by ourselves. (Open Systems Group, 1984, p. 181)

Vickers here stressed again that conflicts in his first sense (conflictual situations) are inevitable in human societies and that these have to be managed over time:

> The mark of a successful individual or a successful society is that it manages to sustain *through time* a host of different relationships, keeping each in accord with some standard of expectation, while containing all within the resources available; and developing all these standards in the process. (p. 180)

He made it obvious that *skills* are needed to manage conflicts in this way and argued that progress requires that such skills be much improved. In effect, then, Vickers was arguing that we *can learn* how to manage conflicts better, and we *can teach* how to carry out such management more effectively.

LEVELS OF CONFLICT

Vickers accepted that society sets wide limits within which we can argue (as he put it vividly, "universities may engage in venomous infighting") without involving authority—the first level. Every society also has set rules or laws for the regulation of conflicts above a certain level of seriousness. A second level of conflict is thus contained by such rules. The political system then provides a means for changing such rules—and a third level of conflict therefore exists related to the changing of the rules by which second-level conflicts are contained. That much is interesting, but Vickers added something else that was not so obvious: "But the histories of most democracies include periods when the pressure to change the rules used highly irregular procedures, from civil disobedience to armed revolution" (Open Systems Group, 1984, p. 182). Those in authority at the third (political) level are thus reminded that their powers to decide are subject also to societal constraint.

TYPES OF CONFLICT

Conflicts about how to achieve agreed ends that, as Vickers pointed out, form such a large part of studies of decision making, were for him quite subsidiary to conflicts about how a situation should be seen and valued. This position was clearly related to Vickers's fundamental view that our differing value systems lead us to see things in different ways: "All major conflicts involve differences in the values which different parties attach to different aspects of a situation common to them all, differences which often lead them to different definitions of the situation itself" (Open Systems Group, 1984, p. 183). Thus Vickers's study of the management of conflict was tightly integrated with his major innovatory idea in which values and perceptions are linked within the concept of an appreciation system.

MODELS OF CONFLICT

Here Vickers was concerned to put most models of conflict in their proper place: perhaps useful but hardly adequate. He was concerned to make it clear that to be useful any model had to include human *communication*. He argued,

> Human conflict is an exercise in communication even when it is prosecuted with bombs and bullets. And it [communication] can have the chance of being adequate only if it can be prosecuted at a level much higher than bombs and bullets. (Open Systems Group, 1984, p. 185)

Although he was not overenthusiastic about the level of political dialogue that he saw around him, he nevertheless thought that the process worked.

At this stage, it seems to me, Vickers had reached a point at which he could claim to have clarified the issue sufficiently for his readers to return toward his central aim: *a better understanding of the threshold between the two types of conflict*—conflictual situations and the hostilities that break out when they cannot be resolved.

THE RESTRAINTS AND ASSURANCES OF MEMBERSHIP

Vickers began this process of explaining the nature of the threshold by referring again to the constraints that he saw as the sources of conflict in our societies: can, must, and ought. He pointed out that persons engaged in conflicts are usually, to some extent, related by their common membership of certain systems. This gives them some assurances about each other's potential behavior, because of the very constraints that are the sources of conflict: what they can and cannot do; must and must not do; and ought and ought not to do. Any serious analysis of the bonds that tie us together with feelings of common membership of systems has to lead to Vickers's own conclusion: "But constraints based on *self*-expectations and assurances based on trust in the *self*-expectations of others differ from the other constraints and assurances . . . in ways of the utmost importance, which are often overlooked" (Open Systems Group, 1984, p. 186).

He then continued, crucially in regard to these self-expectations, that *"they and they alone create those bonds of responsibility, loyalty and mutual trust without which human societies neither function nor cohere in the face of any serious challenge to their integrity* [italics added]." Again the similarity to O'Connell's views on the requirements for a peaceful society are striking. It has to be repeated that Vickers was not sanguine about our capabilities to match up to the demands of our time.

FORCE AND VIOLENCE

Vickers realistically argued that, if conflicts could not be constrained by the assurances of membership, they could only be contained by coercion—the threat of injury. Authority sometimes had to use force to maintain the conditions under which communication was possible. He stated, nevertheless, that

> not all forms of threat, whether mutual or unilateral, are banned by the rules of most societies, but most are so banned, because threats between fellow members are in themselves inimical to the constraints and assurances of membership and are likely to escalate into more extreme threats or into attempts to put the threat into action. (Open Systems Group, 1984, p. 187)

The main mechanisms for containing and resolving conflict, Vickers argued, were the rules and roles that had evolved for this purpose in a particular society.

MUTUAL PERSUASION

In this section of his article, Vickers returned to his concern with the communications between the parties in a conflict. He noted that debate serves to articulate the parties' views of the situation but stressed that it also affects the way the situation is evaluated by the parties. Thus he argued that debate "also makes clear and so confirms or varies how each party views and values its relation with the other, the restraints acknowledged by it and by the other and the assurances on which each can still rely" (Open Systems Group, 1984, p. 191). But the debate is concerned not only with the specific conflict under consideration but with the future relationship between the parties. In Vickers's view:

> This second level of debate tends to grow more important as the debate proceeds and often ends up overshadowing the original issue. The constraints and assurances of membership may or may not contain the conflict over the specific issue. And if they do, the constraints and assurances of membership may be stronger or weaker as a consequence. The second [weaker assurances] is usually by far the more important result. (Open Systems Group, 1984, p. 191)

The scene is thus set for Vickers to specify his ideas on the threshold.

THE THRESHOLD

Vickers summarized the argument he had put forward in a series of propositions. These are set out, in part, in Table 1. The crucial point that Vickers seems

TABLE 1:   Summary of Vickers's Propositions on the Management of Conflict

1. Conflict is endemic in human affairs and its management is the most characteristic human function and skill.

2. The management of conflict includes and depends on containing it within the threshold beyond which it will become self-exciting and destructive of *the resources for resolving and containing conflict.*

3. This threshold is largely set by the constraints and assurances that the contestants feel as implicit in their common memberships.

4. These memberships are multiplying, as the systems in which people are organized (political, economic, social, and other) become more numerous, more unstable, and more interrelated.

5. All conflicts, whatever effect they may have on the conflictual situation, affect the relations of the parties in that and other contexts, notably by weakening or strengthening the constraints and assurances that they feel as implicit in their common memberships. So the management of conflict needs to be even more concerned with preserving these relationships than with the actual conflict.

6. This involves articulating a common appreciation of the multiple objective relations that these subjective relations are required to support, but it is not achieved or maintained by that alone.

to be trying to bring to our attention is that the consequences of how we deal with any particular conflict do not relate to that conflict alone. What we do in any particular conflict has implications for our relationships with other parties across a much wider range of issues. If we damage our relationships in a particular conflict by setting in train a self-reinforcing process of degeneration, we also reduce the chances of being able to deal successfully with the next conflict—which will inevitably arise. We are on the threshold, as Vickers sees it, when we begin to lose sight of the whole system and its future to pursue our goals in the current conflict by whatever means are available.

Vickers's conclusions follow on logically from the argument set out in the table. He stated again that all human conflict involves various forms of communication, from the lowest level of force and violence through to the highest form of common appreciation, and, further, that "bad communication, like bad currency, drives out the good; so the management of conflict is properly concerned with banning lower levels of communication so far as may be" (Open Systems Group, 1984, p. 192). Here we see again a clear connection with the proposals being put into action by mediators in conflict situations (Woodhouse, 1992).

Finally, Vickers stressed that in our complex modern societies we have multiple memberships. In the former Yugoslavia the people presently at war lived together and cooperated in many different ways. In Vickers's view, total failure of the management of conflict results in the parties becoming exclusively attached to a *single* system rather than holding multiple overlapping memberships. This leads to those who are not members of this single system (for example, an ethnic grouping) becoming redefined as enemies. Hence Vickers pointed out "the peculiar virulence of civil war, wars of succession and all such struggles" (Open Systems Group, 1984, p. 192). Although he was writing well before the present conflict in Yugoslavia, such insights surely help to explain to present-day West Europeans some of the reasons for the inexplicable brutality they have seen as people in the former unitary state have retreated to single ethnic entities.

Yet if we return to the question with which we began—the generation and maintenance of peace in the international system—we have to bear in mind Vickers's warning about the effectiveness of the restraints and assurances of membership in systems of different sizes: "This, the membership factor, operates with very varying degress of potency in human systems of different types and sizes. . . . It is normally far more potent in small systems united by a common objective . . . than in a diffuse political society" (Open Systems Group, 1984, p. 189). To what extent then can Vickers's ideas be accepted as applicable to the management of conflict in international society as a whole during the transition period following the end of the Cold War?

TRUST BUILDING IN INTERNATIONAL SOCIETY

The dangerous developments that Vickers (1968, 1970) warned of are still in operation, and it has to be accepted that the consequent global problems are even more daunting than when he was alive. Rogers, for example, has pointed to three factors of enormous importance. First, there is the deep polarization between the islands of wealth and the sea of impoverished peoples. As he remarked, "Just one-fifth of the entire global population uses around three-quarters of the wealth and physical resources" (Rogers, 1993, p. 2). And these people are predominantly in the industrialized North, whereas the poor are in the South or so-called Third World. This problem of the maldistribution of resources and resource use is increasingly compounded by the second factor—our growing realization that there are limits to human activity. At a global level most of us have become familiar with concerns among governments over ozone depletion and global warming. The third factor is less well understood by the general public in industrialized countries. In Rogers's (1993) view, within this ecologically limited planetary system "we are faced with the primary legacy of the Cold War, world-wide militarisation. Although the excesses of military confrontation are past, they leave behind a massive array of weapons, postures and attitudes" (p. 3). Although arms in themselves may not cause conflicts, they can certainly exacerbate conflicts that do occur. Thus any solution to our international problems must include more effective demilitarization.

Dealing more effectively with the worldwide militarization left over from the Cold War era will require attention to a wide range of the postures and attitudes noted by Rogers, for example, in our views on the legitimacy of the use of force in international society. It will also, I believe, need a massive reduction in armaments and arms production, unparalleled growth that Vickers believed had resulted from positive feedback in a "self-exciting system in which defence departments, armament makers and research and development centres . . . stimulate each other in the endless pursuit of innovation in attack and defence" (Vickers, 1983, p. 124). Some have argued that the spread of advanced weaponry such as nuclear weapons will be stabilizing as deterrence systems develop around the world, but there seems to be a much stronger argument that, on the contrary, proliferation is likely to increase the dangers of such weapons being used (Sagan, 1994).

Unfortunately, we do not have sufficient understanding of how Gaddis's "long peace" actually came about to help us design a new peace for the next century. In his overview of a series of analytical contributions designed to elucidate the reasons for the long peace, Kegley (1991a) noted first that the peace that operated between the great powers nevertheless allowed a great deal of destructive warfare in the Third World. So even if we could explain this phenomenon, it would not necessarily apply to a peace throughout the world system of states. Indeed, a number of the contributions, such as that on crises by the eminent authority Michael Brecher, stressed the dangers there were of warfare breaking out even between the major states.

Kegley (1991a) himself emphasized the need for multifactorial explanations. As he expressed it:

> The discovery of cogent explanations is exacerbated by the fact that the long postwar peace has been produced by the simultaneous operation of many inter-acting causes. The quest for a deterministic interpretation that rests on a single cause is bound to prove futile . . . none alone adequately accounts for and thereby explains the prolonged peace. (p. 5)

One has only to compare the commonly held view that nuclear weapons kept the peace between the two superpowers with the view that these two empires behaved as empires do and had no intention of threatening the core of the other (Blachman & Puchala, 1991) to see the difficulties of explaining the long peace.

Yet it is also true that some individual identifiable factors undoubtedly played a part in the generation of the peaceful period that followed the Second World War. Gaddis argued in his original article, for example, that the two superpowers evolved "rules of the game" in their interactions. He asked how order could emerge from a system in which, unlike that within a single country, there was no government authority to impose legal rules. He felt experience had shown that the system resembled "the conduct of games, where order evolves from mutual agreement on a set of 'rules' defining the range of behaviour each side anticipates from the other" (Gaddis, 1986, p. 132). Although the rules were not explicit, Gaddis suggests five examples (pp. 132-141): respect spheres of influence, avoid direct military confrontation, use nuclear weapons only as an ultimate resort, prefer predictable anomaly over unpredictable rationality (e.g., accept the status of Cuba or Berlin), and do not seek to undermine the other side's leadership.

In Gaddis's view such tacit rules

> have played an important role in maintaining the international system that has been in place these past four decades: without them the correlation one would

normally anticipate between hostility and instability would have become more exact than it has in fact been since 1945. (p. 133)

So, as we would have expected from the views of O'Connell and Vickers outlined earlier in this article, peace came about in part because of the increasing predictability of, and therefore reliance that could be placed on, the other party's behavior. What is of interest here is the extent to which such processes might be used to help build a new international system for the next century. Will the processes of integration or those of fragmentation, which Gaddis (1991) has more recently argued have to be understood to map out the future of the post-Cold War world, predominate in the decades ahead?

THE DEVELOPMENT OF INTERNATIONAL LAW

It is, of course, possible to argue that international society lacks central control and is therefore anarchic. Yet as James Rosenau (1992) noted in his study of "Governance, Order, and Change in World Politics":

> Such an implication seems highly questionable. As one observer puts it, noting the authority that attaches to many treaties, international legal precedents, and international organisations, "the international system (in spite of its lack of an overarching regime or world government) is several steps beyond anarchy." (pp. 7-8)

In his contribution to the essays on the long peace, Johnson (1991) was surely correct to argue that "international law assumes and depends upon at least a floor of consensus and orderly behaviour among nations, and it seeks to raise the level of that floor and extend it under all nations" (p. 293). As he also noted, in the 20th century, "International law on the resort to war has followed the main line of 'perpetual peace' theory toward the establishment of international peace through international order" (p. 292). This tradition has roots in European thinking of the 17th and 18th centuries. Within this tradition war is seen as an evil. The means needed to abolish this evil were taken to be the formation of an international league of states with an armed force to keep the peace, and the settlement of disputes by arbitration rather than force. In the 20th century, the tradition has found expression in, for example, the League of Nations Covenant, the 1928 Pact of Paris, and the United Nations Charter. Such positive international law expressed in binding commitments by states, however, is only part of what is taken to be international law. There exist also customary international law and *lex ferenda* (something thought desirable to enact into positive form), which also embody international norms and control behavior to some extent. These together form part of the mechanism by which international law evolves.

It is certainly true that international law has changed this century in its treatment of war. As Geoffrey Vickers (1983) wrote of war in his last book:

> This form of collective struggle remained an accepted form of political action throughout the world until the carnage of the First World War revealed the extent

to which technology had increased its costs in life and treasure and the uncertainty of its outcome. (p. 51)

Hedley Bull (1966) explained in his article, "The Grotian Concept of International Society," how the view was taken in the 19th century that states had the right to make war and that the law was mainly concerned with regulating its conduct. As Bull argued, "The central Grotian assumption is that of the solidarity, or potential solidarity, of the states comprising international society, with respect to the enforcement of the law" (p. 614). Writing in 1966, during the Cold War, Bull was not certain that the 19th-century view, which was much more sceptical of the degree of solidarity that states could achieve, was not the more realistic. As he expressed it then: "Although the solidarity exhibited in international society may increase in the future . . . it can still be argued that in the twentieth century the Grotian conception has proved premature" (p. 632). That point must still be borne in mind as we struggle to create a new world order after the Cold War period. Yet, although some wars may be inevitable, many surely result, in part, from our far-too-ready resort to threats and violence—in direct opposition to Vickers's view on how conflicts should be managed. The important point for us now, as Johnson (1991) concluded, is that the existence of norms concerned with avoiding war are evidence of a wish to achieve such avoidance in international society and that "positive international law comes into being by a process of value-centered debate and interaction and by the formal acceptance of the results of this process in a treaty, agreement, convention, or some other form of international agreement" (p. 302).

Rosenau (1992) attempted to describe how perceptions, behavior, and order at the international level might be linked:

> The numerous patterns that sustain global order can be conceived as unfolding at three basic levels of activity: (1) at the ideational or intersubjective level of what people dimly sense, incisively perceive, or otherwise understand are the arrangements through which their affairs are handled; (2) at the behavioural level of what people regularly and routinely do, often unknowingly, to maintain the prevailing global arrangements; and (3) at the aggregate or political level where governance occurs and rule-orientated institutions and regimes enact and implement the policies inherent in the ideational and behavioural patterns. (p. 14)

Rosenau stressed, in a manner of which Vickers would surely have approved, that the "the degree of orderliness that marks global affairs at any period in history, is a product of activity at all three of these levels." In short, what is being described by these authors looks like a changing setting of appreciation systems and then its codification in reformed institutions.

CHANGING INTERNATIONAL INSTITUTIONS

In 1988, as the ending of the Cold War began to appear possible, a discussion was held in Moscow on the future of the United Nations (UN). Maurice Bertrand presented a paper on the consequences of the changes under way as the world moved from a bipolar to an interdependent system. Bertrand argued that part of the problem was conceptual; it was, as we have seen, just difficult for people to move away from modes of thinking conditioned over the preceding 40 years. Yet he concluded that the then current system—based on East-West opposition, massive nuclear arsenals of deterrence, the South used as space for superpower military-strategic rivalry, political and economic mechanisms based on irrational small state structures and numerous underused international organizations—could appear increasingly absurd. If progress of the kind that was clearly then under way continued, Bertrand (1989) concluded that

> a new reality based on the mutual control of a very reduced level of armaments, plans of security and development of poor regions, a real global market, coherent regional or sub-regional political structures of comparable dimensions, a world institution able to usefully contribute to the maintenance of security and to the management of interdependence

could, as he put it, "appear as being more in line with the interests of peoples of all countries" (p. 67)

In his analysis of the possible process of change and of the problems to be confronted, he argued that "among all world problems, the one concerning institutional change is the most confusing" (p. 59). In Bertrand's opinion, this resulted in part from widespread dissatisfaction, and many differing proposals were therefore being put forward for reform. Moreover, the powerful states realistically chose to do their main business by ad hoc mechanisms such as summits rather than use the current system of world organizations. Worse still, the existence of "taboos" on the discussion of important issues limited what could easily be done to reform current organizations. In view of these difficulties, he argued for a two-stage process of reform. In the short- to midterm he suggested concentrating on the UN. There, he felt, "the problem consists of defining priorities, to concentrate on them the limited resources of the Organization, and to reorganize the Secretariat consequently" (p. 64). Such action would lay the basis for the longer term reform concerned with tackling the issues of representation of states and peoples, regional structures, and an integrated approach to the problems of human society as a whole.

Clearly, if the UN cannot come to grips with our immediate problems, the more difficult issues are unlikely to be solved satisfactorily either. Although the problems of reforming the UN so that it may more effectively generate a peaceful new world order go well beyond the question of arms control (Russett & Sutherlin, 1991), in the remainder of this article I will concentrate on the UN Conference on Disarmament (CD) and its efforts to deal with the problem of arms control and disarmament through negotiation of specific agreements and the development of wider regulatory regimes.

The U.S. diplomat, Ambassador John Hawes, who has worked on numerous arms control issues, recently attempted to set out some guidelines for future progress. Like many other commentators he stressed the significance of the end of bipolar dominance, stating that the basic elements of arms control will not change—stabilizing arms competitions and reducing threats of surprise attack. But it will have much greater geographical scope, engaging states that have been, at most, marginal participants to date. *Arms control forums will be more broadly multilateral* [italics added]. (Hawes, 1993, p. 1)

In this new environment, Hawes stressed, in terms that parallel Vickers's ideas on conflict management, the need is to shed adversarial attitudes and to engage in a flexible process of building confidence step by step as opportunities arise.

To assist this process, Hawes put forward a series of eminently sensible proposals such as very careful prenegotiations and understandings of different parties' positions prior to the opening of formal negotiations. This will clearly be a more complex task with many new states involved in the new multilateral agenda. In the end though, formal negotiations will often be necessary and many of these will take place in the main multilateral negotiation forum—the Conference on Disarmament. How well equipped is this organization, or how well equipped could it be for the task ahead?

The CD is located in Geneva and is the successor to the Conference of the Eighteen-Nation Committee on Disarmament and the Conference of the Committee on Disarmament that functioned from 1962. The CD started work in 1979 and significant changes were made in the rules under which its now 39 members worked (Bertasalegui, 1992). Membership of the CD is limited and prior to the end of the Cold War was very much based on political blocs (East, West, and nonaligned). There has been a trend toward a more regional orientation of states recently, and there has always been a liberal attitude to participation by states that are not members of the CD. However, further expansion of membership is one of the important issues that have to be dealt with soon.

The presidency of the CD rotates every 4 weeks and the powers of the president in relation to the member states is restricted. The CD Secretariat is headed by the permanent secretary-general who is also the personal representative of the secretary-general of the UN. The CD reports to the UN each autumn and receives an input in regard to its future work from the General Assembly each January. Clearly, this system links the work of the CD in the spring and summer with the autumn/winter meeting of the General Assembly (and its First Committee) in New York.

Decision making in the CD on both procedural and substantive issues has to be by consensus. This led to an effective block on any substantive output during the Cold War period. Since the end of the Cold War, however, the CD has succeeded in agreeing the exceedingly complex Chemical Weapons Convention. Thus future successes are probable. Meetings of the CD plenary sessions are open to nongovernmental organizations and documentation of these meetings is available. Meetings of the ad hoc subcommittees that carry out the detailed business of the organization are not open to the general public. The yearly agenda of work usually involves the setting up of about four or five subcommittees from its original "Decalogue" of topics (see Table 2) on the basis of the previous year's work and input from states and the General Assembly.

TABLE 2:   The Conference on Disarmament's "Decalogue" of Arms Control Issues

1. Nuclear weapons in all aspects
2. Chemical weapons
3. Other weapons of mass destruction
4. Conventional weapons
5. Reduction of military budgets
6. Reduction of armed forces
7. Disarmament and development
8. Disarmament and international security
9. Collateral measures, confidence-building measures, effective verification
10. Comprehensive program of disarmament leading to general and complete disarmament under effective international control

Curiously, little research has been carried out into the operations of the CD. Yet in a special publication by the United Nations Institute for Disarmament Research (in Geneva) published in 1992, it was not difficult to find strong criticism of the CD. Ambassador Marin-Bosch of Mexico commented,

> The CD must now decide where it wants to go. . . . It cannot continue with its annual ritual of discussing for weeks the text of a non-negotiating mandate for most of its agenda items. Its members will have to find ways and means to explore some different paths, since the inertia of old habits is at times the CD's worst enemy. (Marin-Bosch, 1992, p. 9)

Ambassador Wagenmakers of the Netherlands, in a somewhat more favorable account, nevertheless voiced similar criticisms (Wagenmakers, 1992). Despite this, Wagenmakers argued that even during the unproductive Cold War period the CD helped to develop common understandings on difficult issues.

A similar point was made by Ambassador Azikiwe of Nigeria in reference to events following the Cold War. In his opinion, "The significant lesson to be derived from the recent changes is that rapid progress in inter-State relations takes place in a climate of trust, confidence, goodwill and transparency" (Azikiwe, 1992, p. 13). A related argument, which also reflects Vickers's views on the dangers of the use of threats, was made by Young and Osherenko (1993) in the conclusion to their wide-ranging study of regime formation: "Our research suggests that power is one of many factors relevant to regime formation. . . . It indicates . . . *that blatant or unsophisticated attempts to bring power to bear in the course of institutional bargaining are apt to backfire*" [italics added] (p. 258). Despite the criticisms, Ambassador Azikiwe saw no alternative to the CD:

> In spite of the fact that the CD operates on the basis of consensus, and has rather complex and sensitive terms of reference, it has achieved modest results. There is no substitute for a multilateral negotiating body like the CD, as global issues require the active and continuous participation of many countries. (Azikiwe, 1992, p. 14)

As he saw it, the international community had an "unprecedented opportunity" and the CD just had to face up to its part of the task because "effective disarmament measures provide a core around which a new world order should be built" (p. 13).

Ambassador Kamal of Pakistan reported that consultations among members of the CD had, over the past few years, led to an improvement in procedures (Kamal, 1992). In regard to the further reform of the CD, Ambassador Kamal focused first on the agenda. He thought that 13 years on from its initiation the "Decalogue" had to be revised. He suggested that regional issues, confidence-building measures, nuclear proliferation, and transparency of armaments required consideration. He also pointed to the question of membership and the consensus rule as requiring reconsideration.

It was against this background of consideration of reform that the UN secretary-general followed up his well-known general document, *An Agenda for Peace* (United Nations General Assembly, 1992a), with his report *New Dimensions of Arms Regulation and Disarmament in the Post-Cold War Era* (United Nations General Assembly, 1992b). This stressed the need for a new approach to arms control based on integration with other aspects of security, globalization to include all states, and revitalization to seize the unique opportunity available. The report was forwarded by the secretary-general to the CD in January 1993 (Boutros-Ghali, 1993). Its conclusion stated,

> Over the past two years the Conference on Disarmament has engaged in a process of self-examination. The time has come to proceed from exploratory discussion to practical actions. In my opinion, a comprehensive approach is needed to address the structure, functions, method of work and working agenda of the Conference on Disarmament. (p. 12)

The challenge of change could hardly have been expressed in a clearer manner.

The CD's response was in three parts (Deyanov, 1993): a report on its consideration of the secretary-general's report; the plenary session documents with individual states' viewpoints; and a report on the CD's consideration of its agenda, composition, and methods of work. This final report contained a review by the president of the CD that indicated the way in which consensus was developing on key items. For example, in regard to membership he stated that the need for expansion was widely recognized, and indicated that "a substantial majority of those in favour of a larger expansion supported the figure of approximately 20" (R. Deyanov, personal communication, March 3, 1993, Report CD/1184, p. 7). In regard to the agenda, "a wide majority of delegations supported or were prepared to accept changes in the agenda" (p. 8), and specifically: "Some trends . . . can be identified with certainty. Many delegations have stressed the importance of two items on the present agenda, 'Nuclear Test Ban' and 'Transparency in Armaments' " (p. 9). The president also noted the general opinion of the need to reduce the number of agenda items—something that would allow improved practical consideration of specific issues of current importance.

In January 1994, the president of the CD intimated that it would begin work for the session on the following items: nuclear test ban, prevention of an arms race in outer space, effective international arrangements to assure non-nuclear-weapon states against the use or threat of use of nuclear weapons, and transparency in armaments (Presidential Statement, 1994). The mandate for the Ad Hoc Committee on the crucial first item, the negotiation of a nuclear test ban, conveyed a sense of some urgency (Conference on Disarmament, 1994): "The Conference directs the Ad Hoc Committee to negotiate intensively a universal and multilaterally and effectively verifiable comprehensive nuclear test ban treaty" (p. 1). Such a treaty is widely considered necessary to assure a successful review of the Non-Proliferation Treaty in 1995 and as a symbol of agreement to proceed to complete nuclear disarmament. Recent reports indicate that there is considerable pressure to reach agreement on this item quickly. Equally, the process of reform is being pressed by conference members.

CONCLUSION

Although the pace of change varies in different regions of the world (Jervis, 1991), we can see that, even at the international level, conflicts can be managed and peaceful cooperation developed. As the UN secretary-general stated in regard to arms limitation and disarmament:

> Openness and transparency are crucially important as part of the process of building confidence. Their significance must be emphasised, particularly at regional and sub-regional levels, *in order to make military behaviour more predictable and to reassure States of the non-threatening intentions of potential rivals* [italics added]. (Boutros-Ghali, 1993)

In a wider sense, despite the current despondency about the demise of initial hopes for a new world order, the events in the CD illustrate that progress is being made. International institutions are beginning to reform and new norms and modes of behavior are being shaped to deal better with the problems of international society following the Cold War. I would argue, indeed, that the current success of multilateralism and trust building in the CD shows us that a peaceful international system in the 21st century is achievable and that the hopes of the founders of the UN for a system based on solidarity can be realized. Furthermore, it is surely clear that the insights of Geoffrey Vickers into how we should manage our inevitable conflicts have much to offer those who are attempting to carry this process forward.

REFERENCES

Attallah, N. (1994, March 6). Denis the Menace. *Observer Magazine*, pp. 40-45.
Azikiwe, E. M. (1992). Disarmament and the new world order. *UNIDIR Newsletter*, 5(1), 13-15.

Bertasategui, V. (1992). Methods and procedures of the Conference on Disarmament. *UNIDIR Newsletter, 5*(1), 3-7.

Bertrand, M. (1989). The process of change in an interdependent world and possible institutional consequences. In J. P. Renniger (Ed.), *The future role of the United Nations in an interdependent world* (pp. 39-70). The Netherlands: Martinus Nijhoff.

Blachman, M. J., & Puchala, D. J. (1991). When empires meet: The long peace in long-term perspective. In C. W. Kegley, Jr. (Ed.), *The long postwar peace: Contending explanations and projections* (pp. 177-202). New York: Harper Collins.

Boutros-Ghali, B. (1993, January 6). Letter dated December 24, 1992 from the Secretary General of the United Nations to the President of the Conference on Disarmament (Report No. CD/1176). Geneva: Conference on Disarmament.

Bull, H. (1966). The Grotian conception of international society. In H. Butterfield & M. Wright (Eds.), *Diplomatic investigations* (pp. 613-634). London: Allen & Unwin.

Conference on Disarmament. (1994, January 25). *Mandate for an ad hoc committee under agenda Item 1* (Report No. CD/1238). Geneva: Author.

Dando, M. R. (1991). The impact of Gorbachev's perestroika programme on Western Europe. In T. Woodhouse (Ed.), *Peacemaking in a troubled world* (pp. 167-195). Oxford: Berg.

Deyonov, R. (1993, March 3). Letter dated February 25, 1993 from the President of the Conference on Disarmament to the Chairman of the First Committee of the General Assembly (Report No. CD/1190). Geneva: Conference on Disarmament.

Gaddis, J. L. (1986). The long peace: Elements of stability in the postwar international system. *International Security, 10*(4), 99-142.

Gaddis, J. L. (1991). Toward the post-Cold War world. *Foreign Affairs, 70*(2), 102-122.

Hawes, J. (1993). *Arms control: A new style for a new agenda* (CISSM Paper No. 2). College Park: University of Maryland, Maryland School of Public Affairs, Center for International and Security Studies.

Jervis, R. (1979). Deterrence theory revisited. *World Politics, XXXI*, 287-324.

Jervis, R. (1991). The future of world politics: Will it resemble the past? *International Security, 16*(3), 39-73.

Johnson, J. T. (1991). International norms and the regulation of war. In C. W. Kegley, Jr. (Ed.), *The long postwar peace: Contending explanations and projections* (pp. 290-303). New York: Harper Collins.

Jones, E. (1974). *Encyclopedia of world geography*. London: Octopus.

Kamal, A. (1992). The perspective of the Conference on Disarmament. *UNIDIR Newsletter, 5*(1), 18-19.

Kegley, C. W., Jr. (1991a). Explaining great-power peace: The sources of prolonged postwar stability. In C. W. Kegley, Jr. (Ed.), *The long postwar peace: Contending explanations and projections* (pp. 3-22). New York: Harper Collins.

Kegley, C. W., Jr. (Ed.). (1991b). *The long postwar peace: Contending explanations and projections*. New York: Harper Collins.

Lewer, N., Milisic, Z., Gillard, S., & Beckett, G. (1994). *Bosnia-Hercegovina: Problems for conflict intervention*. Bradford, United Kingdom: University of Bradford, Department of Peace Studies.

Marin-Bosch, M. (1992). The Conference on Disarmament at thirty. *UNIDIR Newsletter, 5*(1), 8-10.

O'Connell, J. (1994). *Can peace be studied?* (OPPS Paper No. 37). Oxford: Oxford Project for Peace Studies.

Open Systems Group. (1984). *The Vickers papers*. London: Harper & Row.

Presidential Statement on the Agenda and Organization of Work for the 1994 Session of the Conference on Disarmament. (1994). CD/1239.

Rogers, P. (1993). A jungle full of snakes: Responding to North/South conflict. In J. Tansey & C. Tansey (Eds.), *A world divided: Militarism and development after the Cold War* (pp. 1-25). London: Earthscan.

Rosenau, J. N. (1992). Governance, order and change in world politics. In J. N. Rosenau & E-O. Czempiel (Eds.), *Governance without government: Order and change in world politics* (pp. 1-29). Cambridge: Cambridge University Press.

Russett, B., & Sutherlin, J. S. (1991). The UN in a new world order. *Foreign Affairs, 70*(2), 69-84.

Sagan, S. D. (1994). The perils of proliferation: Organization theory, deterrence theory, and the spread of nuclear weapons. *International Security, 18*(4), 66-107.

Sivard, R. L. (1993). Wars and deaths. In *World military and social expenditures* (15th ed., pp. 20-21). Washington, DC: World Priorities.

Thatcher, M. H. (1990). Shaping a new global community. *Quarterly Review, 19*, 9-18.

United Nations General Assembly. (1992a, October 23). *An agenda for peace.* A/C.1/47/7.

United Nations General Assembly. (1992b, October 27). *New dimensions of arms regulation and disarmament in the post-Cold War era.* A/C.1/47/7.

Vickers, G. (1968). *Value systems and social processes.* London: Tavistock.

Vickers, G. (1970). *Freedom in a rocking boat.* London: Penguin.

Vickers, G. (1983). *Human systems are different.* London: Harper & Row.

Vickers, G. (1984). The management of conflict. In Open Systems Group (Eds.), *The Vickers papers* (pp. 126-141). London: Harper & Row. (Original work published 1972)

Vickers, J. (1991). *Rethinking the future: The correspondence between Geoffrey Vickers and Adolph Lowe* ("On coercion and conflict," p. 70). London: Transaction.

Wagenmakers, H. (1992). The balance sheet: The results of the Conference on Disarmament. *UNIDIR Newsletter, 5*(1), 10-13.

Woodhouse, T. (1992). *Improving the good instrument: Active mediation and conflict resolution in the new world order* (Occasional Paper No. 24). Perth: University of Western Australia, Indian Ocean Centre for Peace Studies.

Young, O. R., & Osherenko, G. (1993). *Polar politics: Creating international environmental regimes.* Ithaca, NY: Cornell University Press.

10

Autonomy, Interdependence, and Moral Governance

Pluralism in a Rocking Boat

SCOTT D. N. COOK

Drawing on key themes in the work of Sir Geoffrey Vickers, this article outlines the need for a moral perspective that can address the pluralistic social realities of the dawning 21st century. The trends of globalism and localism are traced out against the material advances that our technologies make possible and the often conflicting moral claims to a share of that wealth that our distinct but increasingly interdependent cultures make inevitable. We have come to see these moral claims as entitlements of membership in society and have designed an array of institutions that we hold responsible for their fulfilment. This status quo, however, is systemically unstable, unsustainable, and, therefore, morally unjustifiable. To achieve an acceptable form of stability (in terms of human systems, the virtuous mean between chaos and stagnation), we must, at the very least, learn to manage both conflicting moral claims and conflicting standards of morality—we must develop a system of moral governance that can enable us to act responsibly within our increasingly pluralistic moral world. Some requirements of such a system are outlined.

The meaning of stability is likely to remain obscured in Western cultures until they rediscover the fact that life consists in experiencing relations, rather than in seeking goals or "ends."

—Geoffrey Vickers
Freedom in a Rocking Boat

The past 150 years or so have set Western civilization apart from all other cultures past and present in two very remarkable ways. The first is technological: Our abilities to shape and control the world in which we live have grown at such an accelerating rate that our technologies have become a central and essential feature of our culture. The degree to which our normal daily lives have come to depend on an ever more elaborately intertwined net of technologies is unmatched. Indeed, the world we have made, as distinct from the world we are given, has become to such an extent the world in which we live that we can no longer regard our technologies as mere aids or adjuncts to our lives: Rather, the way we live our lives and the forms our common life takes are now both impossible and inconceivable without our technologies.

Second, along with the growth in the pervasiveness and centrality of technology in our culture, there has been a parallel and intimately related escalation in our expectations. What we expect to be in place, working, and reliable simply for our daily lives to function unproblematically is truly remarkable. To fulfil the expectations that are implied by the way we live an ordinary day requires not only our expanding technological net but also an expanding network of institutions to provide and maintain those technologies and an even more subtle and more crucial network of concepts and regulations about how these institutions *ought* to operate. Within the first hour of rising in the morning, as Ihde (1990) observed, our normal daily routine betrays expectations that there will be available to us, with little or no bother, an electric power grid to run our alarm clocks, radios, shavers, and so on; a plumbing system that provides water and carries away waste; gas to power the water and home heaters; information from print and broadcast media; and a kitchen equipped to store and prepare foods that themselves have been transported to our homes from around the world. And as Vickers (1970) reminded us, we also expect, although rarely consciously, that there are in place institutions that can provide and maintain all these things, and that there are publicly held standards and agencies that will guarantee the safety and quality of what is available and see to the fairness of their distribution and price.

Only 150 years ago most of these expectations would have been unthinkable, even for the wealthiest. Today they are not only the norm in the West but they are treated largely as entitlements of citizenship: We believe that they are things that ought to be provided to us simply by virtue of our being members of our society. Add to this the mammoth volume of goods and services that we believe ought to be available to us as consumers, and the scope of our escalating expectations becomes remarkable indeed.

Still, the relationship between what our technologies place within our reach and what we expect to be within our grasp is problematic in several senses. There are four that are particularly germane to the topic at hand. First, the prices we in the developed world have paid have not always been sufficient by themselves to sustain the fulfilment of our expectations. What has helped to fill in the gap has been a lower set of expectations and higher prices for their fulfilment for those in the developing world. This fact is part of the history of colonialism and its dismantling. It is also part of the current differences in view concerning the fair distribution of wealth between the Northern and Southern Hemispheres.

Second, in recent years the prices we in the West have been willing to pay have in some cases been going down as our expectations and practices have continued to expand. At times we have even become publicly unconscious of the need to pay. In recent years in the United States, there has been a persistent public demand for such things as clean air, functional highways, and an educated, competitive workforce—at the same time there has been a series of tax revolts and defeated bond measures that have shut off funds needed to pay for these things. At times this disinclination to pay has not been a timid phenomenon but has been tied to a public ethos of righteous indignation. In California, State Senator Jarvis chronicled his successful call for a series of tax repeals in the 1970s in a popular book titled *I'm Mad as Hell* (Jarvis & Pack, 1979). We rarely see the disparity between complaining about potholes in the roadways and repeatedly refusing to pay to fill them. (There is a profound message in the mere fact that the United States burns more petroleum and pays a lower price for it than anyone else on the planet.)

Third, the status quo is unsustainable. Our accelerating rate of technological change teamed with our escalating expectations cannot, as Vickers frequently reminded us (1980, in particular), be sustained indefinitely—particularly, I should think, when linked to so problematic an understanding of how the bills ought to be paid. It is a painful irony that one of the least questioned expectations in the West has been that there will be continual change, even accelerating change—and "change," meanwhile, is conceived almost without exception as synonymous with "improvement." Many of my university students are not able to imagine an alternative to our reaching for one bigger and better goal after another.

Fourth, these issues are centrally and inescapably *moral* issues. Our technologies make many marvelous things possible. However, we rarely if ever are able to put these marvels equally within the reach of everyone. Therefore, every technology carries with it the question as to who will benefit from it, to what degree, when, and at what cost, borne by whom. Such questions are clearly administrative and political ones, but they are also always moral questions. And the expectations we treat as entitlements of citizenship constitute, in practice, tacit moral claims as to what we hold our fair share of technology's bounty to be and what we see as a fair price to pay for it. If the expectations are unrealistic and unsustainable, as I believe they are, then our tacit moral claims are unsupportable and need to be replaced.

AN ESCALATION OF VOICES

As the 21st century unfolds, the public debate about who ought to get what is guaranteed to be carried out in multiple voices that reveal not only vastly differing views about how the wealth *ought* to be shared but even more significantly differing notions as to how conflicting claims ought to be resolved. We face dealing with both more claims for a fair share and more sets of standards for how to measure fairness.

The reasons for this are reflected in two major, and in a way contrary, trends that are responsible, perhaps more than any other factor, for the shape of public life in the last half of the 20th century, particularly in its moral and political dimensions. The first we now call *globalism*. Thanks in large measure to growth in technologies of communication, transport, and commerce, it has become possible or more efficient to accomplish on a global scale things that previously were only possible or efficient on a local or regional scale. The rise of the Pacific Rim, the appearance at center stage of first the multinational and then the transnational corporation, and the formation of economic and political alliances such as the European Union (EU) and the North American Free Trade Association (NAFTA) are clear evidence that the world in many ways has been getting smaller and more of a piece.

Over the same 50 years, we can trace a second and equally important trend in the growth of what might be called *localism*. This is nowhere more apparent than in the increase in the number of countries in the world. At the end of the Second World War, there were some 40 independent nations. As the 21st century unfolds, the number is growing well beyond 200. Whereas the driving force of globalism has been technological, administrative, and economic efficiency, localism has been, and continues to be, driven by numerous factors such as language, ethnicity, religion, history, geography, dominant forms of livelihood, former colonial ties, and so on by which we diversely define our *peoplehood*. Moreover, within the United States and Europe this multiplicity is seen in immigration patterns and in the growing value placed on the diversity of communities. In other words, as technologies have knit us closer together, we have placed ever greater value on forms of peoplehood that divide us into smaller and smaller units.

These two trends taken together have placed public life in an arena that is both increasingly cross-cultural and increasingly multicultural. And as we cross and mix cultural boundaries, we cross and mix values systems, including moral systems: Different cultural groups hold differing views as to what is morally important, morally acceptable, and morally right.

With the advent of the 21st century, we face a growing number of players on an increasingly unified stage making often contentious demands for a voice in deciding how the world's wealth is to be divided up. These demands are contentious not only because they entail conflicting claims as to who ought to get what but because they entail different standards for deciding what a fair share ought to be: The world that our technology has made increasingly singular has become increasingly pluralistic in its understanding of how technology's bounty ought to be parceled out. Yet it is within this arena that the sorts of public moral questions identified above must be answered—indeed, we cannot fail to answer them because in practice our answers will be the product of either design or default on our part. The only thing we can fail to do is to answer them responsibly.

Moreover, our current state of affairs is systemically both unstable and unsustainable. It is unstable because the ideas and institutions by which we have traditionally sought stability have assumed a single standard for the resolution or containment of contending claims, and this single standard seems no longer at hand. It is unsustainable because the trends of increasing globalism and localism—like our escalating expectations that accompany them—cannot increase indefinitely: At some point they must give way either to chaos or to a new mode of stability that can only be chosen and designed by us.

How, then, do we address claims of entitlement responsibly when they are made in a context that has multiple standards for weighing such claims? This effort, I believe, must entail (among other things) a substantial reconceptualization of three interrelated themes that have played a powerful role in shaping Western thought and public life for at least the past three centuries: our understanding of the relationship between the individual and the community, and the moral responsibilities that obtain between them; our notion of what can be taken as the common good or common interest; and our sense of how moral systems ought to operate. This reconceptualization will be difficult to bring about and will take years longer than we may like, but it is work we cannot afford to ignore. It is the reshaping of our understanding of moral systems, moreover, that will likely be the most difficult to accomplish; however, it is also the most essential because it is our sense of how morality ought to operate that enables us to evaluate and regulate the other two.

AUTONOMY AND THE ECLIPSE OF RESPONSIBILITY

Addressing the issue of responsibility in a pluralistic context has been made particularly problematic by the understanding of the nature of the moral relationship between the individual and the community that has become dominant in the West. In practice this understanding has taken the form of an increasingly autonomous and entitled individual whose rise has virtually eclipsed the idea of responsibility as a defining element of the moral person.

The moral relationship between individual and community is a very old theme in human history. In the West, this theme, which figures prominently in Socrates, Plato (1961), Augustine (1963), Hobbes (1651/1991) and others, has become in recent centuries particularly problematic, as Vickers (1980) notes, through the rise of the Enlightenment concept of the autonomous individual, which has carried with it an eclipse of the notion of individual responsibility. MacIntyre (1981) has explored this fashioning of the modern autonomous individual in some detail, seeing in it, much as Vickers had, the seeds of a kind of moral rootlessness. Taylor (1989), meanwhile, has tied the moral malaise of contemporary individual identity to the collapse of the primacy of reason, which the Enlightenment project had promoted as a great liberator of the individual and which until this century had been accepted as such virtually without question.

In keeping with this evolution of concepts, over the past two to three centuries the West has developed *in practice* a form of this relationship that is without precedent in any other culture or age. We have come to treat moral prerogatives as resting primarily with an increasingly autonomous individual, but we have simultaneously placed more and more responsibility for securing those prerogatives onto the community, particularly in the form of our public and private institutions. This has created an unusual and dangerous disjunction between moral entitlement and moral responsibility: Individuals can now claim vast entitlements while assuming only a scant portion of the responsibilities associated with creating them and guaranteeing their fulfilment. The extent to which we have created a growing system of legal, commercial, and administrative institutions to secure and safeguard the entitlements of individuals is a telling measure of the extent of our belief in the individual's moral primacy, yet we are also now able to shunt off moral responsibility to an expanding array of institutional *others*.

Seeing the autonomous individual, as contrasted with the community and its institutions, as the primary (or exclusive) holder of moral prerogatives has supported the conceivability and consequently the viability of the escalating expectations mentioned above. We believe citizenship ought to carry with it an ever-expanding set of entitlements in part because we believe we have moral claims to them.

It was as autonomous individuals, not as communities, that we laid claim to the entitlements of citizenship in the American and French Revolutions. Even when the growing power of our public and private institutions in the 19th century gave rise to the notion of their having certain legal (if not moral) rights, this seemed conceivable only by treating those institutions as fictive individuals. Today it is the same predilection that makes social programs aimed at communities so persistently problematic as matters of public deliberation (in the United States, affirmative action is a prime example).

This tendency is intensified by the existence in our public lives of multiple communities, including the multiple institutions through which we enact much of our public lives. Through multiple community memberships we can appeal to varying sets of standards for assessing responsibility—often in ways that affect neighbors who may not share those memberships or standards but with whom public resources, for example, may need to be shared.

Several aspects of this situation can be seen, for example, in the case of the Clinton administration's health care initiative, which is at its core one of assessing who is entitled to health care coverage and who ought to assume responsibility for guaranteeing it. In this case, the broad resistance to funding a program through taxation reflects a resistance to the individual assuming responsibility in covering costs. Conversely, the resistance to the notion of health care alliances representing people not otherwise covered reflects a discomfort with the notion of entitlement claims being made for a community rather than for individual employees. The idea of an individual having limited options as to which physician, clinic, or hospital he or she can use, meanwhile, continues to strike many Americans as a violation of a fundamental freedom of choice or right to choose. In this case, it seems almost as if responsibility were by definition applicable only to public and private institutions, and that the moral entitlements of the individual ought to be exercisable without limit and guaranteed by rights that are inalienable.

For Vickers the rise of the autonomous individual entailed an "eclipse of responsibility" in an essential sense. "Literally," Vickers (1980) argued, "an autonomous person is one who makes his own rules and sets his own standards. He is at the opposite pole from the responsible person" (p. 27). Because we have so substantially shunted off responsibility to our institutions, reconnecting the counterpoles of moral prerogative and moral responsibility requires a reconceptualization of the relationship between the individual and the community. It seems to me that what is called for is an understanding of the individual and the community as mutually constitutive, an understanding that sees neither as claiming priority over the other either ontologically or morally.

Ontologically, in the West at least, the dominant view is of the individual as primary to the community. This is not only a matter of seeing the community as modeled on the individual but of understanding it to be made up out of individuals, as a wall may be made up out of bricks. This is certainly the ontological stance of the bulk of our economic and political theories that model systemic phenomena on the likes of economic man and the voter. Such views tend to ignore the fact that each of us draws our identity to a remarkable degree from the communities to which we belong. Our language, patterns of life, forms of association, and even (or especially) our likes, wants, and desires are shaped by where and among whom we happen to live and choose to live. And these happenstances and choices are deeply reflected in how we live, including how we spend money and vote.

Our understanding of the moral dimension of the individual-community relationship is in keeping with our ontological sense of it. If communities are believed in fact to boil down to individuals, then, the reasoning would go, individuals must also be where moral matters ultimately rest. As noted, we certainly treat issues of moral entitlement and prerogative as though they were by definition fundamentally about individuals. At the same time we have construed the automony that we accord the individual as entailing freedom from constraints, including the constraints that come with assuming responsibilities. However, the individual so conceived, Vickers (1973) argued, is not "fit to live in the modern world" by virtue of not being "capable of handling the ethical problems involved at the level now required" (p. 15).

This picture changes dramatically when we see individuals and communities as mutually constitutive. Such a perspective—as suggested in the work of Mead (1934), for example—casts neither the self nor the society as prior to the other. Ontologically, as suggested above, this means seeing the individual as constituted through membership in particular communities. In this sense, as Vickers (1968) argued, even those things we take as the most intimate elements of who we are as individuals, such as "hope, fear, love, hate, ambition, loneliness, obligation, wonder," are at least "partly shared" through "forms of interaction—not only human speech, but all the arts of human intercourse, of mutual support, influence, coercion, manipulation" (p. 32). To love, to fear, to hope—each means to engage in interaction with the human world.[1] And the specifics of those interactions—especially the where, when, and with whom—give particular shape and meaning to them. Because most of our forms of interaction are not shared with all the world but rather with specific others with whom we happen to or choose to associate, it is in the sharing of these particular forms of interaction that we constitute both ourselves and our communities.

Morally, this means seeing neither the individual nor the community as a primary holder of either moral prerogatives or moral responsibilities. Rather, it means seeing moral matters as being about the arrangement of affairs among individuals who constitute the community through those affairs. There is a sense of this in the recent work on communitarian ethics—in, for example, the centrally important work of Etzioni (1988, 1993). Many communitarians, however, take as their focus the balancing of contending needs, rights, and concerns of the community with those of the individual. This is inimical to the idea of the two as mutually constitutive: It suggests that individuals and communities each have moral interests and that those interests can be in conflict or in balance. By contrast, when the individual and the community are seen as mutually constitutive, they are no longer treated as potential counterpoles and questions of moral interests are not seen as being about the need to avoid contention and seek a balance between them. Rather, moral matters are seen in terms of the stability of the social system of the community (where stability is understood as the dynamic mean between chaos and stagnation). Such terms as *individual rights* or *community needs* are not ultimately about individuals and communities but about the stability of the interactions among people who make up those communities. To be autonomous, to be responsible, to be entitled—each means to engage in interaction with the human world; each is a form of interaction within that world. Questions of morality, then, are at root about the shape those interactions take, not about interests possessed by potentially contending counterpoles.

Throughout Vickers's work, autonomy is treated as the assumption of responsibility, not freedom from it (Vickers, 1980, in particular). Significantly, Vickers also addresses autonomy as much less a matter of what individuals may or may not possess but more as one about the arrangement of affairs within the social system of the community. It is only to the extent that we arrange those affairs with responsibility as a prime concern that we begin to meet Vickers's criterion of being "sufficiently responsible to deserve a corresponding measure of autonomy" (Vickers, 1980, p. 9).

Ultimately, our inherited Enlightenment concept of the autonomous individual contains the seeds of its own downfall, for there is little if anything in the concept itself that provides for the stability of the social system of the community, on which the exercise of autonomy so conceived is nonetheless utterly dependent. Similarly, Vickers's sense of responsibility is not captured by the notion of balance between two counterpoles, for the idea of contending interests alone does not enable us to see the matter in terms of systemic stability. If we are to bring responsibility out of eclipse, it must be seen not in terms of what individuals and communities possess but in terms of how individuals and communities can mutually constitute themselves in responsible ways, including ways that provide for the stability of the individual/community system itself.

In practical terms, this suggests that we must learn to connect public discussions of rights, entitlements, autonomy, and the like directly and immediately to discussions of moral responsibility. In the U.S. health care case, the issue of who ought to pay is typically cast in terms of economic and administrative efficiency.

Important as these matters are, they can never substitute for, nor resolve, questions of moral responsibility, but they can and often do eclipse them.

Public deliberation on questions of moral responsibility seems particularly important now that the fulfilment of our expectations and the stability of those social institutions that that fulfilment requires rest on an increasingly interdependent multiplicity of communities. At the same time, such deliberation seems to be made increasingly difficult by the fact that those multiple communities do not always share a common standard for gauging the common good.

INTERDEPENDENCE AND
THE ECLIPSE OF THE COMMON GOOD

The need to reconceptualize what we mean by common good or common interest is no less problematic than recasting our understanding of autonomy and responsibility. What we take to be for the common good or as maximizing "social utility" has often figured in our understandings of what we believe to be morally desirable or obligatory. It has received a contemporary exploration, for example, as the notion of "common ground" in the work of Robert Bellah and his colleagues (Bellah, Madsen, Sullivan, Swidler, & Tipton, 1991) in their discussion of the "Good Society."

It seems that, as the world grows more and more interdependent, as commerce, policy alliances, entertainment, the arts, and so on cross more and more community boundaries, we owe it to ourselves and to the successful functioning of those enterprises to seek those areas where we have common ground, where we can agree that our efforts serve a common good. To do otherwise would be to ignore the reality of those interests we do hold in common and to undermine the potential for crafting new understandings of common interest essential to stability and responsibility.

At the same time, in a world where the daily practices of public life increasingly cross several community boundaries, to the extent that we have, in fact, become interdependent, we cannot any longer assume that what one individual or community regards as a common good is similarly valued or valued at all by others. And this is a matter not only of making different evaluations but of having different standards for making them.

This can be seen, for example, in the public discussion in the United States of the topic of the family. It is a recurrent theme that the family is in danger, in crisis, that it is disintegrating. There is a profound and telling amount of agreement on this point, agreement that cuts across ethnic, racial, geographic, and economic communities. In essence, many people hold that the institution of the family is in trouble, that it would be for the common good for the situation to be improved and that public resources ought to be committed to help address the situation. It would be a major mistake, however, to assume that this common ground in identifying the problem also indicates a common experience or conception of the family across the communities that see it as threatened. Indeed, preferred forms of family structure, location, cohesion, and so on vary widely through the range of communities that make up U.S. society. These variations are far from irrelevant to questions of how public policies ought to be crafted, public resources committed, and public institutions located and operated. The problem is neither effectively nor responsibly addressed by placing our faith in common ground alone. This is no less true for scores of other issues of public concern. It is at the root, for example, of labor, emigration, and welfare programs within the EU.

Such issues will continue to demand a central place on the public agenda. Because they will need to be addressed to a growing extent through our institutions, addressing them responsibly will require a level of stability in the governance of those institutions that will make responsible decisions and responsible parceling out of public resources possible. Traditionally, we have sought this stability by reference to moral standards we believed to be universally held or universally applicable. This, it seems, is no longer an option open to us. If we are to achieve the stability necessary for responsible governance, we need to recast our understanding of both the moral relationship between the individual and the community and what we see as the value of the common good as against valued differences; we need to do this in ways that enable us to deal with multiple standards.

It may seem ironic that the interdependence that transportation, communication, and commerce have made part of our daily lives has also eclipsed the notion of common good as a reference and standard by which we might regulate those essential interactions in a responsible way. But ironic or not, it is an inescapable feature of the world we now inhabit. We can no longer rely on the notion of common good alone; we must also learn to deal with our differences.

GOVERNANCE AND CONTENTIOUS MORAL PERSPECTIVES

The converging themes above call for a reassessment of our sense of how moral systems ought to operate. They point to the need for a system that can deal with multiple standards for evaluating public issues. That is, they call for a system that is at its core pluralistic. The traditional perspectives on how we ought to live life that we inherit from moral philosophy have not been particularly helpful in this regard. Indeed, they have contributed to our inability to talk across community lines to the degree we now need to. If moral philosophy is to be helpful in public discussion of moral issues and in establishing stable governance, it must, I believe, develop a coherent understanding of moral pluralism. To explore why it has not and how it might now do so, it is necessary to sketch out, at least roughly, what is traditionally meant by moral absolutism and moral relativism and to see how a generally unexamined juxtaposition of absolutism and relativism has shaped much of recent public discussion of moral issues.

Moral absolutism, roughly, is the view that to any one question about moral right or wrong there can be one and only one acceptable answer. Is abortion justifiable? Is affirmative action fair? What do I do in a culture where I am expected to give a bribe to get needed services? For these and all such questions (in general or in individual cases) the moral absolutist would argue that there can be only one possible answer that is morally justifiable, one that can be discovered and defended through reason (because of this focus on a single answer, this position is also referred to by many as moral *monism*). There have been and are many philosophers who hold to this position. It is also the position of many nonphilosophers. It is the position implied by any one of us when we say (or when our actions indicate) that "my answer to this moral question is not just *my* answer but *the* answer."

There are a number of things that are entailed in the absolutist perspective, even if they are not always acknowledged by absolutists. One, which critics are fast to point out, is the denial of moral legitimacy to any other view. Saying "*my* answer is *the* answer" entails saying "if you don't agree with me, you are wrong." The other is the idea that there are certain principles or standards (such as rights, social utility, or justice) that, when used as tools of reason, will enable us to figure out the morally right thing to do in all cases. That is, absolutism holds that moral systems ought to function through the application of reason and the use of certain principles or rules. It is possible, from the absolutist perspective, for someone or some culture to subscribe to the "right" position on a moral issue but not to have an acceptable justification for it because they do not employ the "right" principles or do not use reason properly in reaching or defending their views. The absolutist, then, tends to be absolute both in terms of what constitutes an acceptable answer and how such answers ought to be reached.

When critics point out certain perennially intractable moral issues or the grand diversity of moral systems across human cultures, the moral absolutists are not shaken. "It may be true," they say, "that we have yet to discover the one true answer to certain moral questions, but that does not mean that such an answer cannot be found! Indeed, look at human history: Is there not moral progress there? Do we not see humankind coming together on more and more issues? It is no accident that slavery is all but gone: We figured out that it was morally unacceptable and convinced one another of it." As to the diversity of moral positions and moral systems, the orthodox absolutist might say, "Because there can be only one morally right answer to any moral question, all others are simply wrong. People who hold those views may do so out of foolishness or evil or honest ignorance, but whatever the explanation, they are still, at bottom, simply wrong."

These aspects of absolutism tend to have a stultifying effect on public deliberation concerning moral issues. In the face of multiple standards for addressing moral entitlements, for example, an orthodox absolutist would see one standard as superior to all others. In practice, this all too readily creates a counterposing of views that provides no means for deliberation.

The way the abortion issue is cast in the United States, for example, virtually forecloses the possibility of useful public deliberation on the matter. It is seen not only as a battle between two camps that find each other to be morally repugnant but as being about absolute standards (life and choice) that must be defended at all costs; it is not seen to be about differing, legitimate issues of public concern that deserve to be discussed and debated. Because the two camps deny all moral legitimacy to each other's positions and standards, no avenue exists for public deliberation. The tragedy is that the subsequent unproductive clamoring of definitionally irreconcilable counterpoles has become an exemplar in American culture for how public moral issues ought to be dealt with. Conversely, as it is not currently popular in many public spheres to say, "I am right, you are wrong. My view is the only morally acceptable one," there are very few *public* moral absolutists. I suspect, however, that there are many *private* ones. And this constitutes another way in which public moral deliberation is silenced.[2]

Moral relativism offers quite a different view. The moral relativists, broadly speaking, say that to any one moral question there can be any number of acceptable answers, depending on where and who you happen to be. That is, morality is seen as relative to context—to society, religion, community, and the like, where the standards of moral conduct can and do vary.

In some societies, when business people take up the time of prospective clients in presenting their goods and services, it is expected that they will show respect and gratitude by giving the prospective clients gifts. To fail to do so can be seen as unethical. In the United States, it is usually seen as a bribe and considered as morally unacceptable (and in many cases illegal). A moral relativist would say that this shows how morality can vary from one culture to the next, both in terms of what is considered right and wrong and in terms of the standards for determining it. (In this case, for example, the U.S. position might be justified by appeal to the maintenance of a fair market and the mitigation of undue influence. In another culture, the issue might hinge on a standard of respect for the time and social position of the prospective client.) The moral absolutist would say that, although cultural norms may differ, such gestures are either morally right or morally wrong, that there is no way for both to be morally justifiable. For the absolutist, this is a matter of confusing empirical fact with moral and rational acceptability. For the relativist, it is evidence that moral standards are social variables, not products of a universal human reason or overarching principles. The debate goes on.

If we are to accept a relativist position, critics say, there are implications that need also to be accepted, but that, like the implications of absolutism, are not always acknowledged. Chief among them is that, ultimately, moral relativism provides neither formula nor footing for guiding action and informing critique regarding moral matters within the public sphere. Because right and wrong can vary depending on who and where you are, there is nothing inherent to relativism per se that places a limit on how small a circle one might appeal to in justifying one's actions. Many moral relativists offer arguments as to what constitutes a meaningful and justifiable circle, but there is no agreement on the issue. Thus, as the critics note, one can conclude there could be as many moral systems as there are people in the world. To the extent that this is true, moral relativism abdicates the traditional function of moral systems of providing for the responsible resolution or containment of differing views among people, particularly those who are members of the same community. If one believes that any answer to a question of public moral concern is an acceptable one, that "everyone is entitled to his or her opinion," then one has no basis for defending any of those views (or one's own) from attack by yet others. In this way, orthodox relativism effectively forecloses public moral discourse because it leaves all parties unable to say no. In effect, whereas absolutism tends to squelch public moral deliberation, relativism abandons it.

Although moral relativism may pass in good times as a kind of warm and comfortable tolerance of diversity, in more difficult times it leaves us powerless to speak or to devise responsible action. This latter state, which I call *abject relativism,* amounts to a particularly frightening form of self-imposed silencing. Where current public commitment to diversity appeals to relativism, it runs the risk of spreading this silence. Indeed, I am afraid that diversity is publicly embraced by some prominent figures who privately find it quite abhorrent precisely because at some level they recognize its silencing powers.

The debate between absolutism and relativism has been fueled by a tendency to see the two as a dichotomy constituting the extent of our options for dealing with the moral dimension of life, particularly public life. Conventional thinking seems to leave us with the notion that if we do not subscribe to absolutism's one answer then we open the door to relativism's any answer, and vice versa. As a philosophical colleague of mine recently put it, "What other option could there possibly be?"

This question is not raised in a vacuum. Many traditional views about moral action and moral systems have been very much under reevaluation in recent years within moral philosophy. MacIntyre (1990) has assessed what he sees as key competing visions of moral inquiry within the Western tradition. Williams (1985) and Rorty (1989) have argued, in very different modes, that we now need to recognize that philosophy can make only limited contributions to the understanding and guiding of moral action. Midgley (1991), meanwhile, has insisted quite compellingly that philosophy can still be a powerful force in understanding the necessity of making moral judgments. In these and other recent critiques, the categories of absolutism and relativism have received a great deal of attention. They now seem to many not nearly as firm or as coherent as they once did. All this work suggests that the question "What other option could there possibly be?" is best taken as a call to explore new territory, not as a rhetorical signaling of retreat to the familiar. This search for other options within moral philosophy, like the themes of increasing interdependence and multiplicity in our public lives, points to the need for a pluralist option.

PLURALISM IN A ROCKING BOAT

The current state of our public lives and institutions leaves us feeling as though we are in a rocking boat made ever more unstable by appeals to points of reference we once regarded as the only possible sources of stability. However, it is within this rocking boat that we must learn to deal with the increasingly pluralistic world around us. Consequently, we need a conceptually and publicly viable moral perspective that can help us act responsibly within the pluralistic world in which we now find ourselves. Neither absolutism nor relativism can provide this. How would a pluralist perspective differ? A pluralist perspective would see for every moral question the possibility of a number of morally acceptable answers, but not *any* number: Some answers would be rejected as morally unacceptable. The pluralist needs to be able to say no. In taking this stance, the pluralist would avoid the stultifying dogmatism of the absolutist and the potential abject immobility of the relativist.

If the case for a pluralist perspective were to be fought solely on empirical grounds, it would win over absolutism and relativism hands down. Even a modest glance at the history of human groups reveals a great variety of moral systems. There is indeed very little in the practices of human cultures to suggest that we have been striving for the absolutist's one answer. On the other hand, our history is filled with instances in which we have committed our minds, resources, blood, and lives to saying "this will not do." Historically, we have not developed social systems with a capacity for the relativist's any answer. The greatest experiment of all, the living of life, profoundly argues that we are in practice pluralists.

However, the issue before us is not simply to recognize that our actions and habits have resulted in multiple moral systems but to understand how we can act responsibly in the face of multiple standards for determining what is morally right. There are three things, at the very least, that a pluralist perspective can embrace that help accomplish this: a shift in focus from principles to practice; an understanding that shaping moral practice entails crafting moral communities; and a recognition that stability within and across moral communities is a matter of experiencing relations, not one of imposing a single standard for all.

A shift in focus from principles to practice is at the core of the pluralist perspective. In addressing a moral question, the primary aim from this perspective is not to discover *the* answer to the question (and all others like it) through the reasoned application of abstract principles. Rather, the primary aim is to fashion a shareable understanding of the question among those for whom it is a relevant concern and to devise a shareable understanding of what are morally acceptable actions with respect to it. It is in forming such understandings among those concerned that the essence of the moral enterprise lies for the pluralist. The question for the pluralist is not What is right? but How do we act responsibly? There are a number of things entailed in this.

For the pluralist perspective, the fact that different groups of concerned people can form different understandings of a moral issue, including different views of what is a justifiable action, belief, or position concerning that issue, is not in itself problematic. The fact that Americans regard as bribe what people from some countries regard as an obligatory expression of respect is not a problem for the moral pluralist: As long as the members of each community have fashioned a shareable understanding of what the practice of giving such gifts means and when it is and is not acceptable to do so, the pluralist perspective would see no need to appeal to anything beyond these facts. The practice is wrong for Americans, right for the others. The situation is not problematic for the pluralist as long as it is unproblematic for those concerned.

Traditionally, we may be tempted to ask if the mere fact that each community considers its practice morally acceptable makes it so. Is it not possible that some positions are simply wrong? This temptation is a mistake from the pluralist perspective in two respects. First, to go beyond saying that each position is moral for the community that created it would require appeal to a universal, over-arching standard by which those (and presumably all) communities could be judged—and for the pluralist no such standard exists. (In fact, the only source of such a universal standard would be from the moral absolutists—of which there are several different camps, each disagreeing with the others and each offering its own brand of universal standard.) Second, it would require shifting focus back to principles and away from practice. What is morally problematic for the pluralist must arise out of practice, not solely out of reasoning about principles.

This does not mean in the slightest, however, that the pluralist perspective accepts as moral all practices of all communities under all circumstances. As noted above, the pluralist needs to be able to say no. But here again, the no must be seen to arise out of practice. The pluralist would not look at the practices of another community in the abstract and declare them immoral. However, if the pluralist were involved in some interaction with another community that held conflicting views, then the interaction would make the issue morally problematic *in practice*. If there were a community somewhere in the world that believes it is morally obligatory to practice head-hunting, I do not feel I can say in a universal or abstract sense that they are acting immorally. I could and would argue that I do not agree with them. And if I found myself in interaction with them, I would certainly do my best to change their minds, particularly if I did not trust the way they were looking at my head. I would have become one of those concerned about the practice, and my objection would be aimed at the world of moral practice, not at the domain of concepts.

Trying to change one another's minds or to come up with a workable understanding of our differences (that is, to engage in public moral deliberation) is what happens or *ought* to happen whenever we cross community boundaries and find ourselves facing multiple standards for determining moral right and wrong. This is the core imperative of the pluralist perspective. It follows from the shift from principles to practice: The shift moves the origin of moral problems away from abstract concepts and toward concrete practices, and it moves the primary focus of addressing problems from a conceptual domain to one of public deliberation about and through practices among those concerned. It should be noted that this shift in primary focus from principles to practices does not require that we abandon principles but rather that we change their role. When engaging in public moral deliberation we certainly can and often do appeal to principles, as may our interlocutors appeal to theirs. What is not in keeping with the pluralist perspective is to insist that our principles are the only applicable ones. There is a world of difference, particularly in the ears of our interlocutors, between saying "this is important to me" and saying "this is the only acceptable thing for us to talk about."

Public deliberation about what is morally important to us also transpires within single communities. In debating, discussing, and interacting around moral issues, communities fashion shareable understandings of what practices are acceptable, unacceptable, and obligatory. And they fashion shareable understandings of what standards are appropriate for making those determinations. These understandings often draw strongly on what is inherited from past generations and also include consideration of current issues and concerns about the future. The specific understandings a community fashions are in a sense the moral artifacts of that community; they are the examples and ideas about acceptable and unacceptable practice through which that community engages in the ongoing business of public moral deliberation about concrete questions of practice at hand. In this way, public moral deliberation is not only how we give shape to moral practice within our communities; it is also one way by which a chosen or circumstantial group of people constitute themselves as a moral community. As Bernstein (1983) argued, this sort of "solidarity, participation, and mutual recognition that is founded in dialogical communities" must be grounded to issues of practice. (For one view of how this would apply to group formation, stability, and learning in general, see Cook & Yanow, 1993.)

Moreover, within a single community we can and often do find public deliberation that entails appeal to multiple standards. This can happen in times of change or turmoil when, for example, conflicting views about such matters as military involvements or social equality come before the public agenda. If those issues are seen as being about immutable and incompatible standards, the deliberation can be stifled, unproductive, and divisive for the community, as in the U.S. abortion case. When there is a shift to what are and are not acceptable practices, the deliberation can move ahead, as has occurred in the United States in the matter of gays in the military. In another sense, there can also be a plurality of standards within a single community where there is a more or less shareable understanding that different standards should apply to different domains. This point has been argued quite strongly by Stone (1987) who observed, for example, that the U.S. public much more readily accepts euthanasia as a means of alleviating suffering in animals than they do in the case of humans. But here again, the standards become tools for shaping a common understanding through public deliberation about particular practices.

When we face multiple, conflicting standards in practices that cross community lines, the obligation that the pluralist perspective sees for engaging in public moral deliberation is also an exercise in crafting moral communities. If we are to engage in practices with others across moral systems, to do so responsibly requires that we fashion common understandings of what is morally acceptable and unacceptable. This does not mean that we must ultimately adopt a single view or a single standard (although in some cases we may). It does mean that we must understand what one another's moral expectations and standards are and that we must build a common understanding of what practices we will and will not engage in with each other. To the extent that we reach these understandings, we are fashioning shareable moral artifacts that we hold in common and thus are crafting a sort of moral community, even if a small and ad hoc one. But it is only within such communities and through such shareable understandings, including operational understandings of differences, that we can reach our most stable form of interaction and governance.

To the extent that we cannot do this, engaging in practices with one another (commercial, political, adminstrative, etc.) is skating on moral thin ice. When we face such situations, it seems that we must either choose not to participate in those interactions with other communities or each community (or individual) must act on its own moral understandings alone, and, presumably, be willing to assume full responsibility for the consequences.

The shift from principle to practice does not mean that our commitment to our moral views must be weakened: Saying "this is what we (or I) most deeply and passionately believe, what we are willing to live by and die for" does not require that we say or believe that those convictions are somehow privileged over the convictions of others. (When we think it does, perhaps we owe it to ourselves, if not to our neighbors, to ask ourselves why.) Also, it is by saying what we deeply and passionately believe and by interacting with other individuals and communities in keeping with our beliefs that we engage in, and contribute to, a pluralist deliberation. Public moral deliberation in a pluralist mode is about dealing with what we have in common along with what we do not. In keeping with Hannah Arendt's (1958) insistence that human plurality is "the basic condition of both action and speech" (p. 175), the pluralist perspective would hold that public life rests ultimately not in a contest of interests but in action and speech among equals about differences. Withholding our deeply held convictions from the public deliberation silences that discussion and erodes the integrity of the public realm. The idea of moral communities does not, for the pluralist, *resolve* moral issues but *enables* responsible deliberation and action concerning them.

The notion of moral communities built around a primary focus on practice as a way of enabling responsible interaction within and across moral systems entails seeing morality as essentially concerned with concrete relatedness, rather than abstract concepts. This aspect of the shift from principles to practice has become a significant theme in recent work in ethics. Noddings (1984) and Manning (1992), for example, both argued that questions of moral right and wrong are ultimately not matters about how moral concepts and arguments hang together but about how people are connected to one another. This is not only a point about how moral thinking might proceed, it is one about the origins of the concerns and considerations that constitute moral life. It is also, I would argue, one about how we can establish responsible relationships with others who hold both different ideas of what is morally right and different standards for determining it. Learning how to craft moral communities that respect both our common ground and our differences can bring a measure of stability to those social institutions through which we aim to fulfil our expectations of public life. This stability, as Vickers (1970) argued, will likely elude us until we rediscover "the fact that life consists in experiencing relations, rather than in seeking goals or 'ends'" (p. 128). Experiencing relations with others who hold to different goals and ends is a source of instability only if we forget that it is out of experiencing relations and not seeking "ends" that we can craft a responsible life within an interdependent world.

The development of a publicly viable pluralist perspective is *necessary* if we are to address moral issues responsibly, given the multiple standards for determining moral acceptability that have become fixtures of our interdependent world. Absolutism and relativism are incapable of providing for the stability of governance in our social institutions that is now required to address claims of entitlement in a world of multiple communities in any way that we are likely to regard as morally acceptable. We must learn that a single moral North Star can no longer enable us to navigate a responsible course.

Whether it is *possible* to put a pluralist perspective in place as part of public moral deliberation is another question. It is, I believe, a question that no one at this point can answer. My argument, accordingly, has not been about what is *possible* but what is *necessary* if we wish to act responsibly. In any case, it seems to me that the question of what responsibility requires ought to come first—if for no other reason than that within the domain of human systems, what is possible is often revealed to us by what we come to see as necessary.

The pluralist perspective cannot resolve all the challenging moral concerns that are certain to come before the public agenda as the demands of stable governance face the ever more interdependent world of the 21st century. However, it can put us in a far better position to talk with one another, and it may even encourage us to listen.

NOTES

1. In making this point I have been influenced by my collaboration with Dr. John Seely Brown on parallel issues of group epistemology.

2. A variation of this can be seen in the case of the 1992 Republican convention where some speakers presented absolutist right-wing views (a conception of family values, for example, that excludes most forms of family). Major party figures subsequently distanced themselves from those speeches. The real issue, however, was not what was said: The speakers' views were well-known to the party, which had invited them to speak. Rather it was the public expression of absolute rather than tolerant views that prompted the distancing. This, in turn, effectively silenced any further discussion of those views, especially within the party itself.

REFERENCES

Arendt, H. (1958). *The human condition*. Chicago, IL: University of Chicago Press.

Augustine, S. (1963). *City of God*. London: Oxford University Press.

Bellah, R. N., Madsen, R., Sullivan, W. M., Swidler, A., & Tipton, S. M. (1991). *The good society*. New York: Alfred A. Knopf.

Bernstein, R. J. (1983). *Beyond objectivism and relativism: Science, hermeneutics, and praxis*. Philadelphia: University of Pennsylvania Press.

Cook, S.D.N., & Yanow, D. J. (1993). Culture and organizational learning. *Journal of Management Inquiry*, 2(4), 373-390.

Etzioni, A. (1988). *The moral dimension: Toward a new economics*. New York: Free Press.

Etzioni, A. (1993). *The spirit of community: Rights, responsibilities, and the communitarian agenda*. New York: Crown.

Hobbes, T. (1991). *Leviathan*. New York: Cambridge University Press. (Original work published 1651)

Ihde, D. (1990). *Technology and the lifeworld*. Bloomington: Indiana University Press.

Jarvis, H., & Pack, R. (1979). *I'm mad as hell: The exclusive story of the tax revolt and its leader*. New York: Times Books.

MacIntyre, A. (1981). *After virtue*. Notre Dame, IN: University of Notre Dame Press.

MacIntyre, A. (1990). *Three rival versions of moral enquiry: Encyclopaedia, genealogy, and tradition*. Notre Dame, IN: University of Notre Dame Press.

Manning, R. C. (1992). *Speaking from the heart: A feminist perspective on ethics*. Lanham, MD: Rowan & Littlefield.

Mead, G. H. (1934). *Mind, self, and society*. Chicago, IL: University of Chicago Press.

Midgley, M. (1991). *Can't we make moral judgments?* New York: St. Martin's.

Noddings, N. (1984). *Caring: A feminist approach to ethics and moral education*. Berkeley: University of California Press.

Plato (1961). *The collected dialogues* (E. Hamilton & H. Cairns, Eds.). Princeton, NJ: Princeton University Press.

Rorty, R. (1989). *Contingency, irony and solidarity*. Cambridge: Cambridge University Press.

Stone, C. D. (1987). *Earth and other ethics: The case for moral pluralism*. New York: Harper & Row.

Taylor, C. (1989). *Sources of the self: The making of the modern identity*. Cambridge, MA: Harvard University Press.

Vickers, G. (1968). *Value systems and social process*. New York: Basic Books.

Vickers, G. (1970). *Freedom in a rocking boat*. London: Penguin.

Vickers, G. (1973). *Making institutions work*. London: Associated Business Programmes.

Vickers, G. (1980). *Responsibility: Its sources and limits*. Seaside, CA: Intersystems.

Williams, B. (1985). *Ethics and the limits of philosophy*. Cambridge, MA: Harvard University Press.

11

Conditions for Social Responsibility

LYNTON K. CALDWELL

This article explores the relationship between cultural integrity, diversity, and social responsibility. The obligations and opportunities of responsible citizenship in a complex diverse society pose a difficult political issue that modern societies scarcely recognize. It is not clear, the article concludes, how large and diverse a society can become and yet remain sufficiently cohesive to behave responsibly by any meaningful standard.

Responsibility, both individual and social, was a major integrating theme in the writings of Sir Geoffrey Vickers.[1] His concern for responsibility as a condition for the integrity, stability, and moral quality of society was set out explicitly in his book *Responsibility: Its Sources and Limits* (1980). This concern also infused his other writings, notably in the collection published as *The Vickers Papers* (Open Systems Group, 1984). He believed that responsibility required a pattern of mutual expectation and trust among individuals that collectively formed an identification and acceptance of moral standards and values that he called "an appreciative system." He was well ahead of his time in recognizing that human relations, especially at the societal level, were systemic. He saw nature (including human nature) as interactively systemic, not a disconnected random aggregation of individual organisms. Publication and reprinting of many of his writings by Intersystems (e.g., the Systems Inquiry Series) and by the Open Systems Group was indicative of his systemic view of the workings of the world, both natural and human.

Vickers's work was based on this appreciation of the complex systemic character of human society and the necessity for taking this reality into account in the analysis, planning, and management of human affairs. This article is obviously indebted to Geoffrey Vickers's examination of the basis of responsibility in its various aspects. I hope it may therefore be regarded as a codicil or footnote to Vickers's more extensive works. Its purpose is to explore the following questions: Is systemic social responsibility a realistic concept? In what sense, if any, can societies be responsible, and, if so, under what conditions? *Social responsibility*, as the term is used here, includes the responsibility of the individual to the society of which he or she is a part and also the collective responsibility of a society to whomever or whatever is affected by its actions. A responsible society implies responsible individuals.

This article raises questions that may not be answerable with our present understanding of human motivation and behavior. But it may point the way toward investigations into some aspects of human behavior wherein our understanding is far from complete. Vickers's insights open the way toward ascertaining the societal problems of responsible conduct that, if unattended and unresolved, threaten the prospects for the sustainability of society as a form of human association.

MEANINGS OF RESPONSIBILITY

A claim of responsibility does not necessarily imply responsible action. An admission of personal responsibility may, in fact, be an act of altruism shielding another person who is truly responsible for an act of commission or omission. Political terrorists, as a warning to their adversaries, have claimed responsibility for acts of violence causing injury and death to innocent individuals. Responsibility for particular acts of violence may be claimed by terrorists, whereas rival claimants may also declare themselves responsible, with the true identity of the perpetrator remaining in doubt. But in a broader sense, was the *act itself* responsible behavior? Whole peoples and nations have been held responsible (i.e., accountable) for acts of their rulers. Collective responsibility may be an arbitrary indiscriminate judgment in circumstances where not all individuals are, or could be, equally responsible (e.g., infant children). Responsibility is thus a word of many meanings; the Oxford Reference Dictionary lists five! In any sense it is rarely absolute and is often relative and circumstantial. To make sense of any of its meanings one must be able to specify *for what, who, why, how, when*, and *where*.

Therefore, responsibility as a concept does not connote any singular relationship, nor is the objective or action for which responsibility is established necessarily good. Individuals and governments may be responsible for acts widely judged to be criminal. An action, morally justified in the mind of the actor, may be judged immoral by persons not sharing his rationale. For example, political or religious fanatics may intend injury or punishment to those who do not share their faith. In what sense could such intent to injure or destroy be regarded as responsible? Ought single-purpose fanaticism devoted to realizing an abstract ideal be considered responsible?

Responsibility *for* something caused or prevented is distinguishable from responsibility *to* something or someone. The first meaning relates to causation; the second implies accountability. Responsibility *for* action guided by a moral imperative takes account of the consequences of action or inaction regardless of how those consequences are evaluated or by whom. These differences are merged when someone may be held accountable *to* someone *for* something, understanding that the someone may be an individual or group, an institution, or an entire society. However, responsibility may also be to an ideal, an ethos, or a social cause. Thus the meaning of responsibility differs significantly as its context differs materially between the perspectives of legalists, legislators, executives, philosophers, theologians, and general public, and in relation to differing circumstances of time and place.

Whatever its meaning in any situation, the concept of responsibility is consequential, that is, responsibility *to* or *for* anyone or anything is linked to its consequences whether known or unknown. Can a person therefore be responsible, or be fairly accounted responsible, for an act judged to be irresponsible because its outcome is unknown? Perhaps, if cause and consequence are linked without qualification. When a person is declared responsible for an irresponsible act, the implication appears to be paradoxical. That is, if the actor clearly performed the act but did not know or care about its outcome and was unable or unwilling to undo or mitigate harm done, he or she was responsible *for* what happened but did not act responsibly *to* whoever or whatever was affected. Responsibility *for*, whatever its qualifications, may be a matter of fact (as in assigned duties in an organization) but the fact may be complex and may include contradictory considerations. The considerations indicating responsibility *to* may be no less complex. They may or may not be establishable as facts. Responsibility of someone *to* someone or something may be no more than opinion. It may also be regarded as a philosophic question belonging to that realm of speculative thought called moral philosophy, for example, responsibility to future generations. But responsibility, whether *to* or *for*, is nonetheless a human value and expectation indispensable to mutual trust, to the integrity of society, and hence to legitimate government.

CHOICE AND NECESSITY

In the realm of philosophy the concept of moral responsibility is linked to opinions about free will and determinism. These opinions, scholarly or popular, tend to bias answers to the philosophic question of whether or under what conditions humans can be truly morally responsible. Pertinent also are assumptions regarding the imperatives and limitations of both free will and moral responsibility. These assumptions are fundamental to how human behavior is explained and evaluated and were so regarded by Geoffrey Vickers.[2]

Mankind, being a mutually dependent social species, finds sustainable freedom only within the confines of a particular subsocial system. In the natural world man is systemically connected to family, occupation, community, tribe, nation—and in modern society to many other groupings. Vickers found that a moral imperative underlies a sense of responsibility. The moral obligation to act responsibly is internalized within the individual as a communal or cultural attribute. The attrition of morality in the contemporary world has been accompanied by a decline in commitment to responsibility. But not all students of responsibility agree with this conclusion. The impulse to act responsibly is clearly instilled by culture. Whether there is also a genetic factor and what is the nature of its influence are presently debatable but cannot be wholly dismissed.

Different conclusions follow from different beliefs regarding the forces shaping human behavior. Opinion polarities believe human actions to be determined either *wholly by nature* (e.g., by genetic and related physiological parameters) or *primarily by culture*. Bruce N. Waller (1990) in *Freedom Without Responsibility* appears to reject nature (i.e., biology) as a source of a sense of responsibility: "The position being championed in this book is that our contemporary, nonmiraculous, naturalist (determinist) world system leaves no room for moral responsibility—though it leaves quite adequate space for individual freedom." Waller further asserts that "our natural world is quite compatible with individual free will but is fundamentally incompatible with moral responsibility . . . individuals can be and often are free [but no one] . . . is ever morally responsible: no one ever justly deserves blame, praise, punishment, or reward."[3]

Waller does not deny that morality and immorality are valid concepts. He merely defends the proposition that they have no innate relationship to responsibility. There appears to be an assumption by Waller that culture, which influences concepts of morality and responsibility, is outside of nature. Nevertheless, some of the deductions of biosociology seem to indicate innate genetic tendencies toward altruism and functional responsibility.[4] Kinship has been identified as a factor in altruism that does not extend beyond a close blood relationship. But the relative frequency of homicide within familial groups raises doubt about the relationship of altruism to responsibility and the extent of genetic factors in either aspect of behavior. With many mammals (e.g., bears, lions, elephants, and deer), mothers manifest a concern for their young that resembles responsible behavior. If this is a response to innate instinct, is it accurate to call it *moral*? In some species, but not all, orphan animals of the same species may be adopted.

Does altruism indicate a sense of responsibility? In certain herd species, behavior resembling responsibility for ill or injured members has been observed. I will not argue that these mammalian behaviors are analogous to a human sense of altruism or moral responsibility. Indeed, this type of nurturing is not found in those humans who abandon, neglect, sell, or abuse their children. In Western society, such behavior is generally seen as immoral, and when it occurs it seems to be a weakening or breakdown of a social system and of social responsibility.

Perhaps the most radical denial of the influence of culture on behavior was made by the French biologist Jacques Monod (1971) in his essay entitled *Chance and Necessity*. He argued that science had confirmed the Cartesian conclusion that man is a machine. In his view life began by mere physicochemical chance. Thereafter, the behavior of living species, man included, was a result of convergent necessities. Freedom of choice is an illusion. Given the forces impinging on human behavior, events could not be other than what they are. Monod firmly separates ethics and values from knowledge, with the consequence that the concept of responsibility has no place in his philosophy.

There are other biologists, however, notably Theodosius Dobzhansky (1956), whose viewpoint parallels that of Geoffrey Vickers. Although evolutionary biology sets limits (and also provides opportunities) for human cultural development, it does not confine man to being little more than an automaton. Human cultures develop on a biological base. But the variety of human cultures past and present supports a strong inference that *choice* is a major causal factor in cultural development. Apart from man's biological endowment, environmental factors set limits and opportunities in which cultural choices are made. Within limits, humans can adapt to or alter their environments, including socioeconomic environments. Responsibility derives from this ability to choose. Societies may, in effect, choose their futures intentionally or inadvertently through response to developments within their environments, the social environment included. Complex cultures may recognize various responsibilities, not all of which are mutually compatible and which among other consequences may lead to personal and social conflict. Thus there are limits to the influence of responsibility on the coherence of a society.

Vickers believed that biological evolution "only sets limits to what can survive but throws no light on what within those limits actually does develop" (G. Vickers, personal communication, March 26, 1980). A biosocial predisposition toward certain values may reinforce a cultural choice in opposition to an alternative based solely on culture (i.e., on institutionalized authority). Sophocles' *Antigone* dramatizes the power of a moral imperative to limit the freedom to choose among conflicting responsibilities. Antigone responds to a moral imperative to bury her dead brother even though the legal authority of her city prohibits her from doing so. She must choose between two conflicting responsibilities. She does not regard herself free to choose whether to honor the dead or to obey the law. Her sense of moral responsibility does not give her that freedom. The theme of moral responsibility to the dead is almost universal in human culture. Its great antiquity is inferred from burial practices in the Stone Age. Moral responsibility in this situation may express a predisposition in the human species that is shaped and activated by culture.

Accordingly, I share the viewpoint of Geoffrey Vickers that moral responsibility in some actual and activating sense is a fundamental characteristic in human society. Yet it is not expressed equally in all cultures or even by all individuals within the same culture. Where it fails to form part of the foundation, that social order risks dissolution or degradation. In few cases, if any, does moral responsibility appear to be uniform across a large aggregation of humans. Nevertheless, its diverse influence on the quality of human life may be inferred from the records of history and the human impact on its ecological life support base.

LAW AND ETHICS

The mores or folkways of human society include its sense of morality and its ethical values. Opinions differ on whether some moral principles are universal, possibly innate. James Q. Wilson (1993), in *The Moral Sense*, identifies four universal moral predispositions: sympathy, fairness, self-control, and duty.

These moral values are expressed in socially responsible behavior, and when contrasted with their opposites, they clearly have a survival value for the society. A more compelling case for innate or biosocial predisposition can be made in the universal aversion to murder and incest, expressed in moral principles. Among many species of animals biological inhibitions to intraspecific killing have a survival value for the species, influencing behavior without moral rationalization (Lorentz, 1966). In human society, these aspects of behavior interact in attitudes and conduct that are described as responsibility and are made explicit in codes of conduct reinforced by social institutions.

The concept of responsibility in human society is reflected in its laws and also tacitly in its mores. These laws and mores are expressed through a structure of obligations and rights. In nonliterate traditional societies, and to some extent in all societies, law is derived from mores institutionalized as custom. In complex, technologically advanced multicultural societies, written law may be elaborated and multiplied and become a province of technicians, lawyers, and judges beyond comprehension by the great majority of the people affected. Under these circumstances, it may be difficult to ascertain in what sense and to what degree government is behaving responsibly *to whom* or *for what*.

The responsibility that governments may have *to whom* and *for what* is basically determined by the assumptions, expectations, and values inherent in the dominant ethnicity of a society (i.e., its mores). These characteristics of a culture are ultimately formalized through codes of law and ethics. For example, in modern Western society, the negotiable legal contract has been the conventional instrument for establishing and enforcing reciprocal responsibilities. Nevertheless, the concept of reciprocal rights is found in other cultures. Often defined by custom or in written codes having the character of law (e.g., in European feudalism or in rules governing commercial transactions), contractual obligations were recognized in some societies centuries before modern trade and labor contracts were developed. And political theorists, notably J. J. Rousseau, proposed the social contract and the general will as organizing principles for society. The contract, however, assumed a conditional obligation freely assumed by individuals. This atomistic view of the autonomous individual as the measure of all things was in the judgment of Sir Geoffrey Vickers a cause of the decline of a sense of responsibility in Western society.

Other legal devices have been invoked to enforce individual responsibility. In Western society and in other cultures as well, the principle of tort liability has been a legal device for establishing and inducing responsibility, although more often invoked to punish failures of responsibility. Particularly in the United States, a de facto moral principle has become conventional, that an injured party is entitled to compensation from someone. Application of this principle in tort litigation has sometimes resulted in what might be regarded as a travesty on responsibility; obligation to compensate has too often been exacted by courts from persons who although neither directly or knowingly involved in an alleged injury were nonetheless compelled to pay (in actuality, because they could financially afford to do so). To the extent that litigation becomes a widespread way to enforce legal accountability it risks undermining a sense of mutual responsibility throughout society, and it thus weakens the bonds of community necessary for the existence of societal responsibility. As far back in time as the Roman Republic, Cicero viewed the law as a bond that held society together in a common polity. It is at least debatable whether today's complex multiplicity of statutes, regulations, and court decisions tends to unite or divide people in multicultural or highly diversified societies. Laws become more abstruse, technical, and inaccessible to the unaided individual, and ethical principles as often divide societies as unite them.

Geoffrey Vickers observed with dismay that the integrity of Western society has been decreasing as the assumptions and values that emerged in the so-called Enlightenment of the 18th century have to a large extent displaced the customary and communal systems of obligations and duties that characterized medieval and ancient societies (see Vickers, 1970, 1977/1984c). The American and French Revolutions broke with the derivation of law from immemorial custom and consensus, adopting instead a philosophy of political invention derived from rational principles. These reasoned principles, however, were based on theories and propositions described as self-evident but were, in fact, no more testable than was belief in the divine right of kings. Moreover, they contained potential contradictions as, for example, between liberty, equality, and fraternity. The medieval order of communal obligations and conditional rights gave way to an assumption that autonomous individuals, not communities, were or should be the building blocks of society. Freedom, liberty, and the rights of the individual, derived from natural law, became basic elements in a new consensus. The new dispensation, deduced from nature and rationality by the political philosophers of the Enlightenment, may have had a liberating influence on human creativity, but it did not provide a reliable foundation for social responsibility.

The philosophy of the Enlightenment proposed that social consensus (and by implication social responsibility) be derived from right reason that was capable of apprehending natural law. Freedom from unquestioning adherence to tradition was necessary in addressing new issues that accompanied advances in science and technology. Many of the political commentators and statesmen of the Enlightenment saw that a society governed by reason required this rational quality in its governors, and that its exercise should be guided by a quality called *virtue*, which has a close affinity to the concept of personal responsibility. Virtue dropped out of common usage early in the 19th century. It did imply a high regard for duty and responsibility in the administration of public affairs. In England, the concept was epitomized by Sir William Jones in an ode, *In imitation of Alcaeus,* who declared that a state was constituted by "high minded men / Men who their duties know / But known their rights / and knowing dare maintain" (Jones, 1807).

This idealistic declaration is hardly consistent with the rough and tumble politics of mass democracy wherein high-minded politicians have not been characteristic. Rights and duties are now largely defined by statutory law and politically appointed judiciaries rather than by intuitive judgment guided by a sense of virtue, perhaps an inevitable development in a complex and diverse society. For questions of public policy where scientific evidence is relevant (and emotional commitments are not inhibiting), findings based on testable scientific inquiry and professional judgment may indicate a direction for responsible social action. But even here, ethical and ethnic differences over the validity and implications of scientific evidence may create political circumstances under which responsible action cannot be taken.

ETHNICITY AND DIVERSITY

In its most simple sense *ethnic* characterizes a group of mankind sharing a distinguishable common cultural tradition. The term *ethnicity* represents a high consciousness of a particular cultural tradition: of a commitment to beliefs, myths, and patterns of behavior that distinguish one culture from others. Ethnic characteristics may be defined by language, race, religion, art, and in an exaggerated form, an excluding or a competitive introverted relationship to other ethnicities.

A vital ethnicity is not neutral. It may or may not be overtly proselytizing and yet may acculturate other ethnicities. Notable examples are the wider influence of Greco-Hellenistic, Indian, and Chinese civilizations. The militant geopolitics of Christianity, of Islam, and of Western civilization were marked by their displacement of other cultures by persuasion, by forced conversion, and by colonization. As with American pop culture, acculturation may resemble a contagion spreading around the globe, permeating, modifying, or suppressing diverse cultural traditions.

Often, however, a superimposed culture is an overlay, with elements of the displaced culture surviving. But too often, as in some island societies of the South Pacific, cultural integrity is destroyed and the basis of social responsibility is shattered. Similar disintegration has occurred among some American Indian societies and peoples of the Arctic. Japan has thus far been the most successful society in achieving cultural syncretism. Ethnicity may be socially bonding, but diverse ethnicities may be socially divisive. Ethnicity may factor in an important way in human conflict between and within political systems organized as nations, multinational states, or empires. Where ethnocentric societies are geographically separated or widely spaced, diverse cultures may coexist with relatively little conflict attributable to ethnic differences. But division and conflict may arise within societies of common ethnicity. Political rivalries and religious differences have arisen in many societies, sometimes signaling societal disintegration. We will presently consider the relationship between cultural integrity, diversity, and social responsibility. But for the moment attention will be focused on the ethnic basis of social responsibility.

Is there a valid basis for distinguishing cultures or societies as more, or less, responsible? Also, is societal responsibility synonymous with the collective responsibility of all members of a society? I doubt that an unqualified answer is valid for either question. Ethnic aggression by a society is certainly attributable to its leadership, which of course implies followers. For leaders to lead there must be some measure of collective consent or support (Bennis, 1990). Not all individuals in a society may approve of the actions of the individuals who are in positions of control; some actions may be opposed. And yet the assumptions and values prevalent in a society do influence its collective behavior. The prevalence of an aggressive social ideology, expressed through such concepts as Marxism, manifest destiny, or the White man's burden, justifies an assumption of social (i.e., collective) responsibility without regard to individual commitment.

One concept of social responsibility postulates society—political or religious—as more than the sum of autonomous individuals. Human systems— political, religious, or economic—persist beyond the lives of individuals, sometimes for centuries or millennia. Yet over time a society conceived as a system may change its institutional arrangements and, to the extent that the formal changes reflect changes in prevailing assumptions and values, they may be regarded as changes in ethnicity. The institutional changes effected by the Reformation in Northwestern Europe or by the French and Russian Revolutions marked changes in the culture characterizing those societies. Causes and consequences in each case were the breakdown of societal consensus, a fracturing of communality, and efforts to establish a new consensus, by force if necessary. Failure of such efforts has left a society largely bereft of any sense of collective responsibility. This may be the condition of Russia after seven decades of state-sponsored indoctrination.

The breakup of Christendom as an institutionalized system was followed by an increase in diversity within one aspect of ethnicity: a common religion. Christianity had never been a wholly unified faith. Sectarianism characterized Eastern Christianity, and in the West the Reformation led to doctrinal reinterpretations that nevertheless continued to retain certain religious beliefs, expectations, and values. Other changes in culture followed the removal of a superordinate theological order. Max Weber (1958), in *The Protestant Ethic and the Spirit of Capitalism*, argued that the Reformation led not only to a different form of institutionalized Christianity; it also opened the way to a new economic order that incorporated a new version of individual and social responsibility. Individualism became a new social reality, contrasting with the communalism of the Middle Ages that institutionalized certain individual rights and duties and collective responsibilities under feudalism and the church, but that had little place for individual autonomy. Seigneur, vassal, serf, and cleric were bound by a system of reciprocal rights and duties that, in the medieval context, could be regarded as a responsible society. Much the same might be said (with qualifications) for the caste system in India. Rulers in these societies were responsible for social stability and public order.

It is easier to determine what people, as a society, are responsible *to* than what they are responsible *for*. In traditional societies, reciprocal rights and duties were institutionalized by custom, and subsequently by written law intended initially to codify societal consensus. Obviously, it is easier to enact and enforce law under conditions of ethnic consensus than under various degrees of ethnic diversity in which interpretations of responsibility are equally diverse. Modern societies present a paradox of increasing degrees of ethnic diversity simultaneously with the growth of unifying technologies and assumptions, some of which, in effect, are also disunifying. This contradiction results significantly from the widespread assumption of individual autonomy being the context within which rights and duties are defined and allocated.

Social diversity has many different aspects but tends to fall into either of two, distinguishable on the one hand by complementary or mutually compatible diversity, and on the other by diversities that are competitive and may indeed be incompatible where ethnic distinctions are strong. In many pluralistic and relatively large societies these diversities have coexisted, as they also do in nature. *How* these diversities coexist peaceably is a matter of great importance to the stability and security of a democratic society.

To the extent that societies are multicultured and sectoralized they are unlikely to share many common standards and values. Their diversity is expressed in differences, and these differences are likely to be multiplied in societies characterized by autonomous individualism within a context of structured group diversity. Mutual advantage may be sufficient to hold a society together if cultural differences are not too great and as long as divisive factors do not arise that are stronger than is a willingness to live together as a community. A multicultural society in which all or nearly all values and behavioral preferences are diversified is unlikely to be able to act collectively and responsibly when a potentially divisive issue arises. In many critical situations such societies will be ineffectual, inhibited from decisive action by their own inherent divisions.

The motto of the United States—e pluribus unum—expresses the hope and expectation that beyond divisions within the political states, the common allegiance to nation, flag, and civic ideals will be strong enough to provide the bond that will hold a pluralistic society together in a common political order. The historical record does not augur well for the longevity of multicultural regimes. Notable exceptions (e.g., Roman and Ottoman) have been held together by military force. The globalization of information, communication, and commerce may lead to a societal future different from the past and more receptive to diversity within community.

As with concepts of responsibility, diversity takes various forms (e.g., biological, chronological, cultural). Biological diversity is characterized by at least three theoretical but related relationships: niche theory, symbiosis, and competitive exclusion. Diversity in ecological relationships is tolerable and sustaining in some circumstances, and destabilizing and transforming in others. Niche relationships separate species, whereas symbiosis syncretizes them, thus avoiding conflict. Interspecific competition by contrast leads to conflict or displacement. For example, introduction of alien species may disrupt relatively stable ecosystems (e.g., rabbits in Australia or zebra mussels in the North American Great Lakes). Competitive exclusion in species or ecosystems can result in extinction of native species so that biological diversity is only temporarily increased and is ultimately reduced. See, for example, Begon, Harker, and Townsend (1990, pt. 2); Gauze (1971); and Hutchinson (1978, chap. 5). But what does diversity, ethnically or ecologically, have to do with responsibility in any sense? In the world of nature, the meaning of responsibility is limited to causation and this limited interpretation would not be an appropriate choice for describing a relationship between humanity and nature, of which humans are a distinctive part. Hurricanes and volcanoes may cause loss of life and property, but these natural events are hardly morally responsible for the catastrophes that they cause. Introduction of the mongoose to isolated islands may wipe out native ground-nesting birds, but the mongoose incurs no moral responsibility. Those persons who liberated the mongoose in a vulnerable environment are, however, responsible for the consequences. Also, people who knowingly put themselves in the path of predictable natural calamities may be accounted as responsible for their own misfortune. However, their behavior is not socially responsible because it places a burden and risk on rescuers when disaster strikes.

Are there significant analogies between the effects of diversity in human society and in nonhuman species? The question is debatable, meaning that there may be both affirmative and negative answers. There are obviously great and numerous diversities among the many forms of animal life. Ecologists have differed regarding the influence of species diversity on the stability of ecosystems. In and among human societies, ethnic or cultural diversity can be shown to entail presumed benefits and possible risks. There is, however, a fundamental difference between the effects of diversity in biological and cultural systems. As Geoffrey Vickers observed, "human systems are different" (Vickers, 1983). That difference lies in the self-conscious and purposive character of human societies and in the ability of humans to forecast a chain of consequences following deliberate choice. Thus responsibility, in any sense beyond causation, becomes a moral question, and it is the freedom to choose (to the extent that freedom exists) that makes the exercise of that freedom a condition for social responsibility. But for the individual, as with Antigone, when an imperative of moral responsibility commands, there may be no real freedom of choice.

Complementary or mutually compatible ethnic or functional diversities may strengthen a society, increasing its efficiency, durability, and prospects for social responsibility. Functional diversity or division of labor within a common ethnic base has obviously been beneficial to the advancement of distinctive civilizations. Competitive cultural diversities, however, may cause social tension and instability. An expansive, aggressive, centralizing social system organized politically and militarily may diminish or destroy ethnic diversity. The aggressive global expansion of Europe after the 15th century was responsible for the suppression or elimination of numerous traditional cultures. European culture was enriched by borrowings from these cultures, but the world was culturally diminished by their extinction. One legacy of imperial conquest and colonization was a condition of social instability and conflict within the invaded countries, which continues today to defeat social and political responsibility in the culturally fractured so-called less developed or developing world.

To what extent can a society behave responsibly in relation to moral values, or for the actions of its individual or institutional members, in the absence of agreement on the meaning of responsibility, or a common set of basic behavioral or ethical principles? From historical experience the inference may be drawn that collective institutions, especially governments, will have difficulty in behaving responsibly in a social order wherein diverse ethnicities are competitive, incompatible, in conflict, or in disintegration. It may, of course, be argued that a responsibility of government is to mediate among diverse values and to develop a modus vivendi that will enable diverse ethnicities to live peaceably together. But this prospect is based on the proposition that divergent values are not irreconcilable or that leaders among ethnicities will not exploit differences to advance personal ambition—optimistic assumptions having little support from the record of history.

CITIZENSHIP AND PROFESSIONALISM

Although an active, socially responsible, participative citizenship remains an ideal, especially throughout the English-speaking world, the administrative state is a reality. In an ever more complex, populous, and diverse society the actual process of governance has devolved on professional bureaucracies and the judicial courts. Vickers recognized the risks and also the necessity for professional judgment, and he addressed some of his concerns in an article on "The Changing Nature of the Professions" (Vickers, 1974/1984a), and in an earlier article and a later book on judgment (Vickers, 1961/1984b, 1965). Responsible judgment, which he regarded as an art, required a dialogue between the professional experts and a wider nonexpert public. Professional responsibility required more than technical conclusions, important as they might be to coping with the problems of a complex and dynamic society. The responsible role of the professional involved a contribution of "special skills in understanding and designing to the making of policy in a field wider than his own" (Vickers, 1974/1984a, p. 288). Responsible professional judgment is made in a social context wider than a narrowly focused instrumental or technological context. In the present world, however, specialization and technical skills have been professionalized in many fields. Codes of ethics have been adopted in such professions as medicine, engineering, law, and public administration. However, they characteristically address conduct specific to the profession even though they are intended to codify responsibility to the larger society. The perspective of the narrower professional-technical viewpoint is essentially linear, in contradiction to the multilinear complexity of the actual world. In *The Technological Society*, Jacques Ellul (1964) described the dominance of technique over considered judgment in modern society. In this society purpose was subordinated to process, and a technological imperative displaced considered choice. In such a society the concept of social responsibility would be anomalous. In fact, however, Ellul's technological society described a powerful tendency, not a conclusive condition. Even in the most technology-oriented societies, public choice has rejected some feasible technologies on grounds of strong countervailing social values. Rejection of commercial supersonic transport in the United States, the establishment of the U.S. Office of Technology Assessment, and the now widespread adoption of environmental impact assessment are cases in point.

The responsibilities of citizens and of trained professionals may in some circumstances be incompatible. Professional indoctrination can lead to arrogance of opinion among practitioners in a wide range of specialisms (e.g., architecture, education, engineering, forestry, medicine, among many others). The phenomenon of whistle-blowing occurs when an individual feels an imperative to assert responsibility as a citizen over responsibility to an organization or a profession. A trained professional may believe that he or she knows what is best for society. Responsibility to his or her profession and its code of conduct may seem to him or her to be consistent with professional responsibility within society. Assured of the rightness of his or her professional judgment, how is his or her interpretation of responsibility to be understood when professional opinion and public opinion conflict?

Concepts of responsibility may not always be consistent within a profession. Changes in scientific information and changes of values, perceptions, and priorities in society may render traditional professional principles socially obsolete. In the U.S. Forest Service, for example, a cleavage has arisen between (a) adherents to the traditional professional principle that the basic purpose of forestry was to produce board feet of commercial timber and (b) the upholders of a newer principle of conserving biological diversity and preserving natural forest ecosystems.

In the theory and practice of democratic governance, policy set by expert opinion without broader citizen involvement may not meet the test of responsibility to society. The principles of participatory democracy require active citizen involvement in decisions affecting society generally. But here a dichotomy is present. A professional expert is, in theory, responsible for giving his best judgment on an issue of his competence, regardless of predominant public opinion. The answer to the question of whose responsibility should prevail may depend more on ideology or philosophical theory than on factual information. The strength and effectiveness of democratic government depends on responsible citizenship that is activated through social institutions, notably through the appropriate structuring of political action. In the United States, governments were structured with the intent to make them responsible to the electorate. The American constitutions, state and federal, were infused with theories of the 18th-century Enlightenment. As nearly every circumstance of American society has changed radically since the 18th century, it is at least questionable whether its governmental structure, although changed in detail, is adequate to cope with the emerging problems of the 21st century. This question may apply to many other political systems today. The techniques of governance have clearly advanced over the years, but the art of government is not yet one of mankind's highest achievements.

The official theorist of 18th-century democracy in America was Thomas Jefferson, who declared that government to be strongest of which every man feels himself a part. But Jefferson believed that broadly participative citizen government was possible only in relatively small communities, essentially agrarian and culturally homogenous. Although he vastly increased the territory of the United States by purchase of Louisiana from the French, he saw risk in this expansion. The survival of democracy in a country of great size required that governance be concentrated in the smallest, most local unit of government. In his autobiography he wrote that "it is not by consolidation or concentration of powers, but by their distribution, that good government is effected" (Jefferson, 1904-1905a, p. 122). And although he thought that territorial expansion would strengthen the bond of union among the States, offsetting local factions, he continued to believe that the only safe repository of political power was at the most local level of political organization. The American states and even their counties were too large for self-government.

Believing the New England township to be "the wisest invention ever devised by the wit of man for the perfect exercise of self government," Jefferson (1904-1905b) urged the division of the counties into wards "of such size that every citizen can attend, when called upon, and act in person." This direct democracy required a high sense of individual citizen responsibility. It implied active citizenship expressed in direct personal participation in governmental decision making and administration. Passive citizenship, limited to paying taxes, voting in elections, and serving when called on in military defense and on juries, was consistent only with representative democracy governed by professional civil servants. The obligations and opportunities of responsible citizenship in a complex diverse society are at the heart of a difficult political issue that modern societies have scarcely faced and scarcely recognized. Yet there have been instances of responsibilities being laid on local jurisdictions by centralized authorities. A notable example was the English civil parish, to which the government in London shifted responsibility at the local level, "self-government at the king's command." See White (1933) and White and Notestein (1915, pp. 241-280). A fraudulent case concerned the alleged local councils or soviets in the Leninist Soviet Union. In the United States today, where the practicality of localized self-government has diminished, a broader based equivalent has been sought in technical innovations such as citizen initiative and referendum. Attempts have been made to simulate the spirit of Jeffersonian democracy through mass participation in televised "town meetings." It is doubtful, however, whether a television town meeting is analogous to the communal face-to-face discourse among citizens in the traditional New England town.

NEED FOR COMMUNALITY

Given the human capacity for holding paradoxical and even contradictory opinions, it is possible for persons to adhere to both individualism and obligation to community. Some commitment to communality is necessary for a society to exist. Yet even a sense of belonging to a community may not extend to a larger society if that community is factional and its members self-centered. It is probably safe to generalize that the relationship between individualism and communality is, at best, ambiguous. Where individualism is deeply ingrained one may expect frequent conflicts between private rights and public interests.

"You owe it to yourself" has become a common expression indicative of what Sir Geoffrey Vickers termed "the autonomous individual," what I have called "the autonomous ego" (Caldwell, 1992, pp. 177-218). It is not obvious how individuals can incur obligations to themselves. To say that one should be responsible to oneself *might* imply an obligation to maintain one's personal integrity, but as a solipsism with no regard to others or to society. In Shakespeare's *Hamlet* the precept of Polonius to Laertes (Act I, scene iii), "to thine own self be true," has little meaning unless it is an admonition to preserve personal integrity with the consequence that "thou canst not then be false to any man." Thus a responsibility to others is implied. There are few autonomous egos in Shakespeare's plays. Even Richard III, surely the most notorious, was hedged about by his status, even in his self-chosen villainy. Assumed autonomy in Shakespeare's characters usually leads to isolation or self-destruction (e.g., Iago and Macbeth) and is a denial of social responsibility.

In our own time, existentialism (and earlier, nihilism) gave autonomous individualism a philosophic rationale. However, anyone who really lived by its precepts was almost surely alienated from society. No society could be sustainable if a critical number of its members tried to live only for themselves. From all that we know of human origins and about the behavior of man's anthropoid relatives, the human species and its distant relatives are in various degrees social; and this is a biological fact with sociological implications. In so-called primitive societies the autonomous individual is lost. Outside of the protection of family, tribe, or community, the prospect for survival is slight. Existentialism is possible only in a society that is able and willing to tolerate aberrant individual behavior. In effect, the autonomous individual is freeloading on society. If he or she contributes to societal well-being and stability, he or she nevertheless feels no obligation to do so.

The term *individualism* implies an inordinate emphasis on the uninhibited exercise of personal choice and action. An *individualist* committed to freedom of personal will may, but need not, take account of the effect of his or her behavior on others. The autonomous ego is therefore responsible only to the extent that it freely elects to accept responsibility. By contrast, *individuality* suggests a personal style or identity that distinguishes, but need not isolate, a person within a larger social ambience. Individuality, therefore, occupies a psychosocial area between rugged individualism with its self-assessed commitment to responsibility and a uniformitarian regimented society in which individuality is regarded as antisocial. In such a society responsibility is construed in terms resembling military codes of obedience, but obedience may be to tacit codes of behavior derived from custom. This is hardly responsibility in the moral sense, yet such a society may be regarded as highly responsible for its acts regardless of their moral quality.

I do not argue that responsibility per se, regardless of circumstance, is a social virtue, or that other values are less important. Geoffrey Vickers's exposition of the systemic nature of the workings of societies provides insight into why a linear, single-track, unqualified pursuit of any virtue leads eventually to its contradiction. Communality carried to excess suppresses creativity, critical judgment, and adaptability. The anarchy of existentialism is the other extreme. When communality and individuality coexist the conditions for social responsibility are enhanced.

STRUCTURE OF RESPONSIBILITY

For responsibility to become characteristic of a society, several conditions must be present. First, agreement on what people should be responsible *for* or *to* should be widely diffused throughout the society. This does not mean that all members of a society should have identical understandings of their responsibilities nor agree on every aspect of societal responsibility. But it does mean that there should be substantial consensus on the meaning of responsibility and on the necessity for responsible conduct. Second, interpersonal and interstatus relationships should be characterized by reciprocal responsibilities and obligations. A responsible society would be characterized by a systemic structure of functions, rights, and duties that accumulate to a collective public morality that, allowing for inescapable exceptions, defines the ethos of the society. Third, these systemic relationships should be in some sense codified, formally through law or precept, or informally through custom. People, individually or collectively, may not behave responsibly if they do not know how. Nihilistic behaviors among the deculturated underclasses of today's greatest cities are cases in point.

The structure of a system of responsibility corresponds closely to the hierarchical and differentiative structure of a society. The exercise of responsibility will differ, for example, between a highly hierarchical or authoritarian society and an egalitarian society in which authority derives mainly from functional differentiation (e.g., expertise and information). In either case, the observance of mutual responsibilities depends heavily on agreement among people regarding their respective roles, rights, and duties. If the behavior of a society is found to be irresponsible, and remedial measures are sought, it seems logical to look at the interpersonal and authoritative structure of the society. Even though there may be a substantial consensus that the society ought to achieve a higher level of responsibility, that consensus is unlikely to be achieved if prevailing beliefs and institutions are maladapted to responsible conduct.

In considering the effect of social structure on social responsibility, the influence of technology should be recognized. In contemporary modern society, the multiplicity and complexity of technologies have contradictory effects, simultaneously enhancing and diminishing communality. A high-tech economy requires a great diversity of specializations, many of which communicate by jargons unintelligible to people not versed in the specific technology (e.g., computers). To the extent that technologies structure working relationships and communication, they affect the ability of a society to be responsible, or to know whether it is in fact acting responsibly. The unprecedented growth of information technologies could enhance prospects for social responsibility, but it does not always lead to this result. The sheer volume of information and the ubiquity of the uses to which it may be put cause uncertainty as to how the free flow of information will affect the prospects for social responsibility. The effect of television appears to be ambiguous. Viewing television is an isolated experience contrasted to collective worship or active participation in public affairs. Nevertheless, conversely, it may be an instrument of public information and could inspire communal responsiveness. Unfortunately, a case can be made that television has commercialized mindless violence and sexual irresponsibility. The ultimate impact of television on social responsibility remains to be seen.

Can a society expand indefinitely and also be responsible? Is there an optimum size for societal responsibility? On this question opinions differ. Biological evolution does not provide an answer, although for thousands of years human communities, familial or tribal, were relatively small. Over the centuries of civilization societies have grown ever larger. If there is a self-limiting factor it has not yet been established as incontrovertible. The influence of size or scale in the structuring of social responsibility as of today is an unknown factor. It may or may not be a significant influence. Size may be significant for responsibility in some circumstances and not in others; culture and technology may be differentiating factors.

CONCLUSION

Drawing on human experience we may identify conditions that appear to be conducive to social responsibility. In aggregate, these conditions seldom, and only briefly, converge in the real world. We may therefore believe that social responsibility is possible in theory but, allowing for exceptions, is uncertain to doubtful as a continuity in real life.

Social responsibility *is* possible when a majority of a defined social group and their leaders are united in concern for the possible consequences of their behavior. Responsible human societies may range from small to large aggregations, but they tend to become less cohesive as their numbers, diversity, and dispersion increase. But even small, relatively isolated, tribal groups under some circumstances may lose a sense of communality and social responsibility. Colin Turnbull's (1972) study of the Ike in East Africa describes an extreme case in point. To be responsible, communities need to have individual awareness of the implications of their collective behavior and must have agreed on criteria for anticipating and evaluating the outcomes that could follow from their attitudes and actions. By these criteria few societies have been continuously responsible in a moral sense to all their members or to other peoples.

Uniformity of preferences and agreement on all issues of policy are not required for the integrity of a society. General acceptance of basic values and agreement regarding the basis for establishing truth are necessary. Diversity of opinions and ways of living are tolerable, and even beneficial, within limits. Those limits, however, are not always clearly identifiable; opinions may differ over how much and what kind of diversity is consistent with integrity. Where difference or disagreement within a society exceeds the level of tacit or willing accommodation, tension and contention result. The relationship between social diversity, communality, and social responsibility merits more attention than it has received. It is not clear how large and diverse a society can become and yet remain sufficiently cohesive to behave responsibly by any meaningful standard.

Unfortunately for constructive change, consistent with social responsibility, these and related issues are now commonly addressed in the news media and political forums by cliché and oxymoron. Invocation of self-evident truths avoids recourse to serious consideration of how truth should be established. No less unfortunate has been the failure of the social sciences to give sufficient attention to the rational basis for beliefs on social-political questions and their implications for social responsibility. The social science disciplines today combine an unacknowledged but tacit acceptance of self-evident truths on many social questions, along with a scientistic approach to methodology in which accuracy is often sacrificed to irrelevant precision. Sociobiology has introduced or revived a perspective on human behavior that draws on methods and concepts from the biological sciences (Wilson, 1981). It reintroduces the nature-nurture controversy but, as yet, has not found a generally acceptable synthesis for human society.

A fundamental question regarding the conditions necessary for social responsibility is, How free are humans to achieve responsible conduct in the moral sense, individually and collectively? If all, or nearly all, human behavior is genetically determined, the margin of real freedom may not be great. Sociobiological theories, although incomplete, cannot reasonably be dismissed out of hand. There seems little doubt today among informed persons that biology does condition and limit some aspects of human behavior. It may be that genetic factors to some degree predispose humans to create cultures in which an imperative for responsible conduct emerges. Yet the variations in human mores and responses to experience provide substance for a strong inference that culture plays a major, and in many ways, a determining role in human history.

We have not yet discovered how, or to what extent, biology influences culture and morally responsible conduct by individuals, institutions, and society. Sir Geoffrey Vickers and I corresponded regarding this question and we agreed that in the indeterminacy of the evidence, we should work on the proposition that human culture can be self-directed toward greater social responsibility, while continuing to enlarge our understanding of the influence of biology on human behavior. In a letter to me, he wrote:

Of course it may well be that human nature, however acculturated, is not capable of sustaining for long societies like the present USA (or UK) or the present USSR. If so, such societies will break down and the world's survivors if any will revert to simpler, smaller organisations, more tribal though not less cultural. I think this is very likely. Equally the present crisis may be a cultural one precipitated by the cult of individual autonomy stemming from the Enlightenment, a cult which would be equally unfavourable to tribal cultures. I think this equally likely and not inconsistent with the other. What I am prepared to fight for to the last is the autonomy of culture and of the historical process by which it develops and changes. The reason I feel so strongly about it is that if we were really dealing with an invariant law of biological nature, we should at least not alter it by misunderstanding it. If on the other hand we are dealing with culture and if this is the supreme artifact of mankind, we cannot help changing it by the way we think about it. And if we deny it we not merely emasculate it but put it outside the realm of conscious debate—as science has already done (most unscientifically) to human history, which is largely the history of culture and its ever accelerating course of dialectic change. (G. Vickers, personal communication, March 26, 1980)

The importance of the concepts of social responsibility to the well-being and stability of society justifies their examination. There is a substantial literature relating to responsibility, especially in its moral context. Yet as with many behavioral concepts, common language seldom reveals the contextual differences from which the word *responsibility* derives particular meaning. To make the intended meaning of responsibility more often evident, linguistic distinctions would be helpful. The Inuit people in the Arctic are said to have many different words for snow in its various aspects, most of which are covered in English by one word. In small, stable, homogenous societies everyone may have a common understanding of words and concepts. In contrast, individuals in populous, culturally diverse societies may find homonyms a cause of misunderstanding and disagreement. English vocabulary has been continually expanded by the addition of new words for new things, but aside from technical jargon it has been conservative in substituting new words to more accurately designate particular meanings formerly carried by one omnibus term.

To preserve the integrity, and even the survival, of a society, it may be necessary to understand and specify the conditions for responsible conduct. Present challenges to societal integrity are evident, and presently unforeseen challenges are probable. We cannot be certain that the ideal of social responsibility, whatever its context, is indefinitely attainable. The interactive relationship between biology and culture is not well understood, and explanatory theories are controversial. The modern world presents a paradox of high achievement in science and technology in contrast to massive failures and contradictions in the arts of communality, governance, and behavioral control. A fundamental question for humanity today is whether its notable achievements will be sufficient to offset its failures. Can modern society save itself from itself? History provides no direct answers, contemporary circumstances having few precedents. But such inferences as may be drawn from the rise and decline of past civilizations offer insufficient reason for optimism. High achievement may occur simultaneously with disintegrative tendencies. Revitalization movements have been valiant, but usually futile, efforts to reverse sociocultural disintegration.

There is a near certainty, however, that continuing failure of a government to ensure public safety and order will exhaust the patience of society sufficiently to cause displacement by a regime perceived to be more responsive to demands for social stability. The consequence may be iron government that will suppress those elements in a society regarded as troublesome or subversive. Responsible government and public order may thus be obtained at the price of individual freedom.[5]

Will the globalization of international economy and the universalizing of culture lead to greater intercultural tolerance and a sense of responsibility to all humankind and for the biosphere? It is presently uncertain if homogenization of culture and economies will occur or, if occurring, to what extent. Would social responsibility become universalized? It is plausible to believe that present trends in international and intercultural relations will make a difference in the character of social responsibility in the future. But what *kind* of difference must be left to future historians to discover.

NOTES

1. The writings on responsibility are many, and their messages are diverse. Sir Geoffrey Vickers addressed responsibility in various aspects, but in particular he was concerned with the relationship between personal responsibility and societal responsibility on which individual integrity ultimately depends. Following is a representative sample of references on responsibility, reproduced in full in the References section: Vickers (1980), French (1992), Horosz (1975), Jonas (1984), Lucas (1993), Roberts (1965), and Waller (1990).

2. For example, see his essay on "Will and Free Will," in Open Systems Group (Eds.) (1984), *The Vickers papers* (pp. 353-363). London: Harper & Row.

3. See Waller, Note 1 above.

4. For different aspects of biology and social behavior see Caldwell (1987, chap. 6, "Biocratic Interpretations of Human Behavior," pp. 111-135), Wilson and Lumsden (1981), and Wilson (1978).

5. The basis for a gloomy assessment is set forth by Heilbroner (1974).

REFERENCES

Begon, M., Harker, J. L., & Townsend, C. (1990). *Ecology: Individuals, populations and communities* (2nd ed.). London: Blackwell.

Bennis, W. (1990). *Why leaders can't lead: The unconscious conspiracy continues*. San Francisco: Jossey-Bass.

Caldwell, L. K. (1987). *Biocracy: Public policy and the life sciences*. Boulder, CO: Westview.

Caldwell, L. K. (1992). Threshold to the post-modern world. In *A time to hear and answer: Essays for the bicentennial season* (The Franklin Lectures, 4th ser., pp. 175-218). Alabama: University of Alabama Press.

Dobzhansky, T. (1956). *The biological basis of human freedom*. New York: Columbia University Press.

Ellul, J. (1964). *The technological society* (J. Wilkinson, Trans.). New York: Alfred A. Knopf.

French, P. A. (1992). *Responsibility matters*. Lawrence: University of Kansas Press.

Gauze, G. F. (1971). *The struggle for existence*. New York: Dover.

Heilbroner, R. (1974). *An inquiry into the human prospect*. New York: Norton.

Horosz, W. (1975). *The crisis of responsibility: Man as the source of accountability*. Norman: University of Oklahoma Press.

Hutchinson, G. E. (1978). *An introduction to population ecology*. New Haven, CT: Yale University Press.

Jefferson, T. (1904-1905a). Autobiography. In P. L. Ford (Ed.), *The works of Thomas Jefferson* (Federal ed., vol. 1, p. 122). New York: G. P. Putnam.

Jefferson, T. (1904-1905b). Letter to Samuel Kercheval, July 12, 1816. In P. L. Ford (Ed.), The works of Thomas Jefferson (Federal ed., vol. 12, pp. 8-9). New York: G. P. Putnam.

Jonas, H. (1984). *The imperative of responsibility: The search for an ethics for the technological age*. Chicago, IL: University of Chicago Press.

Jones, W. (1807). *The political writings of Sir William Jones* (Vol. 2, pp. 20-21). London: Cadell and Davies.

Lorentz, K. (1966). *On aggression* (M. K. Wilson, Trans.). New York: Harcourt, Brace & World.

Lucas, J. R. (1993). *Responsibility*. Oxford: Oxford University Press.

Monod, J. (1971). *Chance and necessity: An essay on the natural philosophy of modern biology* (A. Wainhouse, Trans.). New York: Alfred A. Knopf.

Open Systems Group. (Eds.). (1984). *The Vickers papers*. London: Harper & Row.

Roberts, M. (1965). *Responsibility and practical freedom*. Cambridge: Cambridge University Press.

Turnbull, C. (1972). *The mountain people*. New York: Simon & Schuster.

Vickers, G. (1965). *The art of judgment*. London: Chapman & Hall.

Vickers, G. (1970). *Freedom in a rocking boat: Changing values in an unstable society*. London: Penguin.

Vickers, G. (1980). *Responsibility: Its sources and limits*. Seaside, CA: Intersystems.

Vickers, G. (1983). *Human systems are different*. London: Harper & Row.

Vickers, G. (1984a). The changing nature of the professions. In Open Systems Group (Eds.), *The Vickers papers*. London: Harper & Row. (Original work published 1974)

Vickers, G. (1984b). Judgment. In Open Systems Group (Eds.), *The Vickers papers* (pp. 230-245). London: Harper & Row. (Original work published 1961)

Vickers, G. (1984c). The weakness of western culture. In Open Systems Group (Eds.), *The Vickers papers* (pp. 78-96). London: Harper & Row. (Original work published 1977)

Waller, B. N. (1990). *Freedom without responsibility*. Philadelphia: Temple University Press.

Weber, M. (1958). *The Protestant ethic and the spirit of capitalism* (T. Parsons, Trans.). New York: Scribner.

White, A. B. (1933). *Self-government at the king's command*. Minneapolis: University of Minnesota Press.

White, A. B., & Notestein, W. (1915). The English parish and the New England town meeting. In A. B. White & W. Notestein, *Source problems in English history* (pp. 241-280). New York: Harper.

Wilson, E. O. (1978). *On human nature*. Cambridge, MA: Harvard University Press.

Wilson, E. O. (1981). *Sociobiology: The new synthesis*. Cambridge, MA: Harvard University Press.

Wilson, E. O., & Lumsden, C. J. (1981). *Genes, mind, and culture: The coevolution process*. Cambridge, MA: Harvard University Press.

Wilson, J. Q. (1993). *The moral sense*. New York: Free Press.

Index

and its institutions, 158
and the individual, 157, 159, 160
as building blocks of society, 178
as "world of well," 111
bonds of, 178
breakup, 9
care in the, 99, 111
culturally homogeneous, small, 185
dependence of West on, 60
diversity of, 156
diversity within, 181
human familial, 188
human, tribal, 188
importance of architecture to, 113
moral, 166, 168, 169, 170
moral artifacts of, 167
obligation to, 184-185
physicians, 109
political, 70
sense of, 49, 58
sense of belonging to, 57
social system of, 160
Community action group, 72
Community boundaries, 161, 167
Community care, 111-112, 116
 Glyncorrwg community practice, 113, 115
 Marylebone experiment, 113-114, 115
 models of delivery, 113
 Peckham experiment, 112-113, 115
 Vickers's concept, 108
Community health, 113, 116
 information services, U.S., 102
 trusts, 116
Community, international, 149
 and events in Yugoslavia, 135
Community life, 47
Community medicine, 100, 108, 109, 111, 112, 113
 concepts of, 88
Community, membership(s) of, 60
 multiple, 158
Community needs, 160
Community oriented primary health care, 109
Community practice, concept of, 120
Community responsibility, 95
Community support, 100
Competitive exclusion, 181
Complementary therapies, 113
Complete nuclear disarmament, 150
Complex societies, management of, 36
Comprehensive nuclear test ban, 150
Compromised living, 93
Computers, 188
Concept(s)

of appreciation (Vickers), 44
of appreciative judgment (Vickers), 37
of autonomous individual, 157, 160
of manifest destiny, 180
of order, and Vickers, 137
of reciprocal rights, 177
of responsibility, 174, 175, 184
of social responsibility, 180
of system, and Vickers, 36
of threshold in systems, 138
of time, and Vickers, 137
of White man's burden, 180
Conditions of entitlement in public services, 40
Conduct, responsible, 187, 190
Conference of the Committee on Disarmament, 147
Conference of the Eighteen-Nation Committee on Disarmament, 147
Conference on Disarmament (CD) UN, 146, 147, 148, 149, 150
 Ad Hoc Committee, 150
 "Decalogue" of issues, 147, 148, 149
 membership, 147, 149
 Secretariat, 147
Confidence building, 147, 150
 measures, 148, 149
Conflict(s)
 ambiguity of, 137-138
 and interspecific competition, 181
 and relationships, 141
 between professional and public opinion, 184
 containment of, 57, 140, 141
 exacerbation of, and arms, 142
 human, 139, 179
 in societies of common ethnicity, 179
 levels of, 138
 models of, 139
 personal, 176
 regulation of, 138
 social, 176, 182
 sources of, 138, 139
 two senses, of Vickers, 137, 138
 types of, 139
Conflict management, 34, 133, 135, 136-142, 147
 in international society, 142, 145, 150
Conflict processes, 135-136
Conflict reduction in policy-making, 103
Conflict resolution, 140
 and human societies, 137
Conflicting responsibilities, 176
Conflict-prone international system, 133
Conflictual situations, of Vickers, 138, 139, 141

About the Authors

GUY B. ADAMS is an associate professor of public administration and the director of graduate studies in the Department of Public Administration at the University of Missouri-Columbia. His research has focused on organizational symbolism and culture and on public administration history and ethics. He is a coauthor of *The Tacit Organization* (JAI, 1992) and co-editor of *Policy-Making, Communication and Social Learning: Essays of Sir Geoffrey Vickers* (Transaction Books, 1987) and *Reflections on Research in Public Administration* (Sage, 1994). He has published widely in such scholarly journals as *Public Administration Review, American Review of Public Administration, Administration and Society*, and *Organization Studies*.

MARGARET BLUNDEN is the dean of the Faculty of Business, Management and Social Studies at the University of Westminster in London. She gained both B.A. and M.A. degrees in history from the University of Exeter and a D.Phil. (history) from the University of Oxford. She contributed the introductory article "Geoffrey Vickers: An Intellectual Journey" to *The Vickers Papers* (Harper & Row, 1984). More recently she has worked on defense policy, editing (with Owen Greene) *Science and Mythology in the Making of Defence Policy* (Brassey's, 1988). Her current research is concerned with defense policy and security in Europe and the Mediterranean after the Cold War. Her most recent publication is "Insecurity on Europe's Southern Flank" in *Survival* (Summer, 1994).

LYNTON K. CALDWELL is the Arthur F. Bentley Professor of Political Science Emeritus and a professor of public and environmental affairs at Indiana University. He is active in environmental and science policy research. He received a degree in English with honors in 1934, a Ph.D. degree in 1943 from the University of Chicago, an M.A. degree in 1938 from Harvard University, and an LL.D. degree in 1977 from Western Michigan University. He has served on faculties of the universities of Chicago, Oklahoma, Syracuse, and California at Berkeley, with shorter appointments and lectures at more than 80 other collegiate institutions in the United States and abroad. Services to the public include the U.S. Senate; the Departments of Commerce, Defense, and Interior; the Office of Technology Assessment; the National Institutes of Health; the United Nations; and UNESCO. Scientific bodies in which he has participated include the National Research Council, the National Commission on Materials Policy, the Sea Grant Advisory Board, the Science Advisory Board of the International Joint Commission, and the Pacific Science Congress. He has served on editorial boards of a number of scientific and professional journals and on the Board of Governors of the Nature Conservancy 1959-1965. He is noted as a principal architect of the National Environmental Policy Act of 1969 and the "inventor" of the environmental impact statement.

BAYARD L. CATRON is a professor of public administration in the Department of Public Administration at George Washington University. He earned his doctorate in social policies planning from the University of California, Berkeley. He is well-known for his work in public service ethics, having founded a national ethics network and organized the first national conference on the topic in 1989. Catron is a coeditor of *Policy-Making, Communication and Social Learning: Essays of Sir Geoffrey Vickers* (Transaction Books, 1987) and *Images and Identities in Public Administration* (Sage, 1990). He has published a number of journal articles on public administration theory and ethics.

PETER CHECKLAND is a professor of systems at Lancaster University. After studying chemistry at Oxford (where he was Casberd Scholar of St. John's College and gained a First), he had a 15-year career in ICI; when he left to join Lancaster University, he was the manager of a 100-strong research group in ICI Fibres. At Lancaster, he has led an action research program out of which has come the approach to management problem solving and analysis of organizational information needs known as soft systems methodology, which is now extensively taught and used around the world. Its development is described in *Systems Thinking, Systems Practice* (Wiley, 1981) and *Soft Systems Methodology in Action* (Wiley, 1990, with J. Scholes). He was awarded an Honorary D.Sc. by City University in 1991.

SCOTT D. N. COOK was trained in both philosophy and social science. He received B.A. and M.A. degrees from San Francisco State University, and a Ph.D. degree from Massachusetts Institute of Technology. His research is in the areas of technology studies and applied ethics. His recent publications include *Culture and Organizational Learning* (with Dvora Yanow; Sage, 1993) and "The Structure of Technological Revolutions and the Gutenberg Myth." Under a grant from the U.S. National Science Foundation, he is currently (1994-1996) doing research on aspects of ethics and learning within technological innovation at the Xerox Palo Alto Research Center. He is an associate professor of philosophy at San Jose State University.

MALCOLM DANDO is a professor of international security in the Department of Peace Studies at the University of Bradford, United Kingdom. He trained originally as a biologist at St. Andrews University and gained a doctorate in neurophysiology/behavior. After postdoctoral research work in the United States (University of Michigan, Ann Arbor and University of Oregon, Eugene) and in the United Kingdom, he held a fellowship funded by the Defence Operational Analysis Establishment at the University of Sussex in the study of decision making in crises. He joined the Department of Peace Studies at Bradford in 1979, at which point his work became mainly concerned with issues of arms control and disarmament. Recent publications include *A Violent Peace: Global Security After the Cold War* (with Paul Rogers; Brassey's, 1991) and *Biological Warfare in the 21st Century* (Brassey's, 1994).

JOHN FORESTER received a Ph.D. degree from the University of California, Berkeley in 1977. He was the Lady Davis Visiting Professor at the Technion in Haifa, Israel, where he spent a sabbatical year in 1993-1994. He is a professor of city and regional planning at Cornell University. Interested in the politics and ethics of planning practice, his recent work includes collections of first-person voice accounts of planners working in diverse fields, including most lately planners and architects in Israel. Author of *Planning in the Face of Power* (University of California, Berkeley, 1989), Forester recently co-edited (with Frank Fischer) *The Argumentative Turn in Policy Analysis and Planning* (Duke University Press, 1993) and published *Critical Theory, Public Policy, and Planning Practice* (State University of New York Press, 1993).

NEVIL JOHNSON has held the post of Nuffield Reader in the Comparative Study of Institutions in the University of Oxford since 1969 and is a professorial fellow of Nuffield College. Formerly a member of the Administrative Class of the Home Civil Service, he has written widely on government and administration as well as on theoretical aspects of political science. His books include *Parliament and Administration: The Estimates Committee 1945-65* (1966), *Government in the Federal Republic of Germany: The Executive at Work* (1973 and 1982), *In Search of the Constitution: Reflections on State and Society in Britain* (1977), and *The Limits of Political Science* (1989). From 1967 to 1981, he was the honorary editor of *Public Administration*, from 1982 to 1985 a Civil Service Commissioner, and from 1981 to 1987 a member of the Economic and Social Research Council.

NANCY MILIO received a Ph.D. degree in sociology from Yale University and is a professor of health policy and administration (School of Public Health) and a professor of nursing at the University of North Carolina at Chapel Hill. Her teaching, research, and publications center on policy development, implementation, and evaluation; health policy and strategic analysis; community IT (information technology); and health promotion/education. She has worked with numerous governments (in Scandinavia, Eastern and Western Europe, China, and Australia) and with the World Health Organization as a policy analyst and consultant for 20 years. She was involved in community organization for health during the 1960s. Among her publications are seven books and over 100 articles in 40 health, social science, and policy journals in seven countries. She has been a visiting professor to universities in the United Kingdom, New Zealand, Australia, the Netherlands, Spain, and Brazil.

PATRICK C. PIETRONI (FRCGP, MRCP, DCH) is an associate regional adviser with the British Postgraduate Medical Federation and Council member of the Royal College of General Practitioners. He was formerly a member of the

Medicines Commission and also a senior lecturer in general practice at St. Mary's Hospital Medical School. He is a founder member and past chairman of the British Holistic Medical Association, set up in 1983, and is a practicing Jungian analyst. He is the principal in a National Health Service Health Centre, which, as part of a research project, incorporates complementary therapies, audit, community outreach, and education and self-help programs. As a result of this research work, the Marylebone Centre Trust was set up in 1988 to both promote and develop the experimental work of the Health Centre with education and training programs, the aim being to encourage similar models of health care within the National Health Service. He has practiced acupuncture and homeopathy for over 15 years. He has taught yoga and lectured widely on the topic of complementary medicine. He is the author of *Holistic Living* (1986) and *The Greening of Medicine* (1990) and edited, for *Reader's Digest, The Family Guide to Alternative Medicine* (1992).

ROD A.W. RHODES, B.Sc. (Bfd), B.Litt. (Oxon), Ph.D. (Essex), is research professor of politics at the University of Newcastle. Between 1989 and 1995, he was professor of politics and head of department at the University of York; and between 1987 and 1989, he was reader in government and chair of department at the University of Essex. He also held permanent appointments at the University of Birmingham (1970-1976) and the University of Strathclyde (1976-1979) and visiting appointments at the European Institute of Public Administration (Maastricht), the Australian National University, and the University of the West Indies (Jamaica). He is the author of many books and articles, including *Public Administration and Policy Analysis* (Saxon House, 1979); *Control and Power in Central-Local Relations* (Gower, 1981); *The National World of Local Government* (Allen & Unwin, 1986); and *Beyond Westminster and Whitehall* (Routledge, 1988). He has been the editor of *Public Administration* since 1986. Recently, he published four edited collections: *Implementing Thatcherite Policies: Audit of an Era* (Open University Press, 1992) and *Policy Networks in British Government* (Clarendon Press, 1992), both with David Marsh; *Prime Minister, Cabinet and Core Executive* (Macmillan, 1994) with Patrick Dunleavy; and *The European Yearbook of Government and Administration 1994* (Oxford University Press, 1995) with Jens Hesse. In 1992, he was a member of the Higher Education Funding Council's Research Assessment Panel for Politics and International Relations. Currently, he is chair of the Economic and Social Research Council's research program on local governance; and director of the ESRC's Whitehall research program.

ALVIN M. WHITE is a professor of mathematics at Harvey Mudd College, Claremont. He gained an A.B. from Columbia University and received a Ph.D. degree from Stanford University. He edited *Interdisciplinary Teaching* (Jossey-Bass, 1981) and *Essays in Humanistic Mathematics* (Mathematical Association of America, 1993). He was the director of New Interdisciplinary, Holistic Approaches to Teaching Learning, Claremont, 1977-1980, and has been the editor-publisher of the *Humanistic Mathematics Network Journal* since 1987.

SIR GEOFFREY VICKERS was born on October 13, 1894 in Nottingham, England; his father, a man of wide-ranging intellectual interests, ran the family lace manufacturing business. Vickers was educated at Oundle School and went up to Merton College at Oxford University in 1913. He enlisted as soon as war broke out, served throughout the war, and was awarded the Victoria Cross. After the war, he returned to Oxford, where he obtained a degree in classics. Vickers qualified as a solicitor in 1923, and 3 years later became a partner in the City of London firm of Slaughter and May, where he remained until 1940. His work involved him in the legal aspects of large financial operations, often with an international dimension. In 1940, Vickers reenlisted in his old regiment, but spent most of the war assigned to the Ministry of Economic Warfare, where he rose to become director, and was a member of the Joint Intelligence Committee of the Chiefs of Staff. It was for these services that he received his knighthood.

In 1947, Sir Geoffrey Vickers became a member of the newly formed National Coal Board, then one of the biggest industrial enterprises in the world, and remained on that board with responsibility for manpower and welfare until his formal retirement in 1955. In 1951, he also became the chairman of the research committee of the Mental Health Research Fund, a voluntary position that he held for 16 years and that added knowledge and reading of psychiatry, anthropology, sociology, psychology, and ethnology to his existing interests in management, government, and the law, and his emerging interest in systems thinking.

After formal retirement in 1955, Vickers published 87 papers in a wide variety of academic and professional journals, wrote nine books, lectured at universities in North America and Britain, and carried on an impressive intellectual debate by correspondence with academics from many different disciplines throughout the English-speaking world. He died in March 1982.